A Glimpse of Hell

Reports on Torture Worldwide

Edited by Duncan Forrest

for Amnesty International

NYU
Press

AMNESTY
INTERNATIONAL

© Amnesty International United Kingdom and the individual contributors 1996

All rights reserved.

First published in the U.S.A. in 1996 by
NEW YORK UNIVERSITY PRESS
Washington Square
New York, N.Y. 10003

First published in Great Britain by Cassell 1996

CIP data available from the Library of Congress

ISBN 0-8174-2665-8 (hardcover)
ISBN 0-8174-2666-6 (paperback)

Cover and title-page illustration by Hong Seong-Dam, South Korean ex-POC and torture victim

The views expressed are those of the individual authors and not necessarily those of Amnesty International.

Amnesty International and the publisher wish to thank Frank Cass Limited for permission to reprint the extract from *Medicine and War*, Volume 8, which appears on pages 162–5.

Typeset by Ben Cracknell Studios

Printed and bound in Great Britain by Biddles Ltd, Guildford and King's Lynn

---

For more information about Amnesty International please contact:

Amnesty International USA
322 Eighth Avenue
New York, NY 10001

or the Amnesty International office in your country.

Contents

The Contributors

John Denford, consultant psychiatrist (retired); Clinical Director of the Medical Foundation for the Care of Victims of Torture, London

Duncan Forrest, consultant paediatric surgeon (retired); Editor of Amnesty International UK Section Medical Group *Newsletter*; volunteer clinician at the Medical Foundation for the Care of Victims of Torture, London

Gisli Gudjonsson, forensic psychiatrist at the Institute of Psychiatry, London

Gill Hinshelwood, physician to the Medical Foundation for the Care of Victims of Torture, London

Mike Jempson, author, journalist and lecturer specializing in human rights

Dan Jones, Human Rights Education Officer at Amnesty International UK Section

Bernard Knight, Professor of Forensic Medicine at the Welsh School of Medicine; Trustee of the Medical Foundation for the Care of Victims of Torture, London

Andrew McEntee, General Secretary of the Central America Human Rights Group; Chairman of the Lawyers' Group, Amnesty International UK Section

Eric Prokosch, Theme Research Programme Co-ordinator at the International Secretariat, Amnesty International

Piet van Reenen, former Commandant of the Dutch Police Training College; Board member of Amnesty International Dutch Section; legal consultant to the Ministry of Justice in the Netherlands

Morris Tidball-Binz, founder member of the Argentine Team of Forensic Anthropology; researcher in the Americas Region of International Secretariat, Amnesty International

Steve Wright, Director of the Omega Foundation, a human rights organization specializing in military, security and police concerns; Chairman of the Military, Security and Police Group, Amnesty International UK Section

Felicity de Zulueta, consultant psychotherapist at the Charing Cross Hospital, London; member of the Medical Group, Amnesty International UK Section

Foreword

Dear Reader,

This book is frightening because it depicts some of the dreadful acts committed by many governments on the very people they are supposed to protect. It is disturbing because it questions the meaning of human progress and the persistence in our societies of practices that revolt our consciences. It is moving because it makes us confront the pain and humiliation of many men, women and children. But it also points to the resilience of the spirit of resistance to oppression and injustice.

Amnesty International has been reporting about such pain and suffering for thirty-five years. Beyond the reporting, our membership has been taking decisive action to stop the abuses. Here we have commissioned some of the foremost experts in the field to write about the history of torture, the methods used and the torturers and their victims.

When you have finished this book you will want to know what you can do to help stop this happening again. You will want to take action. May I humbly suggest that joining Amnesty International could constitute the first step; its address is on page ii.

PIERRE SANÉ
Secretary General of
Amnesty International

Preface

Amnesty International (AI) has for more than two decades been the engine of international efforts to combat torture. In 1973 it initiated and led a joint non-governmental organization (NGO) campaign against torture. This campaign created the climate for, at first hesitant, United Nations activity in the field, eventually involving extensive international standard-setting. A 1975 Declaration against Torture was followed by codes of conduct or ethics for law enforcement officials (1979) and medical personnel (1982), as well as principles for the protection of any detained or imprisoned person (1988). The landmark 1984 Convention against Torture and Other Cruel, Inhuman and Degrading Treatment or Punishment, initiated by Sweden and the Netherlands in 1977, has its roots in this period.

The organization renewed its campaign in 1984, by which time the UN had begun to try its hand at monitoring implementation. In 1980 the Commission on Human Rights had created a Working Group on Enforced or Involuntary Disappearances and, in 1982, it had appointed a Special Rapporteur on Summary and Arbitrary Executions. So, by 1984, we felt that the time might be right to urge on the UN the establishment of a similar mechanism to deal with the problem of torture (I was Head of AI's Legal Office at the time). (In fact, we had sought some implementation machinery at the time of the 1973 campaign, but the UN was not then ready for so radical a departure from its traditional view that interceding in human rights issues in specific countries was unwarranted interference in their domestic jurisdiction.) The organization's main objective at the 1985 session of the Commission on Human Rights was precisely the establishment of the mechanism. The Dutch delegation to the Commission formally proposed the creation of a Special Rapporteur on the question of torture and the Commission agreed. The Chairman of the Commission appointed the head of the delegation, Professor Peter Kooijmans, to the function. I succeeded him in 1993 after he resigned on becoming his country's Foreign Minister.

Following the methodology of the previously established mechanisms, Professor Kooijmans rapidly developed the techniques of sending allegations of torture to governments for their comments, seeking invitations to visit countries and reporting annually and publicly to the Commission on his interventions, country by country, and on any response received. Especially important were the urgent appeals made when information came in suggesting that individuals were actually being tortured or were detained in circumstances indicating a credible risk of torture. Needless to say, I have continued these activities. What is clear is that this work would simply not be possible without information being supplied by NGOs, and especially important among them, both for quantity and quality of information, is AI. In other words, from my new vantage point, I can confirm what had long been apparent to me, that AI's most important contribution, in its field, to world human rights awareness and action is the reliability of its information, bolstered by effective diplomatic and grass-roots campaigning techniques.

The world will have reason to be grateful for the organization's third international campaign against torture in 1998, for which this publication and the UK Section campaign will pave the way in the United Kingdom. It is a dismal reality that, despite impressive non-governmental and intergovernmental action over nearly a quarter of a century, torture is still a widespread problem. We are becoming increasingly aware of its perpetration, not only on political opponents, but also on ordinary criminal suspects. This campaign will again bring the glare of international publicity to bear on the issue and, it is to be hoped, stimulate new thinking and new ideas on how to combat it.

NIGEL RODLEY
Professor of Law, University of Essex
United Nations Special Rapporteur on Torture

Introduction

Duncan Forrest

> *There can never be any justification for torture. It creates an escalation of violence in the internal affairs of states. It spreads like a contagious disease from country to country. It has lasting effects on the mental and physical health of the victim, and brutalises the torturer.*

From the Declaration of the first Amnesty International
Conference for the Abolition of Torture, Paris, 1973

Why publish yet another book on torture? Hasn't the subject been covered fully already? Is there anything new to say on the subject?

Certainly, it is true that much has been written, not least by Amnesty International (AI), which has produced authoritative works, the *Report on Torture* in support of its 1973 Torture campaign and *Torture in the Eighties* in conjunction with the campaign of 1984. These and many other publications have shown how widespread the practice is. Unfortunately, the world has not stood still, and most of the countries implicated in those books are still actively torturing their citizens; and a few more countries have been added to the list. New military campaigns, civil wars and terrorist groups have sprung up, providing a fertile soil for torture and other cruel, inhuman and degrading treatment and punishment. So now AI is in the position of needing to mount yet one more torture campaign, and this book is being published in order to raise awareness and acquaint readers with aspects of the subject that it is hoped will increase understanding of the subject.

There is a danger, in presenting a book on torture, that its effect could be counter-productive. There is a possibility that readers may feel the *frisson* that undoubtedly exists in contemplating human cruelty, degradation and suffering. One only has to note the queues that form to see Madame Tussaud's Chamber of Horrors or the London Dungeon to see the danger. Visitors to these centres can look unmoved on the displays of appalling instruments of torture, believing that they are looking at the remote past. Yet they should be told emphatically that torture still goes on and that some of the methods are still in use while others have been superseded by methods made possible by modern technology, methods just as painful and inhumane as the rusting 'iron maiden' or thumbscrew.

What should be the scope of the book? Torture used to obtain information, extract confessions or break down a community, that requires a structure and organization, is of course central. Study of 'cruel, inhuman or degrading treatment or punishment' is also essential, though these need not be officially planned, often occurring through lack or neglect of checks and balances and often the random outcome of individual human cruelty, laziness or lack of discipline. Not all cruel activities come within AI's mandate, thus becoming susceptible to AI's campaigning strategies. Though they are relevant to the study of formal torture, 'disappearance', extrajudicial execution, corporal punishment and the death penalty are topics that are too large to be covered in any detail in a book of this size.

In planning to look at the subject from different perspectives, we have called on a number of contributors, each with some specific expertise in one aspect of the subject. This has inevitably led to some repetition, which is not necessarily a drawback. We have tried to put the whole subject into focus by viewing it from different viewpoints.

There is no clear distinction between torture and the limits of legitimate interrogation. What some would regard as normal treatment others would regard as excessive use of force, physical or psychological. This depends to a great extent on the culture in which one is brought up. The lack of a clear dividing line becomes important when we consider how easily a culture of torture can develop in a community unless strictly kept in check by an incorruptible judiciary supported by effective legislation and good policing. There is no doubt that torture thrives in countries where there is corruption, disregard of the law and a weak or corrupt judiciary. No country on earth can relax its guard against the possibility of torture spreading into interrogation methods. Effective legal constraints are essential to guard against the encroachment of excessive coercion in the interrogation of suspects. In Chapter 4, Gisli Gudjonsson shows how fresh legislation in Northern Ireland and England and Wales was necessary two decades ago to defuse dangerous situations where interrogation was shown to be excessively coercive. Many other countries need to introduce effective legislation to restore the rule of law. Recent examples, notably Chile and South Africa, have shown that a change in government can successfully change the pattern of torture.

Questions which are constantly being asked – what makes a torturer?

and why is torture so deeply ingrained in human history? – must be faced however uncomfortable the answers. Felicity de Zulueta in Chapter 6 describes research that sheds a chilling light on the potential for individuals to become torturers.

Apart from legalized torture, cruel, inhuman and degrading treatment and punishment thrive in countries where there is a cultural tradition of harsh discipline in home and school. In such countries, brutality in police stations and prison are often accepted without question by the citizens.

It is inevitable, given the subject, that this book will appear as one of almost unrelieved gloom. Every page reminds us that human society does not seem to have improved. There is hope, however, as is seen clearly by those who treat torture survivors. They find evidence that some, though not all, torture survivors can rise above their experience and demonstrate that the human spirit is capable of great resilience and nobility. Chapters 10 and 12 describe the possibilities of restoring some sense of humanity to victims who seem to have lost everything. Perhaps we can draw the lesson that sometimes the torturers are not victorious.

The final chapter outlines possible strategies for keeping torture at bay. The emphasis is on preventing torture rather than just dealing with its consequences.

While it is true that torture remains widespread and good news is very patchy, it is important to bear in mind that even in the most debased society there are many individuals of goodwill who deplore the use of torture and work to eliminate it. It is these people who, with the support and solidarity of individuals and organizations worldwide, need to be empowered to overcome those for whom torture is a way of life and convince and mobilize those for whom it remains a matter of indifference.

The purpose of this book is to ensure that the plight of torture victims and their courage do not go unrecognized, and to stir people of goodwill to action. Perhaps by drawing attention to the subject in all its diversity, it may bring about a small step in that direction.

CHAPTER 1

Law and Torture

Andrew McEntee

Article 1

For the purposes of this Convention, the term 'torture' means any act by which severe pain and suffering, whether physical or mental, is intentionally inflicted on a person for such purposes as obtaining from him or a third person information or a confession, punishing him for an act he or a third person has committed or is suspected of having committed, or intimidating or coercing him or a third person, or for any reason based on discrimination of any kind, when such pain or suffering is inflicted by or at the instigation of or with the consent or acquiescence of a public official or other person acting in an official capacity. It does not include pain or suffering arising only from, inherent in or incidental to lawful sanctions.

UN Convention against Torture and Other Cruel, Inhuman
or Degrading Treatment or Punishment, 1984

Throughout recorded history, and surely before then, men, women and children have torn and battered the flesh of other men, women and children, without intending to kill them, and subjected them to pain and mental anguish sufficient to unbalance their minds. Some of those incidents will have occurred in spite of laws outlawing such behaviour, some of them will have happened with the full backing of the law, and some of them will have resulted in punishment of the perpetrators and redress for the victims. But how many of these incidents would be classified as 'torture' under contemporary international human rights law?

More often than not, the word 'torture' is invoked in everyday, non-legal usage to describe activity which international human rights law does not, in fact, define as 'torture', no matter how excessively violent the activity or how much pain and suffering is caused. Hence, a proper working definition of 'torture' is central to its use in a legal setting, and this will be one of the key points dealt with below.

Law for the victim: a shield and a sword

Clearly, the aim of this chapter is to provide an introduction to the relationship between torture and the law. However, this necessarily goes beyond laying out the printed letter of the law. While we must hope that the law will usually be an effective shield against torture in the first place, we have to accept that this will not always be so, and make every effort to ensure that it is designed to be an effective sword in the hands of victims and courts, whether for punishment of the torturer or compensation and medical treatment for the victims. An essential aspect of the law against torture, then, is that it should provide effective procedures for prevention and enforcement, otherwise the law is quite pointless.

Law's opinion of violence against the person

This is not the place to go into the historical context of torture, in particular those contexts where it has been a lawful activity in the hands of agents of the state, such as its use by the Greeks and Romans in gathering evidence or punishing wrongdoers, or its role in the civil and ecclesiastical courts of Europe in the Middle Ages. That is dealt with in Chapter 2. The focus of this chapter is on contemporary standards, particularly regarding developments based on international law since the end of the Second World War.

Violent acts by one person against another, falling short of taking life, can be described by everyday legal vocabulary in various ways, such as 'trespass against the person', 'battery', 'assault', 'grievous bodily harm', or even 'wounding in self-defence' and 'judicial corporal punishment'. Clearly, then, the laws of a state can view some violence as permissible, if not actually laudable.

Further, some violent acts against the person take place in circumstances which are governed by the special legal regime of the law of war, often referred to as international humanitarian law, where the law attempts to mitigate the excessive application of 'legal' violence against person or property. The role of this branch of law in combating torture is as important as that of international human rights law.

Consequently, any lawyer whose personal belief is that violence against the person is never desirable, and certainly never to be encouraged, will nevertheless concede that not all acts of extreme violence are prohibited by law, and that some acts of extreme violence may actually be justifiable in law; acts in self-defence are probably the best-known example.

This is an important point for human rights organizations dealing with torture, as states will often accept that a detainee has been subjected to physical or psychological pressure during, for example, the act of arrest, questioning or imprisonment. Given that torture is not justifiable under international law, such states will often attempt to justify the treatment as being within those international standards for the treatment of detainees which are justifiable.

Torture from a human rights perspective

Consequently, there are certainly four crucial aspects from the human rights perspective. First, to use the term 'torture' only in its proper legal sense under international human rights law. Second, to recognize *de facto* acts of torture or cruel, inhuman or degrading treatment or punishment whenever they occur, no matter what vocabulary a particular law might use in order to describe (or even mask) the activity. Third, to challenge the practice, wherever it occurs, with the full force of the laws at our disposal. Fourth, to be satisfied with nothing less than remedies which give the victims satisfactory redress, and measures which are designed to prevent further incidents, including measures designed to deter. Clearly, any punishment of the perpetrator should take place within the constraints of international human rights standards for the treatment and punishment of offenders (for example, capital punishment should not be an option in sentencing).

Definition of torture and cruel, inhuman or degrading treatment or punishment

Let us turn, then, to consider the definition of torture and its related concept of cruel, inhuman or degrading treatment or punishment, and to consider the extent of the law's reach into the behaviour of both the state and the private individual. The definition of torture must be distinguished from the application of that definition by relevant tribunals; the former will be dealt with immediately below, and the latter will be touched upon in the sections which outline the particular treaties and mechanisms created for supervision, interpretation and application of the law.

The most authoritative definition of torture in international human rights law is that contained in Article 1 of the UN Convention against Torture of 1984, as stated at the beginning of this chapter. The important points to note about the definition are that the pain or suffering must be *severe* and may be either *physical or mental*; the act must be *intentional*; it must involve direct or indirect participation of *public officials*; and it must have a *purpose*. Mental suffering entered the international standard for the first time with this definition.

Torture

The Convention against Torture of 1984 succeeded the 1975 Declaration

on Protection from Torture, and it is worth comparing the definition of
torture which each provides in its first article, given that the definition in
the Declaration was not finally accepted by the General Assembly for
inclusion in the Convention. In particular, the Convention does not
include the Declaration's definitional sentence that 'Torture constitutes an
aggravated and deliberate form of cruel, inhuman or degrading treatment
or punishment.' However, the Convention does highlight more
effectively the purposeful use of torture when inflicted as a means of
punishment for a third person's purported act, or for intimidating or
coercing a third person, or due to discrimination of any kind. It also
establishes state responsibility more clearly where 'consent or
acquiescence' can be shown.

Both instruments rely on the view that torture is an activity which has
an official purpose behind it, and in that sense is distinguishable from
treatment which is without a purpose but is nevertheless cruel, inhuman
or degrading. Beyond the particular stigma attached to a finding of
torture, it may be that the distinction is quite academic, given that each
mode of conduct is forbidden absolutely under international law.

The only other definition contained in international treaties is that in
the Inter-American Convention to Prevent and Punish Torture, which
also takes the purpose approach in defining torture. The definition here is
similar in that it covers physical and mental pain or suffering, and relies on
the role of public officials. However, it is a broader definition in that the
pain and suffering need not be 'severe' as in the UN treaty, but it is
narrower in that it does not explicitly refer to torture which is inflicted on
account of a third person. It is also more explicit in defining the mental
aspect of torture as being the use of methods intended to 'obliterate the
personality of the victim', or to 'diminish his . . . mental capacities', even
in the absence of physical pain or mental anguish.

Cruel, inhuman or degrading treatment or punishment

While the means of distinguishing torture from cruel, inhuman and
degrading treatment is largely settled at the Human Rights Committee
and the regional courts, neither instrument has provided a definition of
'cruel, inhuman or degrading treatment or punishment', and this
inevitably has led to some uncertainty as to where acceptable treatment
ends and cruel, inhuman and degrading treatment begins.

Lawful sanction

The UN Convention against Torture, in excluding 'lawful sanctions'
from the prohibition, opens up a potential loophole for governments, and
it is necessary to rely on separate overlapping standards in an attempt to

Definitions of torture

1975 UN Declaration on Protection from Torture, Article 1 (two parts):

1. *For the purpose of this Declaration, torture means any act by which severe pain or suffering, whether physical or mental, is intentionally inflicted by or at the instigation of a public official on a person for such purposes as obtaining from him or a third person information or confession, punishing him for an act he has committed, or intimidating him or other persons. It does not include pain or suffering arising only from, inherent in or incidental to, lawful sanctions to the extent consistent with the Standard Minimum Rules for the Treatment of Prisoners.*

2. *Torture constitutes an aggravated and deliberate form of cruel, inhuman or degrading treatment or punishment.*

1984 UN Convention against Torture, Article 1 (two parts):

1. *For the purposes of this Convention, the term 'torture' means any act by which severe pain and suffering, whether physical or mental, is intentionally inflicted on a person for such purposes as obtaining from him or a third person information or a confession, punishing him for an act he or a third person has committed or is suspected of having committed, or intimidating or coercing him or a third person, or for any reason based on discrimination of any kind, when such pain or suffering is inflicted by or at the instigation of or with the consent or acquiescence of a public official or other person acting in an official capacity. It does not include pain or suffering arising only from, inherent in or incidental to lawful sanctions.*

2. *This article is without prejudice to any international instrument or national legislation which does or may contain provisions of wider application.*

close it, such as the UN Standard Minimum Rules for the Treatment of Prisoners, or the UN Body of Principles for the Protection of All Persons under Any Form of Detention or Imprisonment, both of which contain standards and procedures for safeguarding detainees.

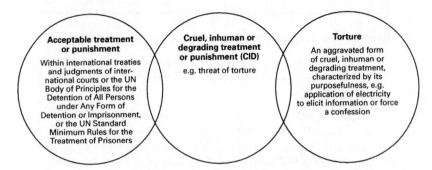

Figure 1.1. Three faces of treatment

The legal nature of declarations and treaties: are they legally binding?

Treaties are binding on the states which have become party to them, and may be relied upon by tribunals such as the International Court of Justice of the United Nations when settling international disputes. Declarations, such as the Universal Declaration of Human Rights, are merely declaratory, and possibly have some moral force, but have no legally binding force against states party to them, although they do provide evidence of the evolution of principles of general international law through being declaratory of existing legal norms. It has been argued that the Universal Declaration of Human Rights was a unique exception to the general rule, as it was born virtually directly from the UN Charter, but this is largely academic given the number of legally binding treaties which have superseded it and addressed the points at issue in far greater detail.

The modern law of human rights is based on the notion that some rights and freedoms are so essential to the lives of individuals that their governments should be under an obligation to respect them, and the

Some terms and definitions used in international law

Declaration: A general statement of principles that, while not necessarily legally binding, may have considerable authority

Convention/Covenant: A formal, legally binding treaty or agreement between sovereign states

Protocol: A formal, legally binding agreement between sovereign states that is normally a supplement to another treaty or agreement

Ratification/Accession: A decision by a sovereign state to adhere to a treaty or agreement and to be bound by its provisions

State Party: A country whose government has ratified or acceded to a treaty or agreement and is legally bound to follow its provisions

Signature: Expression by a sovereign state of its intention to refrain from acts that would defeat the object and purpose of a treaty or agreement, and at some future date to ratify or accede to the treaty

international community is assigned the role of ensuring compliance. Thus, treaty obligations have necessarily displaced the idea that states are allowed to do whatever they like to their own citizens so long as their activities remain inside their own borders. Indeed, in matters of human rights, there are no longer any legal grounds under international law for states attempting to invoke the doctrine of non-interference in their internal affairs.

Can the prohibition against torture ever be set aside?

It has always been accepted in law that not all human rights are absolute and inalienable, and that certain civil and political rights and freedoms may legitimately be suspended by states ('derogated from') at certain times; for example, freedom of movement during times of war, civil conflict or other national emergency. Article 4 of the International Covenant on Civil and Political Rights (ICCPR) explicitly allows for derogation from certain measures 'in time of public emergency which threatens the life of the nation'. Suspension of such rights is not to be undertaken lightly, and states will be called upon to justify their action in international fora.

However, certain human rights guarantees are considered so fundamental as to be absolute and non-derogable under any circumstances, and Article 4 of the ICCPR goes on to stipulate that there may not be derogation from certain of its provisions, including Article 7, which prohibits torture and cruel, inhuman or degrading treatment or punishment. Building on this, Article 2 of the UN Convention against Torture stipulates that 'No exceptional circumstances whatsoever, whether a state of war or a threat of war, internal political stability or any other public emergency, may be invoked as a justification of torture.'

Treaty obligations and the individual

There also continues to be some debate as to how far the scope of the concept of torture should extend in the direction of the relations between private individuals. For example, should treaty prohibitions against torture and cruel, inhuman or degrading treatment or punishment automatically bring condemnation of certain practices carried out by private citizens, such as female genital mutilation or harsh child discipline?

It is a fact of international law that treaties are binding on states rather than individuals, and therefore treaty definitions and procedures do not create obligations for private citizens. However, there is scope for considering to what extent governments should be held accountable for inaction in the face of behaviour which would amount to torture or cruel, inhuman or degrading treatment or punishment if carried out by a public official. In this regard, there is a useful theory of 'horizontal significance' of human rights, whereby governments not only have a duty to refrain from violating human rights, but also have a duty to protect private citizens from similar treatment by other private citizens.

Treaties and mechanisms which address torture

Through a multitude of international declarations and treaties, the United Nations and regional bodies in Africa, the Americas and Europe have set up some far-reaching standards of achievement and mechanisms for the protection and promotion of certain human rights and fundamental freedoms. The following sections will outline the main legal sources dealing with torture, with a snapshot of the mechanisms for enforcement or for provision of remedies.

Main United Nations treaties and mechanisms which address torture

The International Bill of Human Rights

The principles espoused by the 1948 Universal Declaration of Human Rights (UDHR) are given a more precise legal form in two covenants: the International Covenant on Civil and Political Rights (ICCPR) of 1966 (which entered into force in 1976), and the International Covenant on Economic, Social and Cultural Rights (ICESCR) of 1966 (which entered into force in 1976). These three 'instruments', plus their attached Optional Protocols, are known as the International Bill of Human Rights. The Covenants and Optional Protocols are binding on the states party to them.

Article 5 of the UDHR provides that 'No one shall be subjected to torture or to cruel, inhuman or degrading treatment or punishment', as does Article 7 of the ICCPR, except that the latter also provides that 'In particular, no one shall be subjected without his free consent to medical or scientific experimentation.'

The Human Rights Committee

The ICCPR established an independent Human Rights Committee (HRC) in Geneva (though it is resourced by the UN), composed of 18 independent human rights experts, to monitor compliance with the ICCPR by the states party. The ICCPR's First Optional Protocol established a procedure whereby individuals may submit complaints to the HRC that their rights under the Covenant have been violated, but this is binding only on those states which have become party to the First Optional Protocol (80 as of 1995, as against 129 party to the ICCPR itself).

The HRC meets in private and its views are not legally binding. However, the HRC will normally offer its opinion on a state's obligation, and may call for immediate steps to be taken, such as release from detention or provision of compensation for a victim. Since 1990, states have been asked to notify the HRC, within 180 days of receiving its opinion, of action taken, and the annual report of the HRC will publicize abuses in those states which fail to respond or to provide a remedy.

From early on, the HRC has applied a broad interpretation of Article 7, and has held that it protects not only persons arrested or imprisoned, but also children, pupils and patients in educational and medical institutions who are subjected to corporal punishment, including 'excessive chastisement' as an educative or disciplinary measure (General Comment 20 of 1992).

The HRC has also held in this General Comment that the granting of amnesties in respect of acts of torture is incompatible with states' duty to investigate such acts, guarantee freedom from them, and ensure they are not repeated. Neither can states deprive victims of an effective remedy, including compensation and such rehabilitation as is possible.

The HRC now works in a manner intended to be complementary to deliberations of the Committee against Torture, which was created by the Convention against Torture (see below).

UN Declaration on Protection from Torture, 1975

In 1975 the UN General Assembly adopted by consensus a Declaration on the Protection of All Persons from Being Subjected to Torture and Other Cruel, Inhuman or Degrading Treatment or Punishment. This provided evidence for the view that the prohibition of torture was an existing principle of international law.

UN Convention against Torture, 1984

The Convention against Torture superseded the Declaration on Prevention from Torture, and set the most authoritative international legal standard on the subject, particularly in that it adopted a wider definition of torture than previous definitions. For these reasons, it is worth closer inspection than other treaties.

The Convention, which came into force in 1987, prohibits torture in all circumstances, obliges states party to make torture a criminal offence under their own laws, and provides for universal jurisdiction over alleged torturers, including procedures for extradition. It also forbids the return of persons to countries where they would risk being tortured, insists that victims of torture are entitled to compensation and rehabilitation, and prohibits confessions or statements extracted under torture from being used as evidence in court.

The Committee against Torture

The Convention established a Committee against Torture (CAT) in Geneva, composed of 10 independent human rights experts elected by the states party. Subject to the consent of the relevant state, the CAT may examine reliable information which appears to indicate that torture is being practised systematically, and to undertake a confidential enquiry, possibly including a visit to the territory. Also, with a state's consent the CAT may hear complaints from individuals who claim to have been tortured in their country.

Unlike other committees, the CAT has the power to initiate its own investigation rather than await complaints, if it receives reliable information from any person or body indicating systematic torture; it cannot initiate an investigation into less severe forms of treatment or punishment. In considering cases, the CAT is prepared to draw upon the decisions in previous cases of the Human Rights Committee of the ICCPR, but it is not allowed to hear a case already examined through another international procedure.

Like those of the Human Rights Committee, the CAT's views are not legally binding. However, the CAT communicates its views on cases to the parties concerned and requests information 'in due course' on action taken. There is no formal sanction, but the CAT may publicize inaction, and will include its decisions in its annual report. For situations indicating systematic torture, states are asked to inform the CAT of action taken in response to its recommendations. However, this latter procedure is confidential, and the CAT may publish a summary account of the proceedings in the annual report only after undefined 'consultations' with the state concerned.

Optional supervisory mechanisms under the Convention against Torture

While the prohibition against torture is well-established, the Convention allows states to opt out of aspects of its supervisory and adjudication function.

For example, Article 28 of the Convention allows a state party to make a written declaration that it does not recognize the competence of the CAT to examine information indicating systematic use of torture. Of the 86 states which were party to the Convention by 1995, seven had made such a declaration (Afghanistan, Belarus, Bulgaria, China, Israel, Morocco and Ukraine).

Interestingly, there is a reverse procedure to this under Article 22 of the Convention, the article which establishes the right of individuals to complain directly to the CAT that they have been victims of a violation by the state. For a complaint by an individual to be received by the CAT, a state must already have made a separate written declaration that it recognizes the competence of the CAT to consider individual complaints. By 1995, there were consenting declarations by only 35 of the 86 states (note that 80 states have agreed to individual petition to the Human Rights Committee under the First Optional Protocol to the ICCPR).

Incorporation of the Convention against Torture into national laws

Article 4 of the Convention requires that torture be made an offence under the national criminal law of each state party, and that penalties be established consistent with the gravity of the offence. The offence is to include attempts to commit torture, and acts which amount to complicity or participation in torture. Many countries' constitutions stipulate that international treaties adopted by the state are binding, and to be incorporated automatically into national law, and that the courts should treat them as superior to previous lesser national standards. Other countries, such as the United Kingdom, require separate national legislation in order to incorporate the treaty.

In the UK, sections 134 to 138 of the Criminal Justice Act 1988 (CJA 1988) incorporate the Convention, but with a defence where the accused can show that he had 'lawful authority, justification or excuse for that conduct', including under the laws of the country where the conduct occurred. On conviction, the accused is liable to a penalty of life imprisonment.

States' implementation of their treaty obligations is reviewable by the CAT. Given the scope of the Convention, this goes beyond the review of traditional obligations relating to torture in other fora. For example, at its 1995 Session, the CAT queried the Netherlands on universal jurisdiction, and why it had not taken steps to investigate allegations against General Pinochet of Chile during his visit to the Netherlands the previous year.

Universal jurisdiction

When a crime under international law is subject to universal jurisdiction, any state which finds on its territory a person suspected of committing this crime may bring the suspect to trial, no matter where the crime occurred.

Draft optional protocol to the Convention against Torture

In 1992, the UN Commission on Human Rights decided to establish a working group to draft an optional protocol to the Convention against Torture. The protocol is to establish a mechanism whereby UN representatives may visit any place, in any state party to the protocol, where people who are deprived of their liberty by a public authority, or at its instigation, or with its consent or acquiescence, are held or may be held. The protocol is a preventive approach modelled on the 1987 European Convention for the Prevention of Torture (see below).

Special Rapporteur on torture

The Economic and Social Council of the UN (ECOSOC), established by the UN Charter, has itself established a number of functional commissions, including the Commission on Human Rights (UNCHR) in 1946, whose first task was to draw up the International Bill of Human

Rights. The UNCHR meets annually for six weeks to consider reports, proposals and recommendations, and may set up Working Groups or appoint Rapporteurs and Experts to assist its work. The Special Rapporteur on Torture is given the task of studying states' activities in this area of human rights and reporting annually, in his (or her) personal capacity, to the UNCHR. His recommendations may be taken up by the UNCHR and advanced in other fora. He does not have any formal connection with either the Human Rights Committee of the ICCPR or the Committee against Torture of the Convention against Torture.

Main regional treaties which address torture

American Convention on Human Rights, 1969

Following on from the American Declaration of the Rights and Duties of Man, itself merely a recommendation from a conference of American states in 1948 (but pre-dating the UN Declaration of Human Rights), the American Convention on Human Rights came into force in 1978. Article 5 provides that 'No one shall be subjected to torture or to cruel, inhuman or degrading treatment or punishment.' The Convention provides for a Commission on Human Rights and a Court of Human Rights, based in Costa Rica, for the promotion, supervision, interpretation, application and enforcement of the Convention. Individuals, groups of people and non-governmental bodies may lodge a complaint or a denunciation with the Commission regarding violation of the Convention by a state party (Article 44), provided that all domestic remedies have been exhausted (Article 46), and the particular state is agreeable to the Commission receiving complaints (Article 45).

The Convention is a treaty of the Organization of American States (OAS), an intergovernmental body comprising over 30 states from Latin America, the Caribbean and North America. The Commission on Human Rights actually came into existence as an autonomous body of the OAS in 1958, with the function of promoting respect for human rights, and therefore continues to retain its original function over all OAS states, as well as its jurisdiction under the American Declaration of 1948, whether or not states are party to the 1969 Convention. Notably, neither the USA nor Canada has become party to the Convention.

Inter-American Convention to Prevent and Punish Torture, 1985

The Inter-American Convention, which came into force in 1987, is a treaty of the OAS. Article 2 of the Convention defines torture more broadly than the phrase which appears in the American Convention on Human Rights of 1969. Cruel, inhuman or degrading treatment or punishment is not mentioned, let alone defined, in Article 2, but is referred to in the preamble as an 'offense against human dignity'. Article 6 provides that all acts of torture, and attempts to commit torture, are criminal offences which are to be punishable by severe penalties. Article 6 likewise demands effective measures by states to prevent and punish cruel, inhuman or degrading treatment or punishment. In this regard, Articles 12 and 14 introduce the requirement of universal jurisdiction for crimes of torture and cruel, inhuman or degrading treatment or punishment, to allow investigation and criminal proceedings in the courts of the state party, unless it proceeds to extradite the accused for proceedings to take place elsewhere.

Article 8 stipulates that cases may be submitted to relevant international fora once domestic remedies have been exhausted. Generally this will be the Inter-American Commission, which Article 17 acknowledges as responsible for supervising the introduction of measures to prevent and eliminate torture in member states of the OAS.

European Convention on Human Rights, 1950

The European Convention on Human Rights (ECHR) was founded in 1950 by the Council of Europe, an intergovernmental body then consisting of 14 states (now roughly 30 across Western and Eastern Europe), not to be confused with the European Union. The ECHR created two judicial bodies (the Court of Human Rights and the lesser Commission of Human Rights, based in Strasbourg) for the supervision, interpretation, application and enforcement of human rights within the states party to it. In case of a state not abiding by a ruling, the Committee of Ministers of the Council may be asked to decide on action to be taken.

Article 3 of the ECHR provides that 'No one shall be subjected to torture or to inhuman or degrading treatment or punishment', and people who feel that their rights have been violated in this regard by a state party can lodge a complaint with the Commission, provided that all domestic remedies have been exhausted (Article 26), and the particular state is agreeable to the Commission receiving complaints (Article 25).

The Commission has found torture in two cases (*Denmark et al.* v. *Greece* in 1969 and *Ireland* v. *UK* in 1976) but the Court has never found torture to have been practised (it overruled the Commission in the *Ireland* v. *UK* case in 1978).

European Convention for the Prevention of Torture and Inhuman or Degrading Treatment or Punishment, 1987

The European Convention was drafted by the Council of Europe, with full knowledge of the relevant prior UN instruments and their definitions and procedures. It acknowledges in the preamble its legal origins in Article 3 of the ECHR. The key distinctive feature of the European treaty on torture is that it is based on the idea of official visits to places under the control of public authorities where there are also detainees.

Article 1 of the Convention creates a special body, the European Committee for the Prevention of Torture and Inhuman or Degrading Treatment or Punishment (known as the ECPT). The ECPT aims at practical 'prevention', as distinct from the legal 'solution' aimed at by the European Court and Commission.

African Charter on Human and Peoples' Rights, 1981

The African Charter (Banjul Charter), a treaty adopted by the Organization of African Unity (OAU) in 1981, came into force in 1986. Covering a wider range of rights than the European or American conventions, it deals more broadly with economic, social, cultural and peoples' (or community) rights. Article 5 provides that 'All forms of exploitation and degradation of man particularly slavery, slave trade, torture, cruel, inhuman or degrading treatment or punishment shall be prohibited.'

Supervision of the Charter is through the African Commission on Human and Peoples' Rights, which has a general supervisory function and jurisdiction to hear inter-state complaints alleging violation of the Charter (Articles 48 and 49), as well as discretion to receive complaints from individuals, groups or non-governmental bodies (Article 55), provided domestic remedies, if any, have been exhausted (Articles 50 and 56). If no amicable solution can be brokered, or there is evidence of serious or massive violations, the Commission forwards a report, and recommendation if appropriate, to the Assembly of Heads of State and Government of the OAU for consideration.

Towards an International Criminal Court

Following the Second World War, and the experience of the Nuremberg and Tokyo war crimes tribunals, in 1948 the UN General Assembly asked the International Law Commission (ILC) to study the feasibility of creating a permanent International Criminal Court (ICC). The court would be able to hold individuals personally responsible if they had planned, ordered or committed gross crimes under international law, regardless of whether the crimes were committed in war or peace (war crimes, crimes against humanity, or human rights violations), or whether the perpetrators were leaders or subordinates, civilians or members of military, paramilitary or police forces. An ICC would complement prosecutions in national courts, acting when states were unwilling or unable to bring perpetrators to justice.

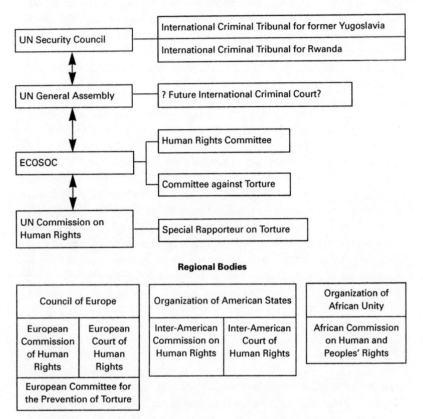

Figure 1.2. Main United Nations and regional bodies that deal with torture

Between 1950 and 1990 the Cold War paralysed most of the ILC's work on the ICC, but over the past five years, fuelled by atrocities in former Yugoslavia and Rwanda, there has been renewed progress. In 1993 the UN Security Council set up an *ad hoc* International Criminal Tribunal to hear cases involving serious violations of international humanitarian law, also called the law of war (see below), in the former Yugoslavia, followed by a similar *ad hoc* tribunal on Rwanda in 1994.

In 1994 the ILC submitted the final draft statute to the UN General Assembly, and an *ad hoc* committee of experts was set up to review the draft. In December 1995 the General Assembly decided to convene a Preparatory Committee in 1996, from March 25 to April 12 and again from August 12 to 30, to provide it with a draft statute by September.

The General Assembly will then decide whether to convene an international conference of states' diplomats in 1997, to finalize a treaty establishing the Court. The Court might then operate by 1998.

> '*In the aftermath of the horrors of the Second World War, and the trials by the victorious powers of the Nazi leaders at Nuremberg, it was generally anticipated by the international community that a new era had begun – an era in which the human rights of all citizens in all countries of the world would be universally respected. It was not to be. The past five decades have witnessed some of the gravest violations of humanitarian law. Those responsible have too frequently escaped trial and punishment by national courts. . . . There was no mechanism devised by the international community for establishing the guilt of the perpetrators and for punishing them. Justice was denied to the millions of victims of murders, disappearances, rape and torture.*'
>
> Prosecutor Richard Goldstone, opening the first hearing of the International Criminal Tribunal for the Former Yugoslavia, November 1994

Torture of soldiers or civilians in time of war

The laws of war, also termed international humanitarian law (IHL), apply to situations of armed conflict. Both human rights law and IHL share core non-derogable rights, such as the protection from torture, but the detailed provisions of IHL generally provide victims of armed conflict with more clearly stated protections than are available through human rights provisions. The greatest convergence between these two fields of international law is to be found in situations of purely internal armed conflict.

The principal sources of IHL are the Hague Conventions of 1899 and 1907, the four 1949 Geneva Conventions (two aimed at preventing wartime violations of human rights, the third designed to prevent mistreatment of prisoners of war, and the other designed to prevent mistreatment of civilians in time of war) and their two Additional Protocols of 1977 (the first dealing with the protection of victims of international armed conflicts, the second with the protection of victims of non-international armed conflicts), and the customary laws of war.

All four 1949 Geneva Conventions contain the same Article 3, which

17

prohibits 'mutilation, cruel treatment and torture . . . humiliating and degrading treatment' (the latter includes rape and other sexual abuse) during *internal* armed conflict. All parties to the conflict, state or otherwise, are bound by Common Article 3.

'War crimes' generally refer to crimes during *international* armed conflict which amount to 'grave breaches' of the 1949 Geneva Conventions and Additional Protocol I, or violation of the customary rules of armed conflict. Such acts include torture, inhuman treatment, and wilfully causing great suffering or serious injury to body or health (which includes rape and other sexual abuse).

Crimes against humanity, including genocide, may be classified as part of IHL, but, since such crimes may be committed in peacetime as well as in armed conflict, it is more useful to treat them as part of human rights law.

A safe rule of thumb on torture is to use the standard of protection under human rights law, because its absolute prohibition against torture, being non-derogable, applies as much in war as in peacetime.

Crimes under international law

Crimes under international law represent a consensus by states that certain acts are so abhorrent that the individuals responsible must be brought to justice even if the acts are not crimes under national laws. Crimes under international law include crimes against peace, serious violations of humanitarian law and crimes against humanity, including genocide.

Torture by non-state entities

Although international treaties are binding only on states party to them, organizations like Amnesty International hold that armed groups not having statehood, such as insurgents or other paramilitary groups, should be expected to adhere to the same standards of treatment of detainees as the governments they are opposing. The closest set of international standards relating to human rights abuses by non-governmental entities appears to be Common Article 3 of the Geneva Conventions which, as explained above, prohibits torture and is binding on all parties to an armed conflict, whether international or internal.

Crimes against humanity

Crimes against humanity are inhumane acts which involve widespread or systematic violations aimed at a civilian population. These crimes include:

*   genocide;
*   extrajudicial executions (unlawful and deliberate killings carried out by order of a government or with its acquiescence);
*   'disappearances' (the taking into custody of a person by agents of a state, when the authorities deny that the victim is in custody, thus concealing his or her whereabouts and fate);
*   torture (including rape);
*   slavery, deportation or forcible transfer, arbitrary imprisonment and persecution on political, racial or religious grounds;

if these acts are conducted on a mass or systematic scale.

Codes of professional ethics

Various codes of conduct for law enforcement officials, and for medical professionals and lawyers, provide rules on how these professions should act in order to prevent human rights violations, and what they should do when faced with violations of the rights of prisoners.

For example, the Code of Conduct for Law Enforcement Officials, adopted by the UN General Assembly in 1979, states that 'No law enforcement official may inflict, instigate or tolerate any act of torture or other cruel, inhuman or degrading treatment or punishment' (Article 5). Also, the 1979 Declaration on the Police of the Parliamentary Assembly of the Council of Europe, 1979, provides that 'Summary executions, torture and other forms of inhuman or degrading treatment or punishment remain prohibited in all circumstances' (Article 3).

For medical personnel, the 1975 Declaration of Tokyo of the World Medical Association states that 'The doctor shall not countenance, condone or participate in the practice of torture or other forms of cruel, inhuman or degrading procedures . . .' (Article 1), and the Principles of Medical Ethics, adopted by the UN General Assembly in 1982, provides: 'It is a gross contravention of medical ethics as well as an offence . . . to engage, actively or passively, in acts which constitute participation in, complicity in, incitement to or attempts to commit torture or other cruel, inhuman or degrading treatment or punishment' (Principle 2).

For lawyers, the 1990 UN Basic Principles on the Role of Lawyers provides that 'Lawyers, in protecting the rights of their clients and in promoting the cause of justice, shall seek to uphold human rights and fundamental freedoms recognised by national and international law' (Article 14). Also, the 1985 UN Basic Principles on the Independence of the Judiciary provides that 'The principle of the independence of the judiciary entitles and requires the judiciary to ensure that judicial proceedings are conducted fairly and that the rights of the parties are respected' (Article 6).

A stronger exhortation for lawyers has been proposed by Amnesty International and the International Commission of Jurists in a Draft Principles for a Code of Ethics for Lawyers, Relevant to Torture and Other Cruel, Inhuman or Degrading Treatment or Punishment: 'A defence lawyer representing a person who alleges that he has been subjected to torture or other cruel, inhuman or degrading treatment or punishment while detained by any authority and for any cause should be prepared to raise such allegations before the competent authorities, unless instructed to the contrary by his client' (Article 1).

CHAPTER 2

Torture through the Ages

Duncan Forrest

When one looks at the history of torture, it becomes necessary to separate cruel, inhuman punishment from systematic, judicial torture being used as a means of obtaining information or confession (Peters, 1985). Obviously, there has always been an urge to make punishment or execution as painful and prolonged as possible, and there are many accounts in the earliest writings of punishment and execution which were often very cruel, for example the accounts of scourging or stoning to death. However, there are no records in the biblical texts of torture being used to extract confessions. Judicial torture has been recorded, though, in ancient Chinese, Egyptian and Assyrian texts.

When we come to the ancient Greek and Roman civilizations, we find that the testimony of slaves in criminal cases was not relied on unless extracted under torture. It was described by Demosthenes as the most reliable method of obtaining a confession. Only late in the Roman Empire was torture freely applied to freemen, though its use was attacked by Cicero. Seneca condemned it as likely to lead to false confessions. St Paul was excused from flogging on the grounds that he was a Roman citizen (Acts 22:22–29).

There is no evidence of the use of torture in the early Christian Church. Heretics were changed by moral persuasion, and, in the case of failure, excommunication or 'infamy' was a sufficient punishment. St Bernard of Clairvaux stated: 'Faith must be the result of conviction and should not be imposed by force.' By the eleventh century, however, heretics were being subjected to torture to force them to recant, or executed by cruel means such as burning at the stake if they failed to do so.

Later in the Middle Ages in Europe, as trial by ordeal or conflict fell into disrepute, torture began to be used in secular courts as well as religious ones. The practice of using torture to obtain strong proof of guilt or a confession became widespread and was more and more relied upon in criminal trials. It was also used after conviction to obtain the names of fellow-conspirators. The practice was most widespread in Italy and

Germany where sophisticated techniques were developed, including the method known in Germany as *Aufziehen*, or elsewhere as *strappado* ('the queen of torments'), a precursor of present-day 'Palestinian hanging', the method of suspending the victim by the wrists tied behind the back. The rack and thumbscrew were also used (Peters, 1985). In England, where the presumption of innocence, and the fact that it was the jury rather than the judge who decided the verdict, made it less often applicable, torture was not so frequently employed. However, when a suspect refused to plead either 'guilty' or 'not guilty', *peigne forte et dure* was employed. In this, the suspect was made to lie on the floor and increasingly heavy weights were piled on the chest, sometimes to the point of death. It was not abolished until 1772. Torture was also used in England in the sixteenth and seventeenth centuries for 'exorbitant offences not subject to the ordinary course of law' – these were under the sanction of the Privy Council or the Star Chamber. The 'rack' in the Tower of London (Figure 2.1) was last used in 1640, 'an engine of the State, not of Law'.

The Papal Inquisition, which flourished especially in Italy, France and Spain from the twelfth and thirteenth centuries, did not always rely on torture to secure recantation. Many inquisitors were, by the standards of the day, humane intellectuals who attempted to determine proof of heresy by questioning. Sentences were to penance, imprisonment or death. Later in the Middle Ages, it was the Spanish Inquisition that became dominant. It was directed mainly against the residual Moorish communities and the large Jewish population. Methods of interrogation and torture were codified. The Grand Inquisitor of Aragon's *Directorium* described the five stages of 'softening up' before torture. The most infamous name in this context is that of Tomás de Torquemada, who wrote *Articles of the Inquisition* on the investigation of crimes, not only of heresy, and described suitable methods of torture (Sabatini, 1924; Swain, 1965). In the early sixteenth century inquisitors were established in the New World and in the Netherlands, and it was only in the early nineteenth century that the Inquisition was finally suppressed.

The Enlightenment in Europe saw the rise of humanitarian opinions as well as the relaxation of the previously rigid social structures. There was condemnation by such figures as Voltaire of torture as a means of extracting information. Jeremy Bentham believed that torture often produced the opposite effect from the intended one. Torture had been outlawed in most European countries by the end of the eighteenth century, beginning with Sweden in 1734, and this came to be one yardstick of a country's 'civilization' – though its abolition may have owed as much to the perception that torture was inefficient as to the belief that it was immoral (Peters, 1985, p. 76).

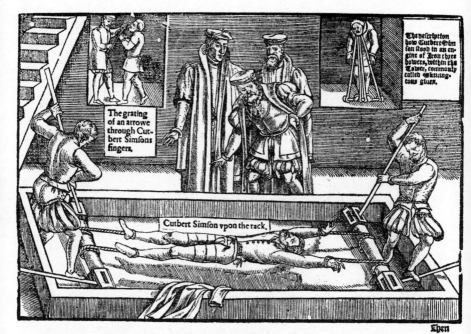

Figure 2.1. Cuthbert Simson on the rack in the Tower of London
Source: *Book of Martyrs* by John Foxe (1610) (by permission of the British Library)

The use of torture in other parts of the world is surveyed by Peters (1985, pp. 92–7). Islamic law, the *shari'a*, does not recognize the validity of a confession obtained by coercion, and in spite of the frequent use of torture in the Ottoman Empire, whose laws permitted it, it was consistently opposed by the *muftis*, who insisted that if the torturer killed his victim he was obliged to pay blood money.

China and Japan conducted cruel punishments and forms of execution. Under the Japanese criminal procedure of *dangoku*, confession was required and, if not forthcoming, the judge was empowered to have the defendant beaten on the back and buttocks with sticks. From the tenth to the sixteenth centuries, the use of torture was broadened and *gomon* (suspension by the wrists tied behind the back) and *romon* were used in serious crime. The latter included whipping on the back, being made to kneel on triangles of wood with stone weights on the knees or being made to sit cross-legged with a rope tied tightly round the ankles and neck.

Torture is first recorded in medieval Russia around 1100. Princes used torture widely, though peasants were legally entitled to compensation. The weakness of the monarchy in the first half of the seventeenth century meant that torture could be used widely by the provincial governors regardless of central laws. The legal code of Alexis I in 1649 distinguished political from other crimes, and torture was a matter of routine, including the use of *strappado*, the knout for beating, and fire. However, in 1801, the young Alexander I declared torture abolished.

In the USA since Independence, the Fifth Amendment of the Constitution has prohibited self-incrimination, thus ruling out the need for torture to obtain a confession. In spite of this, the 'third degree' was routinely used until the 1930s (see page 37).

In many African, Asian and South American colonies, the European rulers continued to turn a blind eye to torture long after its abolition in their homelands.

By the second half of the nineteenth century there was a move towards international agreement on human rights as exemplified by the first Geneva Convention of 1864 and its later revisions, and the establishment of the International Red Cross (Peters, 1985, p. 141). However, in spite of this, torture in its most florid form returned to Europe in the twentieth century, partly because of the separation in many countries of politics from law with subordination of the latter and the supremacy of the state over the individual. Through much of its 70-year history the Soviet Union continued the unabated use of torture, employing increasingly sophisticated methods.

In Germany the process was propelled forward by the concept of the *Untermenschen*, too far below humanity to deserve pity. With a slow, deliberate build-up of public opinion it became possible first to sterilize and then kill (by 'euthanasia') the mentally retarded and, later, non-Aryans, and in doing so to torture and mutilate them before death without restraint. The medical profession played a sinister and prominent role in this process (Burleigh, 1994). It was the revelation of the Holocaust that led to a wave of revulsion throughout the civilized world and prompted the setting up of the United Nations and the formulating of ethical codes. In spite of this, many countries, notably the Soviet Union, carried on with gross abuses, ignoring the new codes, and surviving Nazis passed on their techniques to many oppressive regimes, particularly in South America but also in Greece and Spain.

Most surprising and disturbing was the involvement of France in the 1950s, so soon after the country's suffering under Nazi occupation, in the widespread use of torture in Indo-China and the Algerian revolt of 1954. When rumours of torture reaching mainland France were finally confirmed, the practice was repudiated by the great mass of the population and eventually contributed to Algerian independence in 1962 (Peters, 1985, pp. 132–5).

Less obvious forms of torture have probably never gone away, but disguised under such euphemisms as the 'third degree' or 'moderate physical pressure' have continued to be used in most countries, psychological means as much as physical ones being used to achieve the same ends.

The argument against torture is not entirely won. Voices are still heard justifying it in utilitarian terms, as in the case postulated by Michael Levin, professor of philosophy in New York, who wrote:

> *There are situations in which it is not merely permissible but morally mandatory to torture. Suppose a terrorist has hidden an atomic bomb on Manhattan Island which will detonate at noon on July 4 unless . . . [here follow the usual demands for money and release of his friends from jail]. Suppose, further, that he is caught at 10 am that fateful day, but – preferring death to failure – won't disclose where the bomb is. . . . If the only way to save those lives is to subject the terrorist to the most excruciating possible pain, what grounds can there be for not doing so? I suggest there are none. . . . Torture only the obviously guilty, and only for the sake of saving innocents, and the line between Us and Them will remain clear. There is little danger that the Western democracies will lose their way if they choose to inflict pain as one way of preserving order.*

> Levin (1992)

This argument seems persuasive until we consider further possibilities:

> *A man admits to planting a bomb: torture will save lives. A man is suspected of planting a bomb: torture will reveal it. A man has a friend suspected of planting a bomb: torture will lead us to the suspect. A man has dangerous opinions and might be thinking of planting a bomb: torture will reveal his plans. A man knows the one with dangerous opinions and probably thinks the same: torture will lead us to still others. A man has refused to say where a suspect is: torture will intimidate others who might do the same.*

> Amnesty International USA (1985), quoted in Plachta (1989)

References and further reading

Amnesty International USA (1985) *Torture by Governments*, p. 39. New York: Amnesty International USA.

Burleigh, M. (1994) *Death and Deliverance: 'Euthanasia' in Germany, 1900–1945.* Cambridge: Cambridge University Press.

Davis, R.H.C. (1972) *A History of Medieval Europe.* London: Longman.

Levin, M. (1992) 'The case for torture'. *Newsweek*, 7 June, p. 13.

Peters, E. (1985) *Torture.* Oxford: Blackwell.

Plachta, L.R. (1989) 'Torture and health care professionals'. *New York State Journal of Medicine*, March, 143–8.

Sabatini, R. (1924) *Torquemada and the Spanish Inquisition.* London: Stanley Paul.

Swain, J. (1965) *A History of Torture.* London: Tandem Books.

Trevelyan, G.M. (1973) *History of England.* London: Longman.

CHAPTER 3

Amnesty International's Anti-torture Campaigns

Eric Prokosch

[T]orture has virtually become a worldwide phenomenon . . . the torturing of citizens regardless of sex, age, or state of health in an effort to retain political power is a practice encouraged by some governments and tolerated by others in an increasingly large number of countries.

In short, what for the last two or three hundred years has been no more than an historical curiosity, has suddenly developed a life of its own and become a social cancer. To describe torture as a malignant growth on the body politic is, however, not simply to employ a figure of speech but to announce a program of action to remove it.

Amnesty International (1973, p. 7)

These words from the preface to the first edition of Amnesty International's *Report on Torture* summed up what the organization wanted to tell the world in its first Campaign for the Abolition of Torture in 1972. Contrary to popular belief, torture was widespread. The practice was abominable. It must be stopped.

Amnesty International's first Campaign for the Abolition of Torture (1972–3)

Launched on Human Rights Day, 10 December 1972, with a statement from Seán MacBride, Chairman of Amnesty International's International Executive Committee, that torture must be made 'as unthinkable as slavery', the Campaign for the Abolition of Torture soon became known in the Amnesty International (AI) movement by the acronym CAT. Its approach can be summed up in three words: document, denounce, mobilize.

The documentation of torture was achieved through the research effort leading to the publication of the *Report on Torture* in 1973. Documentation was itself a form of denunciation, because the cruelty of torture was so evident from the descriptions, as in this testimony from a 1972 Turkish case which opened the report:

> *they attached wires to my fingers and toes and passed electric current through my body. . . . After a while, they disconnected the wire from my finger and connected it to my ear. They immediately gave a high dose of electricity. My whole body and head shook in a terrible way. My front teeth started breaking. At the same time my torturers would hold a mirror to my face and say: 'Look what is happening to your lovely green eyes. Soon you will not be able to see at all. You will lose your mind. You see, you have already started bleeding in your mouth.'*

Amnesty International (1973, pp. 9–10)

Mobilization began with the circulation of a petition to the United Nations (UN) and reached its climax at the International Conference for the Abolition of Torture, held in Paris on 10–11 December 1973. The conference adopted numerous recommendations, including the establishment within AI of a central clearing-house for information on specific incidents of torture; the formulation of codes of ethics for medical, police and military personnel; the strengthening of international and national laws on the protection against torture; and the setting up of a register of health professionals to undertake missions to investigate allegations of torture in specific countries.

AI's campaign led to a heightened exposure of the problem of torture in the world news media and a heightened interest among governments, professionals and the public. Several of the events during the campaign and in the years following may be mentioned:

- *AI's petition was presented to the UN with more than a million signatures from all over the world calling on the UN General Assembly 'to outlaw immediately the torture of prisoners throughout the world'. On 2 November 1973 the General Assembly adopted resolution 3059 (XXVIII) expressing grave concern that 'torture is still practised in various parts of the world' and urging all governments to become parties to international instruments containing provisions relating to the prohibition of torture.*

- *Two years later the General Assembly adopted the Declaration on the Protection of All Persons from Being Subjected to Torture and Other Cruel, Inhuman or Degrading Treatment or Punishment (Declaration against Torture). This important document constituted the first international agreement as to the measures which all governments should take to stop torture, including the obligation of states to conduct impartial investigations of complaints and reports of torture, the obligation to bring torturers to justice and the obligation not to use statements extracted under torture in court proceedings.*

- *The issue of torture was discussed in various professions with a view to adopting codes of ethics aimed at stopping it. In October 1975 the World Medical Association adopted the Declaration of Tokyo stating that the doctor shall not 'countenance, condone or participate in the practice of torture', shall not provide 'premises, instruments, substances or knowledge' to facilitate the practice of torture and shall not be present at any procedure during which torture is used or threatened. In December 1979 the UN General Assembly adopted the Code of Conduct for Law Enforcement Officials; its Article 5 states that 'no law enforcement official may inflict, instigate or tolerate any act of torture or other cruel, inhuman or degrading treatment or punishment' and that no law enforcement official may invoke superior orders or exceptional circumstances as a justification of torture. In 1982 the General Assembly adopted the Principles of Medical Ethics relevant to the Role of Health Personnel, particularly Physicians, in the Protection of Prisoners and Detainees against Torture and Other Cruel, Inhuman or Degrading Treatment or Punishment, Principle 2 of which states: 'It is a gross contravention of medical ethics, as well as an offence under applicable international instruments, for health personnel, particularly physicians, to engage, actively or passively, in acts which constitute participation in, complicity in, incitement to or attempts to commit torture or other cruel, inhuman or degrading treatment or punishment.'*

- *The work of the medical profession against torture also took the form of the establishment of centres in different countries for the rehabilitation of torture victims. Further support for victims was provided in December 1981 when the UN General Assembly established the United Nations Voluntary Fund for the Victims of Torture. As of October 1983 some 10 governments had contributed a total of US$518,300 to the fund.*

- *Doctors were also making an increasingly important contribution to the documentation of torture by participating in missions sent by AI and other organizations to investigate allegations of torture. They examined people who claimed to have been tortured and wrote reports stating whether the symptoms observed were consistent with the allegations.*

- *New international non-governmental organizations (NGOs) were formed with the specific aim of combating torture. In France, for example, members of different Christian denominations formed Action des Chrétiens pour l'Abolition de la Torture (ACAT, Action of Christians for the*

Abolition of Torture), an organization aimed at encouraging international action against torture from a religious perspective. National branches were set up in other countries, and an international federation was formed later. The Comité Suisse contre la Torture (Swiss Committee against Torture), known today as the Association pour la Prévention de la Torture (Association for the Prevention of Torture), was formed in 1977 with the specific task of promoting the establishment of an international system of visits of inspection of places of detention as a safeguard against torture. The idea became a reality in 1987 when the Committee of Ministers of the Council of Europe adopted the European Convention for the Prevention of Torture and Inhuman or Degrading Treatment or Punishment, as described below.

While international NGOs multiplied, national human rights organizations increasingly took on the all-important task of combating torture in their own countries, often under extremely repressive conditions. In the 1970s such organizations included the Vicaría de la Solidaridad in Chile and the Free Legal Assistance Group (FLAG) of the Civil Liberties Union of the Philippines. These organizations carried out such activities as documenting cases of torture; filing petitions in the courts on behalf of torture victims; and making information on torture known to international NGOs and intergovernmental organizations which could take action from outside the country.

AI's own work for human rights also developed significantly in the aftermath of the campaign. A campaign department was set up in the organization's International Secretariat and began its full operation in spring 1974. One of its early tasks was to organize actions against torture in specific countries. For this purpose, the organization in 1974 devised an Urgent Action network of AI members around the world to launch immediate appeals on behalf of named individuals under threat of torture. (The operation of the network was extended in 1976 to include death penalty cases and other urgent matters.) In early 1976 AI conducted an intense worldwide publicity campaign against the practice of torture in Uruguay, a precursor of the campaigns against human rights violations in specific countries which would become a large part of the organization's most visible work. Also in 1976, AI published a booklet to promote the elaboration of codes of professional ethics against torture. In 1977 the organization published *Torture in Greece: The First Torturers' Trial 1975* as an example of how the ordinary criminal process could be used after the end of a repressive regime to establish the facts of torture and punish some of the torturers.

The second Campaign for the Abolition of Torture (1984–5)

Despite the campaigning and the achievements, torture did not go away. In the early 1980s there was a strong feeling in the AI movement that a new campaign was needed. When the organization began planning its second Campaign for the Abolition of Torture (CAT II), there was a sense that a new approach must be found. Documentation, denunciation and mobilization would be elements of the campaign, but there must be something more.

The UN Declaration against Torture provided the answer. Through this document, the world's governments had agreed on the measures which must be taken to stop torture. AI's task would be to make these measures known and to call on governments to implement them.

A second, closely related element was furnished by AI's then Secretary General, Thomas Hammarberg, in a speech at an international colloquium on torture in Geneva in April 1983. He said:

> *We have talked about this phenomenon as a 'social cancer'. That expression, however, should not be interpreted to mean that torture is socially inevitable. In fact, it is clear that the existence in a country of torture or not is, to a very large extent, a question of political will.*
>
> *Some governments have referred to 'tradition', 'violent temperament' or the like, when explaining why torture has not been stopped in their countries. The fact is that those governments who decisively attempted to stop torture have succeeded . . .*
>
> *This focus on governments should not be lost. Certainly, there is a need to approach the individual police officer, military official, doctor or judge, but such actions should not be allowed to blur the fact that governments are responsible – politically, legally, morally. The basic international agreements on human rights are directed towards governments.*
>
> **Swiss Committee against Torture (1984, p. 56)**

This theme was taken up in the report produced for the campaign, *Torture in the Eighties*. As stated in the introduction to the report:

> *Torture can be stopped. The international legal framework for its abolition exists, as do the investigative methods to verify and expose it. What is lacking is the political will of governments to stop torturing people. It is as simple and as difficult as that. AI hopes that this new report about torture as well as its continuing campaign against torture will contribute to creating this political will so that our generation can banish torture from the earth.*
>
> **Amnesty International (1984, p. 4)**

The report and the campaign were built around these themes. *Torture in the Eighties* opened with the example of a colonial governor in Cyprus who took action to stop torture by going in person to visit an interrogation centre where torture had allegedly been used. The report analysed various preventive safeguards and remedial measures and gave details on how they should be applied. One chapter comprised case studies from two places, Northern Ireland and Brazil, where improvements had been achieved through public pressure and national and international scrutiny. The entries in the report describing torture in specific countries included information on the extent to which the available safeguards and remedies met the standards set forth in the UN Declaration.

For use in the campaign, AI devised a 12-point Program for the Prevention of Torture (see page 198). This document contained measures from the UN Declaration which AI considered especially important, as well as other measures which had not yet been incorporated in UN instruments, such as the limitation of detention incommunicado. Point 1 emphasized the responsibility of governments to stop torture by stating that 'The highest authorities of every country should demonstrate their total opposition to torture' and that they should 'make clear to all law enforcement personnel that torture will not be tolerated under any circumstances.' The 12-point Program was intended to be both a programme of action and a yardstick of governmental behaviour: the preambulary paragraphs called on all governments to implement the programme and stated that in AI's view, 'the implementation of these measures is a positive indication of a government's commitment to abolish torture and to work for its abolition worldwide'.

CAT II was meant to move on from denunciation to prevention, and the campaign focused on prevention. In the first months of the campaign, AI members around the world wrote letters to officials in some 33 countries where torture and ill-treatment were serious problems, urging them to take appropriate measures as set forth in the UN Declaration and the 12-point Program. Members of the public and AI members were invited to send appeals on a series of strongly documented cases of torture; in most cases the authorities were urged, among other things, to set up official investigations into the allegations, as required under the Declaration. These activities served to promote the measures in the Declaration by making them known to the AI movement and the public. As in so many of its other activities, AI, an NGO, was trying to make human rights a reality by promoting measures which governments had agreed to internationally but failed to implement at home.

Several months after the launching of the campaign in April 1984, the Prime Minister of Spain wrote to AI acknowledging the receipt of 'the ten thousand letters from your members' sent on behalf of a prisoner featured in one of the appeal cases and announcing that urgent legal proceedings were being instituted in the case. But many governments did not reply at all. The pressure on specific countries and cases largely failed to have a perceptible impact. Many governments which used or tolerated torture seemed inured to the international outrage generated by the campaign and to the embarrassment which the exposure of torture must have caused.

As with CAT I, there were important developments during the campaign and in its aftermath. During the campaign, AI sections in different countries had urged their governments to give high priority to the adoption of a UN convention against torture and to work for the establishment of a UN procedure for intervention on cases of torture in all countries, analogous to other UN human rights procedures, in particular the UN Working Group on Enforced or Involuntary Disappearances, established in 1980, and the UN Special Rapporteur on Summary or Arbitrary Executions, appointed in 1982.

During the first year of the campaign the text of a convention against torture was forwarded by the UN Commission on Human Rights through the UN Economic and Social Council to the UN General Assembly, where it was adopted on Human Rights Day, 10 December 1984, as the Convention against Torture and Other Cruel, Inhuman or Degrading Treatment or Punishment ('Convention against Torture'). The General Assembly had originally requested the Commission on Human Rights to draft such a convention in 1977, and an open-ended working group of the Commission had been developing the draft from 1979 to 1984. AI's campaign helped provide the impetus to move from drafting to final adoption.

In the following year, 1985, the UN Commission on Human Rights decided to recommend the appointment of a Special Rapporteur on Torture; the recommendation was adopted by consensus at the UN Economic and Social Council the same year. Unlike the Convention against Torture and the Committee against Torture established under it, which can deal with torture only in states party to the Convention, the Special Rapporteur can send appeals to all countries in urgent cases where torture is alleged and can report on allegations of torture in any country.

These developments were followed by the adoption in December 1985 of the Inter-American Convention to Prevent and Punish Torture, and in 1987 of the European Convention for the Prevention of Torture and Inhuman or Degrading Treatment or Punishment. The latter treaty provides for the establishment of a European Committee for the Prevention of Torture and Inhuman or Degrading Treatment or

Punishment, which carries out visits of inspection to places of detention in states party to the Convention. Together with the UN Committee against Torture and the UN Special Rapporteur on Torture, there are now three international or regional intergovernmental procedures or 'mechanisms' which have been created specifically to deal with the problem of torture.

Since the end of CAT II, more international NGOs have been set up to combat torture. More domestic human rights organizations in more countries have taken action against torture, and their work has grown more sophisticated. The medical work on behalf of torture victims has grown: centres for the rehabilitation of torture victims now exist in all continents.

Challenges in the fight against torture today

As the 25th anniversary of the launching of AI's original Campaign for the Abolition of Torture draws near, the problem of torture may seem much as it did when the organization was planning its second campaign in the early 1980s. Much has been achieved, yet torture persists. Is it not time once again to seek a new approach?

Because torture is secret, its incidence can never be determined precisely, and trends are hard to establish with certainty. In an initial attempt to see whether any trends could be found, I made in 1994 a comparison of the information in the country entries of the *Report on Torture* (Amnesty International, 1975), the second edition of which covered the four and a half years from 1970 to mid-1974, *Torture in the Eighties* (Amnesty International, 1984), covering the three and a half years from 1980 to mid-1983, and the *Amnesty International Report 1994* (Amnesty International, 1994), covering the year 1993. Over the 24 years spanned by these three reports, there had been a substantial increase in the number of countries from which AI received reports of torture or ill-treatment; this was due in part to the substantial growth in the research capacity of the organization since the 1970s. According to my estimate, however, the number of countries where torture is an especially serious problem seems to have remained approximately the same over the 24-year period, between around 40 and 45. Although it is not possible on the basis of the facts available to say that the geographical extent of torture has widened since 1970, it is safe to say at the very least it is not decreasing.

Historically, increases in torture have been associated with periods of political repression, when the authorities detain their alleged opponents and torture them, while decreases in torture have been associated with political relaxation and the removal of repressive regimes, when the secret police apparatus may be dismantled and the reasons for repression no longer exist. Such correlations between torture and political repression were documented in *Torture in the Eighties* and are likely to continue. What is especially alarming today, however, is the increase in examples of torture, including rape, associated with armed conflict. According to my analysis, of the 14 countries where torture now appears to be an especially serious problem (on the basis of entries in the *Amnesty International Report 1994*) but was not so indicated in *Torture in the Eighties*, such increases in torture can be associated primarily with political repression in six countries, primarily with outbreaks of armed conflict in seven countries, and with other factors in one country. During the earlier period, by contrast, out of 10 countries where factors associated with increases in torture were identified in *Torture in the Eighties*, these factors were of the nature of political repression in eight countries, while in two countries increases in torture were associated with outbreaks of armed conflict (guerrilla and counter-guerrilla fighting in one country, an invasion in another).

Torture is not an inevitable companion of armed conflict, but it may happen that when an armed conflict breaks out, the security forces torture their captives for such purposes as obtaining information on the opposing forces, or for intimidation. It is possible, too, that military forces use unlawful force against civilian prisoners when carrying out policing functions for which they are ill-trained. Armed conflict can also engender an overall increase in violence in a country, and an increase in torture and ill-treatment may be a consequence. With armed conflicts so prevalent today, the prognosis must be for more torture.

The task of combating torture in the often chaotic situation of an armed conflict may require new approaches from those human rights organizations whose main experience has been with a more stable political order, albeit a repressive one. New techniques of research and new forms of action may be needed.

Whereas torture was seen in the early 1980s as a feature of political repression, with prisoners of conscience and other political prisoners as victims, since the 1980s AI and other organizations have paid increasing attention to the problem of the torture and ill-treatment of common criminal suspects and social 'underdogs' such as immigrants and members of racial minorities. This is an area deserving far more attention. The task of building up work in this area is likely to involve a series of challenges including obtaining information, involving local NGOs, finding practical ways to strengthen the prevention of torture in the police and prison warden professions, and building public support. Human rights organizations may find that public sympathy for their work against torture declines when the victims are common criminal suspects and social 'underdogs'. The news media may be less interested in publicizing or investigating such cases than in covering political cases. Torture and ill-treatment may be regarded by the public as normal practices, and the victims as people who deserve what they get at the hands of the police. Human rights organizations will need to find ways to overcome these attitudes and uphold the notion that human rights apply to all of us, the 'worst' as well as the 'best'.

The links between torture in political cases and the torture of common criminal suspects also need to be recognized. When a period of political repression comes to an end, the torture of common criminal suspects may continue; and security forces accustomed to torturing common criminal suspects may easily adapt their methods to political prisoners if political repression increases.

These are some of today's challenges facing the worldwide movement to eradicate torture from the face of the earth.

References

Amnesty International (1973) *Report on Torture*. London: Duckworth.

Amnesty International (1975) *Report on Torture*, revised edition. London: Duckworth.

Amnesty International (1984) *Torture in the Eighties*. London: Amnesty International Publications.

Amnesty International (1994) *Amnesty International Report 1994*. London : Amnesty International Publications.

Swiss Committee against Torture (1984) *How to Combat Torture: Report on the International Colloquium on How to Combat Torture*, Geneva, 28–29 April 1983. Geneva: Swiss Committee against Torture.

CHAPTER 4

Custodial Confinement, Interrogation and Coerced Confessions

Gisli Gudjonsson

Introduction

The term 'interrogation' is typically used to describe the interviewing of 'suspects' for the purpose of obtaining a confession. In many cases a confession helps to secure the prosecution and conviction of the suspect and it is sometimes the most important evidence the police have when the case goes to court (Gudjonsson, 1992a). Interrogation and confessions can also occur in contexts other than criminal investigations. For example, interrogation and the extraction of confessions do sometimes occur for political purposes, as well illustrated by the 'show' trials and public confessions in Stalin's Russia (Beck and Godin, 1951) and the interrogation of American military personnel and Western civilians by the Chinese communists (Schein *et al.*, 1961).

The purpose of this chapter is to discuss some salient aspects of police interrogation, custodial confinement and coerced confessions.

Interrogation techniques

The police are responsible for investigating criminal offences, and this includes having to interrogate suspects in order to establish the facts and help secure a conviction. Suspects are often unforthcoming with the information that the police want and may be deliberately deceptive in order to avoid the long-term consequences of making a confession (Gudjonsson, 1992a). The police may try to overcome the suspect's resistance and deception by becoming persuasive in their interrogation methods.

The extent to which the police are legally allowed to use psychological pressure and manipulation varies from country to country. For example, police officers in the USA are currently allowed to use psychological manipulation and deception in order to obtain a confession (Leo, 1992). In contrast, deliberately lying to suspects in order to obtain a confession is generally not allowed by courts in England and Wales (Gudjonsson, 1994a).

Leo (1992) gives a fascinating account of the changing nature of police interrogation in the USA. Prior to the 1930s confessions were commonly obtained by a variety of interrogation methods which focused on physical pain, discomfort and torture. Leo identifies six forms of such 'third degree' methods: 'brute physical force'; 'physical torture'; 'deniable physical and psychological coercion' (e.g. the use of a rubber hose, which did not leave obvious marks, to beat a confession out of suspects); 'incommunicado interrogation' (i.e. isolating the suspect from lawyers, family and friends); 'physical duress' (including food and sleep deprivation); and 'threats of harm'.

According to Leo, the use of these 'third degree' methods began to decline in the 1930s and by the 1980s interrogation methods which relied on physical coercion were replaced by more psychologically oriented approaches that employed deception, trickery and manipulation. Many police interrogation manuals have been produced to illustrate these 'modern' techniques of interrogation. Undoubtedly, the most authoritative and influential manual is *Criminal Interrogation and Confessions* by Inbau *et al.* (1986), the original edition, by Inbau and Reid, having been published many years previously in 1962. Inbau *et al.* give the reader information about the state of the art of interrogation as practised in the USA. The 'nine steps' discussed by these authors can be broadly classified into two different approaches, which can be used in combination. The first approach focuses on providing the suspect with various face-saving excuses for having committed the offence and minimizing the consequences. The other approach focuses primarily on exaggerating the weight of evidence that the police have against the suspect, such as claiming that they have forensic or eyewitness evidence to link the suspect with the offence. I have discussed the ethical problems and dangers associated with the use of these techniques (Gudjonsson, 1992a). I consider these techniques to be potentially psychologically coercive.

Some of the techniques recommended by Inbau and his colleagues have been used by interrogators in England, but their use is declining (Irving and McKenzie, 1989; Baldwin, 1993). The main reason for this change is the introduction of the Police and Criminal Evidence Act (PACE) in 1986 and recent legal judgments where confession evidence was excluded on the basis that it was obtained by oppressive and unfair means and thereby rendered unreliable (Gudjonsson, 1994a; Williamson, 1994).

I discuss the methods used by the Israeli General Security Service to extract a confession from a suspected Palestinian terrorist in Gudjonsson (1995). Here the emphasis was on the custodial features of the confinement, including painful body position, sleep deprivation, hooding and isolation from 'outsiders', rather than on the interrogation techniques used (Landau Commission Report, 1989). These methods are similar to those used by police interrogators in Northern Ireland over 20 years ago (Shallice, 1974). These methods have now long been outlawed in Northern Ireland (though reports of ill-treatment persisted in the 1980s) and custodial confinement is subject to independent scrutiny (Blom-Cooper, 1993). Undoubtedly, these and other similar methods are used and legally sanctioned in many countries throughout the world. They do not constitute humane treatment of detainees and are akin to torture, where the primary aim is deliberately to inflict physical and psychological pain for the instrumental purpose of breaking down detainees' will to resist making a confession. It is naive to think that confessions obtained under such conditions are truly voluntary. Clearly they are not, and the legal criteria used to judge voluntariness and 'free will' are adjusted to suit the purposes of a given legal system. The legal criteria in a given society represent the nature and extent of the pressure and coercion that are openly sanctioned to break down the suspects' resistance (Gudjonsson, 1995).

The English law on confession evidence

Prior to the introduction of the Police and Criminal Evidence Act 1984, and its Codes of Practice (Home Office, 1985, 1991), the admissibility of confession evidence in England and Wales was determined by the Judges' Rules and Administrative Directions of the Police (Home Office, 1978). According to the Royal Commission on Criminal Procedure Report,

> The presumption behind the Judges' Rules is that the circumstances of police interviewing are of their very nature coercive, that this can affect the freedom of choice and judgment of the suspect (and his ability to exercise his right of silence), and that in consequence the reliability (the truth) of statements made in custody has to be most rigorously tested.

(Philips, 1981, pp. 91–2)

Here the legal arguments concerning admissibility of confessions focused on the concept of 'voluntariness'. That is, the statement made by the suspect had to be voluntary, in the sense that it had not been obtained from him or her by 'fear of prejudice', 'hope of advantage', or by 'oppression'. These are imprecise concepts and the criteria for determining them have never been properly clarified. However, it is clear that the concept of voluntariness, as used in the Judges' Rules, focused on those behaviours of interviewing officers that had to be prohibited, which involved threats, inducements and oppression.

The work of Irving and Hilgendorf (1980) and the Royal Commission on Criminal Procedure (Philips, 1981) highlighted the discrepancy between the legal and psychological interpretation of the concepts of voluntariness and reliability. In law, a confession found to be involuntary was by definition also unreliable. In psychological terms, this was not inevitably the case. In addition, the legal criteria for determining voluntariness were not necessarily the same as the psychological criteria. For this and other reasons, the Royal Commission on Criminal Procedure had reservations about retaining the voluntariness rule.

With the implementation of PACE, the concept of 'voluntariness' was replaced by the concept of 'reliability'. That is, confessions are excluded if they are obtained by methods or in conditions which are likely to render them 'unreliable'. Under separate legal headings, confessions can also be excluded if they are found to have been obtained by 'oppression' of the person confessing, as well as if their admissibility into evidence is considered 'unfair'. In England and Wales, confessions are very rarely excluded on the basis of 'oppression'; the two recent exceptions include the case of the 'Cardiff Three' (Tan, 1992) and that of George Heron (Pithers, 1993). Most cases are excluded on the basis of unreliability and unfairness (Gudjonsson, 1992a, 1992b). The current legal position does not address the issue of whether or not the confession is true. Instead, it focuses on the circumstances and nature of the detention and police interview as well as on the individual vulnerabilities of the suspect. Therefore, a confession is sometimes excluded even when it is known or believed to be true (Criminal Appeal Report, 1991). In this respect, English law is similar to American law, although the latter still relies on the legal concepts of 'voluntariness' and 'free will' rather than specifically on 'oppression', 'unreliability' and 'unfairness' to determine the legal issues of admissibility (Gudjonsson, 1992b). The law is different in Scotland and Northern Ireland.

How interrogation can go wrong

I have illustrated a number of ways in which interrogations go 'wrong' (Gudjonsson, 1994a). This happens when:

- *the account obtained by the police is incomplete, misleading, unreliable, or false;*

- *when the circumstances and nature of interviewing are such as to render the statement obtained inadmissible in a court of law;*

- *when justice miscarries on flawed confession evidence, thereby undermining public confidence in the criminal justice system;*

- *when interviewees react to interrogation with hostility and anger, because they believe that they have been manipulated, tricked, or pressured into giving a statement that was obtained by unfair means;*

- *when the police interviewer fails to obtain evidence from interviewees because they feel unduly pressured by the police and refuse to co-operate; and*

- *when interviewees suffer from 'post-traumatic stress disorder' (PTSD) as a result of being interviewed by the police.*

Each of these six areas raises some fundamental issues about the adverse consequences of police interrogation. Two of these areas, which relate to the unreliability of confession evidence and PTSD, are discussed in this chapter.

Unreliable evidence and psychological vulnerability

The reliability or credibility of evidence is determined by many factors which can be classified into two groups: motivational factors and vulnerability factors. Motivational factors refer to the willingness of the person to tell the truth, whereas vulnerability factors are concerned with the characteristics of the person which may, under certain circumstances, render his or her account of events unreliable.

Suspects are often reluctant to tell the truth when they are interrogated by the police because of the fear of the consequences of incriminating themselves (Gudjonsson, 1992a). The police may suspect that they are lying and place them under pressure to give a truthful account of events. This is commonly done by the police confronting the suspect with his or her alleged lies. Problems arise when suspicions that the suspect is lying are unfounded, and police pressure him or her to agree with an account that is misleading or false.

A number of different vulnerability factors may render a person's account unreliable during an interrogation (Gudjonsson, 1992a, 1992b, 1993). In Gudjonsson (1994b), I classified these vulnerable people into three categories: first, suspects who suffer from mental disorder at the time of the interrogation; second, suspects who suffer from an abnormal mental state during the custodial confinement and interrogation, such as severe anxiety, a phobic reaction to the confinement, bereavement, or drug withdrawal, which may impair their ability to cope satisfactorily with the interrogation; and third, suspects with personality characteristics, such as undue suggestibility or compliance, that may make them tend to give unreliable information when they are asked leading questions, placed under pressure, or manipulated psychologically.

There is very little information available about the psychological characteristics and vulnerability of persons detained at police stations for questioning. In a recent study by Gudjonsson *et al.* (1993) for the Royal Commission on Criminal Justice, which reported in 1993, 164 suspects were formally assessed psychologically whilst detained for interviewing at two police stations in south-east England, namely those at Peckham and Orpington. The psychological variables assessed included the suspects' mental state, intellectual functioning, reading ability, anxiety (trait and state), interrogative suggestibility and their understanding of their legal rights.

The findings of the study were as follows. First, the mean IQ score of the sample was only 82 (range 61–131). The performance of some of the detainees may have been impaired as a result of the circumstances in which the assessment took place (that is, a police station where they were waiting to be interviewed by the police). However, their mental state did not appear to be significantly related to their IQ scores (Gudjonsson *et al.*, 1994). This indicates that the police commonly interview detainees who are of low intelligence. Second, the intellectual limitations of many of the detainees were not obvious from a brief interview with them. Many appeared to be able to cover up their intellectual deficits and other mental problems so that these would not have become apparent without psychological testing and a clinical interview. Third, the police identified all the most mentally disabled detainees and provided them with the required legal protection. The police did, however, have problems identifying those suffering from mild or borderline learning disabilities (also known as 'mental handicap' and 'mental retardation') as well as those whom the researchers diagnosed as suffering from depressive illness. Fourth, only a small proportion (7 per cent) of the subjects were diagnosed as suffering from mental illness, although many were in a state of severe anxiety.

Retracted and false confessions

Inbau *et al.* (1986) state: 'Most confessed criminal offenders will subsequently deny their guilt and allege that they either did not confess or else were forced or induced to do so by physical abuse, threats or promise of leniency' (p. 176).

Retracting a previously made confession is very common in England and the USA, and it is naive to think that most such retractions represent genuine false confessions. However, Inbau and his colleagues do not consider the possibility that suspects could possibly confess to crimes they did not commit. They even suggest that 'none of the steps is apt to make an innocent person confess and all the steps are legally as well as morally justifiable' (p. 78). This is a misguided statement to make, considering the very manipulative and coercive nature of their interviewing techniques. There is ample evidence that the types of techniques recommended by Inbau and his colleagues do sometimes result in a false confession (see Gudjonsson (1992a) for a review, and also Ofshe (1989), Gudjonsson and MacKeith (1994), and Gudjonsson (1995)). What is not known is how often false confessions occur during interrogation.

False confessions generally arise from a combination of factors, rather than from a single cause (Gudjonsson, 1992a, 1992c). In addition, there are three psychologically distinct types of false confession (Kassin and Wrightsman, 1985; Wrightsman and Kassin, 1993), which tend to be associated with different vulnerability factors (Gudjonsson, 1992a, 1992d, 1993). The psychological characteristics of the detainee, and his or her mental state, interact with a number of factors, including the nature, seriousness, and circumstances of the alleged offence, as well as custodial factors such as the length of detention, and the type and nature of the interrogation.

It is important to remember that psychological vulnerabilities, such as low intelligence, heightened suggestibility and compliance, and inability to cope with interrogative pressure, do not invariably result in misleading or false information being obtained. Vulnerabilities indicate that under certain circumstances, suspects may give a confession which cannot be relied upon and special caution is therefore required when eliciting information from them. Even when vulnerabilities are marked, they do not invariably or necessarily result in an unreliable statement being obtained.

In Gudjonsson (1992c), I recommended various ways of reducing the 'risk' of false confession happening, which focuses on educational, psychological and judicial levels of approach at the pre-trial, trial and post-conviction stages. The emphasis is on *reducing* the 'risk', since it is unrealistic to expect that false confessions can ever be eliminated altogether. The motivations behind false confessions are often highly complex and some are internally generated (Gudjonsson, 1992a; Sigurdsson and Gudjonsson, 1995).

Post-traumatic stress disorder

There have been several studies into the psychological effects of torture, for example, those of Başoğlu et al. (1994), Daly (1980) and Gonsalves et al. (1993), which show that many survivors suffer from post-traumatic stress disorder (PTSD). No similar research appears to have been conducted into the psychological effects of police arrest, confinement and interrogation. However, a study of the interviewing methods of the British police in Northern Ireland in the early 1970s indicated that some may have suffered from PTSD as a result of their ordeal (Shallice, 1974). Similarly, Hinkle (1961) argues that harsh interrogation techniques can cause serious mental disturbance in some suspects.

Being arrested, detained and interrogated can be a very stressful experience. We found that about 20 per cent of suspects detained for a police interview scored abnormally high on the Spielberger State Anxiety Inventory (Gudjonsson et al., 1993). Furthermore, a clinical interview indicated that about one-third of the sample were in an abnormal mental state which might have interfered with their ability to cope with the interrogation.

The extent to which some individuals may be traumatized by being arrested, detained and interrogated, and the long-term sequelae of the experience, are unknown. MacKeith and I discuss two cases where suspects had been traumatized by being arrested by the police and interrogated (Gudjonsson and MacKeith, 1982). However, it is often difficult to separate the individual effects of the arrest, confinement and interrogation. The humiliation of being arrested and detained may be sufficient to cause PTSD in vulnerable individuals. This can be illustrated by two cases seen by me. Both individuals, a man and a woman, were perfectionistic and their identity was very much associated with being honest and respected. Neither person was charged with any offences by the police, but they were arrested and kept in custody for a number of hours before their innocence could be established. The feeling of shock and humiliation associated with the arrest and confinement resulted in persistent symptoms which were consistent with PTSD. In other cases it has been the police interrogation itself which resulted in PTSD. For example, two alibi witnesses to a major crime were pressured and threatened by the police in an attempt to make them alter their evidence, which they resisted doing. Both subsequently experienced major problems with intrusive thoughts and other symptoms of PTSD concerning the police interrogation, which lasted for several years before they sought treatment.

Conclusions

Confessions made during interrogation often form an important part of the evidence presented in court, although there are great differences in the methods used by police forces in different countries to extract confessions from suspects. The criteria for admissibility of such evidence in court and what is legally sanctioned also vary from country to country.

The rights and protection of persons detained at police stations in England have markedly improved in recent years. This will not by itself eliminate the risk of false confession, because it is doubtful whether the risk of false confessions can ever be eliminated. False confessions form a part of a complicated social process and occur for a variety of reasons and motives.

References

Baldwin, J. (1993) 'Police interviewing techniques: establishing truth or proof?' *British Journal of Criminology* 33, 325–52.

Başoğlu, M., Paker, M., Paker, O., Ozmen, E., Marks, I., Incesu, C., Sahin, D. and Sarimurat, N. (1994) 'Psychological effects of torture: a comparison of tortured with non-tortured political activists in Turkey'. *American Journal of Psychiatry* 151, 76–81.

Beck, F. and Godin, W. (1951) *Russian Purge and the Extraction of Confession*. London: Hurst & Blackett.

Blom-Cooper, L. (1993) *First Annual Report of the Independent Commissioner for the Holding Centres*. Submitted to the Secretary of State for Northern Ireland, 31 January 1994.

Criminal Appeal Report (1991) *Court of Appeal Judgment in the Case of Cherie McGovern*, Criminal Appeal Report 92, pp. 228–35.

Daly, R.J. (1980) 'Compensation and rehabilitation of victims of torture'. *Danish Medical Bulletin* 27, 245–8.

Gonsalves, C.J., Torres, T.A., Fischman, Y., Ross, J. and Vargas, M.O. (1993) 'The theory of torture and the treatment of its survivors: an intervention model'. *Journal of Traumatic Stress* 6, 351–65.

Gudjonsson, G.H. (1992a) *The Psychology of Interrogations, Confessions, and Testimony*. Chichester: John Wiley & Sons.

Gudjonsson, G.H. (1992b) 'The admissibility of expert psychological and psychiatric evidence in England and Wales'. *Criminal Behaviour and Mental Health* 2, 245–52.

Gudjonsson, G.H. (1992c) 'The psychology of false confession and ways to improve the system'. *Expert Evidence* 1, 49–53.

Gudjonsson, G.H. (1992d) 'The psychology of false confessions'. *New Law Journal* 142, 1277–8.

Gudjonsson, G.H. (1993) 'Confession evidence, psychological vulnerability and expert testimony'. *Journal of Community and Applied Social Psychology* 3, 117–29.

Gudjonsson, G.H. (1994a) 'Investigative interviewing: recent developments and some fundamental issues'. *International Review of Psychiatry* 6, 237–45.

Gudjonsson, G.H. (1994b) 'Psychological vulnerability: suspects at risk'. In D. Morgan and G. Stephenson (eds), *Suspicion and Silence: The Right to Silence in Criminal Investigation*, pp. 91–106. London: Blackstone Press.

Gudjonsson, G.H. (1995) 'Alleged false confession, voluntariness and "free will": testifying against the Israeli General Security Service (GSS)'. *Criminal Behaviour and Mental Health* 5, 95–105.

Gudjonsson, G.H. and MacKeith, J.A.C. (1982) 'False confessions: psychological effects of interrogation. A discussion paper'. In A. Trankell (ed.), *Reconstructing the Past: The Role of Psychologists in Criminal Trials*, pp. 253–69. Deventer, The Netherlands: Kluwer.

Gudjonsson, G.H. and MacKeith, J.A.C. (1994) 'Learning disability and PACE protection during investigative interviewing: a video recorded false confession of double murder'. *Journal of Forensic Psychiatry* 5, 35–49.

Gudjonsson, G., Clare, I., Rutter, S. and Pearse, J. (1993) *Persons at Risk during Interviews in Police Custody: The Identification of Vulnerabilities.* Royal Commission on Criminal Justice. London: HMSO.

Gudjonsson, G., Clare, I. and Rutter, S. (1994) 'Psychological characteristics of suspects interviewed at police stations: a factor-analytic study'. *Journal of Forensic Psychiatry* 5, 517–25.

Hinkle, L. (1961) 'The physiological state of the interrogation subject as it affects brain function'. In A.D. Biderman and H. Zimmer (eds), *The Manipulation of Human Behavior*, pp. 19–50. New York: John Wiley & Sons.

Home Office (1978) *Judges' Rules and Administrative Directions to the Police.* Police Circular No. 89/1978. London: Home Office.

Home Office (1985) *Police and Criminal Evidence Act 1984 (s. 66). Codes of Practice.* London: HMSO.

Home Office (1991) *Police and Criminal Evidence Act 1984 (s. 66). Codes of Practice,* revised edition. London: HMSO.

Inbau, F.E., Reid, J.E. and Buckley, J.P. (1986) *Criminal Interrogation and Confessions,* 3rd edition. Baltimore: Williams & Wilkins.

Irving, B. and Hilgendorf, L. (1980) *Interrogation: The Psychological Approach.* Research Studies No. 1. London: HMSO.

Irving, B. and McKenzie, I.K. (1989) *Police Interrogation: The Effects of the Police and Criminal Evidence Act.* London: Police Foundation of Great Britain.

Kassin, S.M. and Wrightsman, L.S. (1985) 'Confession evidence'. In S.M. Kassin and L.S. Wrightsman (eds), *The Psychology of Evidence and Trial Procedures*, pp. 67–94. London: Sage.

Landau Commission Report (1989) *Israel Law Review* 23, 146–88.

Leo, R.A. (1992) 'From coercion to deception: the changing nature of police interrogation in America'. *Crime, Law and Social Change* 18, 35–59.

Ofshe, R. (1989) 'Coerced confessions: the logic of seemingly irrational action'. *Cultic Studies Journal* 6, 1–15.

Philips, C. (1981) *Royal Commission on Criminal Procedure Report.* Cmnd 8092. London: HMSO.

Pithers, M. (1993) 'Uproar greets acquittal in Nikki Allen case'. *Independent,* 22 November, p. 17.

Royal Commission on Criminal Justice Report (1993). Cm 2263. London: HMSO.

Schein, E.H., Schneier, I. and Barker, C.H. (1961) *Coercive Persuasion: A Socio-psychological Analysis of the 'Brainwashing' of American Civilian Prisoners by the Chinese Communists.* New York: W.W. Norton.

Shallice, T. (1974) 'The Ulster depth interrogation techniques and their relation to sensory deprivation research'. *Cognition* 1, 385–405.

Sigurdsson, J. and Gudjonsson, G.H. (1995) 'The psychological characteristics of "false confessors": a study among Icelandic prison inmates and juvenile offenders'. *Personality and Individual Differences,* in press.

Tan, Y.H. (1992) 'Confessions from hostile interviews inadmissible'. Law report, *Independent,* 17 December, p. 28.

Williamson, T.M. (1994) 'Reflections on current practice'. In D. Morgan and G. Stephenson (eds), *Suspicion and Silence: The Rights to Silence in Criminal Investigations,* pp. 107–16. London: Blackstone Press.

Wrightsman, L.S. and Kassin, S.M. (1993) *Confessions in the Courtroom.* London: Sage.

CHAPTER 5

Torture Worldwide

Mike Jempson

Introduction

This chapter is a catalogue of depravity. No amount of explanation or political analysis can justify the gross abuses of human rights illustrated in the graphic accounts of torture that follow. None is offered.

All the information has been culled from the painstaking reports prepared by Amnesty International researchers over the past 10 years, mostly the last five. In some cases people have risked their lives to inform the 'outside world' of what is happening in the torture chambers of the jails, the police stations and the rural areas of their country.

All the evidence lends force to the argument that anyone could become a victim of torture anywhere in the world simply by being in the wrong place at the wrong time. Dissent and non-conformity is not always a determining factor in defining those most likely to be tortured, but torture itself is always an abuse of power.

The terror of torture

The terror of torture is not confined to the individual victim. It could be argued that one of the major purposes of subjecting a detainee to violence is to coerce others into at least tacit support for those wielding power in the torture chamber, whether they represent an elected government, a military regime, a dictatorship or a guerrilla army. The knowledge that torture or death awaits those apprehended by agents of the state is a tried and tested method of cowing others. Reports and rumours of the violence conducted behind closed doors serve as a warning to others that their compliance is demanded by the authorities. The world may have been the intended audience when 12 members of a judicial commission investigating human rights abuses in the Magdalena Medio region of Colombia were assassinated by soldiers and paramilitaries in 1989 (Figure 5.1), but more often the message is for domestic consumption. Not content with torturing, burning alive and then shooting 11 peasant

Figure 5.1. Colombia: members of a judicial board of inquiry investigating killings and 'disappearances' in 1989 were ambushed and shot dead by a paramilitary 'death squad'. A paramilitary leader was imprisoned for his part in the assassination, a rare example of perpetrators being brought to justice.

farmers, all members of the same family (see Figure 8.1, p. 123) near Ilarguta in June 1990, Colombian soldiers dressed the bodies in army uniforms and daubed 'ELN' on their hats (indicating membership of the left-wing National Liberation Army). 'I hope God can forgive the army . . . they have left 48 orphans, seven widows and two unsupported mothers,' said the mother of one of the victims when the soldiers were eventually acquitted of the crime. Once again the authorities were demonstrating the impunity granted to those executing official policy – the annihilation of support for the guerrillas.

To frighten villagers in the Delta region of Ayeyarwady Division into co-operating with them, military authorities in Myanmar (Burma) singled out community leaders and church elders for extrajudicial execution during operations against the paramilitary Karen National Union (KNU) in 1991:

'During the fighting many people fled from their villages. But when . . . they tried to return to home, the government troops accused them of helping the KNU guerrillas. Two men I know were killed at this time. Ta

Tay Lay, who was aged around 40 . . . and another man aged around 20, Sa May Taw . . . Both were farmers and Sa May Taw was a member of the NLD . . . They were both beaten repeatedly with clubs and interrogated. All the bones in their arms and legs were broken. The troops then cut their stomachs with knives and put salt in the wounds. The troops then called out to the villagers: "Look what happens to people who help the Karen rebels."'

The military authorities in Papua New Guinea resorted to similar tactics to intimidate any inhabitants of Bougainville Island who were minded to support the Bougainville Revolutionary Army. In one incident in December 1992, soldiers hacked the arms and legs of Taitus Kungkei, a young man who had been shot and killed during a skirmish with the military. They stood guard over his corpse, which was left outside one of the government-controlled 'care centres' into which villagers had been resettled. Relatives could see the mutilated body but were too afraid to collect it for burial.

Sometimes the 'target audience' for such assertions of power can be very specific. Viorel Baciu is not a Jehovah's Witness, but his father is, and had been harassed by the police in Romania on a number of occasions. Viorel was arrested on charges of murder, rape and assault on 24 October 1988, one day after the murder and three days *before* the rape was reported. During interrogation Viorel was taunted about his father's religious beliefs and accused of being a Jehovah's Witness himself. In December, after spitting and coughing up blood, he was permitted hospital treatment for the injuries he received. Viorel 'confessed' under torture, and though he later retracted the confession and demanded an investigation into his ill-treatment, he was sentenced to 17 years. A prisoner who shared a cell with him at Botosani Prison commented:

'The boy is young and strong, but I think that some people want him exterminated. In the way he's tortured and ill-treated, he won't last long. I saw him with his hands crushed, flowing with blood, bound in chains and beaten, many days in a row.'

Often jailers are concerned in this way to stamp their authority over the inmates. In memory of those killed in Tiananmen Square in 1989, Li Jie, a political prisoner from Jilin Province in China tried to stage a one-day hunger strike on 4 June 1991 at the Lingyuan No. 2 Labour-Reform Detachment, Liaoning Province. To deter others from joining him he was dragged before the assembled prisoners, stripped and held down by common criminals while a senior officer repeatedly held a 50,000-volt electric baton to the inside of his legs. Guards then applied electric batons to his head, neck, shoulders, armpits, chest, stomach and fingers until he went into spasms and lost consciousness.

AI has had numerous reports from Pakistan of the public humiliation of prisoners. Men and women have been made to strip in front of family members of the opposite sex; women have been paraded naked in public; and two Christian women were made to strip and dance naked by police officers at Jaya Bagga police station in Lahore.

Ghulam Mustafa Soomro was strung up to the ceiling at a military camp and beaten repeatedly. Several days later he was taken to the local marketplace in Sita Road, Sindh Province, and stripped along with four other prisoners. Their moustaches and hair were then shaved off and all five were tied to ropes and dragged through the town by an army pick-up truck for two hours. Soomro had been arrested on 7 December 1992 when Paramilitary Rangers from the Kurram Militia searched the house of the government-appointed contractor without a warrant. The origin of the raid appears to have been a dispute involving neighbours. They found two licensed weapons registered in the name of his brother, a senior vice-president of the opposition Pakistan People's Party (PPP).

Such brutal coercion may not encourage respect for the law but it is an effective statement that the population should fear the consequences of upsetting the status quo. In July 1991 a large contingent of police herded villagers from Hadmatiya in Rajasthan, India, into a field and opened fire, injuring 35. The women were then stripped and beaten. It appears that this punishment was intended to deter them from asserting their planting rights against the wishes of a local landowner.

In April 1992 journalists covering the elections in Sanghar constituency, Sindh Province, Pakistan, were harassed by uniformed officials from the provincial government. Four journalists who had been investigating allegations of ballot-rigging were set upon, dragged from their car and badly beaten. Mohammad Ishaq Tunio and Shafi Bejoro were taken off in a jeep, where the beatings continued. Their attackers threatened to kill them and dump their bodies in a canal. On their release they were advised not to make formal complaints or publish incriminating photographs.

In Afghanistan later in the same month Javed Asanahi, a high school teacher accused of looting in the capital, Kabul, was blindfolded and tied to a lamppost. Although he protested innocence of any crime, his captors announced to assembled journalists and photographers that he would be tried by an Islamic court for alleged looting and sentenced to have his hands 'surgically removed'.

Among the many assaults upon Roma people (Gypsies) in Romania was a horrific attack on a house in Hadareni on 20 September 1993. Two brothers, Rupa Lucian and Pardalian Lăcătuş, had taken shelter after being

Figure 5.2. Bulgaria: Roma families have been subjected to illegal detention, torture and ill-treatment by agents of the state and members of the public, just because their lifestyle is viewed with suspicion.

involved in a fight with seven or eight local men in which Lucian Lăcătuş reportedly killed Ghetan Craciun by stabbing him in the throat with a knife. Over 400 Romanians and ethnic Hungarians from Hadareni and other nearby villages surrounded the house and set fire to it. When the brothers tried to escape, one of them was arrested and handcuffed by police, but the crowd took away both men, who were then subjected to a 'lynch mob' beating. They died on the way to hospital. Meanwhile their brother-in-law, Mircea Zoltan, was burned to death in the house, apparently too frightened to risk escaping. The mob moved on to set fire to another 13 houses. The rest of the 170-strong Roma community spent the following week living in nearby fields.

Roma have also regularly suffered public abuse, torture and racist attacks in Bulgaria. Attacks on such 'politically unacceptable' minorities appear to have been at least sanctioned if not actually orchestrated by agents of the state (Figure 5.2). When a group of 20 men, women and children were caught gathering grapes illegally in the village of Glushnik in November 1993, they were locked in a pigsty overnight and villagers were summoned by church bells next morning. Ilia Slavov Banov was hauled from the sty and the crowd beat him with their fists and sticks. He and two others eventually managed to escape, but the rest were taken out one by one and tied to a fence, their hands behind their backs. They included two children aged 11 and 14, and five women who were also threatened with rape. A police sergeant, villagers and their mayor then took it in turns to beat them before they were rescued by the arrival of another police patrol.

A series of disturbing reports from France about killings and shootings by police officers, often involving Arabs or Africans, suggest a somewhat cavalier attitude towards the lawful means of apprehending suspects. The pattern of excessive force used largely against people of non-European ethnic origin reinforces concerns that they are neither welcome nor tolerated by the authorities.

Widespread human rights violations were committed by Iraqi forces following the invasion of Kuwait in August 1990, including arbitrary detention of thousands of civilians, systematic torture of detainees, extrajudicial executions and 'disappearances'. Instead of enforcing those international standards called for during the occupation, after the withdrawal of Iraqi troops in 1991 the Amir of Kuwait declared martial law and introduced a special martial law court, unleashing a terrifying period of arbitrary arrests, torture and extrajudicial killings of those termed 'collaborators', most of whom were non-Kuwaitis. Many of those detained subsequently 'disappeared' and their fate and whereabouts remain unknown.

Though not permitted by law, public beatings by police officers have also been reported in Romania. Andrei Zanopol, a journalist from the magazine *Impartial*, was stopped by plain-clothes police officers in Mazepa, a city quarter in Galaţi, at 8.15 p.m. on Sunday 27 June 1993. They said their warrant was at the police station, then tied him to the railings of a building with wire and began kicking and hitting him. Some neighbours gathered along with police reinforcements. He was taken to the police station and beaten again. He was released in July without charge.

It is not uncommon for individuals to be 'selected' to bear the brunt of official disapprobation in public or to witness brutal displays as a warning to others. On 26 May 1992, the day after her son, a political activist, had been arrested in Port au Prince, Haiti, Claire Edouard was taken from her house and executed by members of the security forces, who insisted that her neighbours be made to watch.

A woman from Afghanistan who had returned to Kabul from exile in Pakistan was picked up with a female relative by *mujahideen* armed guards in October 1993. They were taken to a makeshift military base where they were to be beaten, released and told to leave the city. But first they were faced with evidence of atrocities:

'They told us that we were spies. They showed us a number of containers in the house. They opened one . . . and I saw that there were gouged-out eyes stuck to the side. . . . They told us these were the eyes of those who fought against them . . . there could have been about 50 to 60 eyes. They told us that our eyes would be gouged out if we did not tell them who had sent us.'

However, it would seem that innocent victims of terror are not permitted to display alternative evidence of oppression. In mid-1992 Nahid, a 16-year-old girl, threw herself from the fifth-floor balcony of the flats where she lived to avoid being raped by *mujahideen* guards in Afghanistan. AI was told by witnesses: 'She died instantly. Her father put her body on a bed frame and wanted to carry it in the streets to show the people what had happened to her, but the *mujahideen* groups stopped him.'

Brutal displays are not the only way of terrorizing people. The very fact that torture is known to take place is frightening enough, but in many countries the notoriety of the buildings where torture occurs strikes fear in people's hearts. They may be military barracks like the Mariscal Cáceres base in Tarapoto, Peru; or particular police stations like the 4th police company in Port au Prince, Haiti, known as the 'Caféteria', where many beatings and violent interrogations took place under the military dictatorship; or intelligence headquarters like 'the fourth floor' of the Criminal Investigation Department in Colombo, Sri Lanka; or prisons like the El Khiam detention centre in south Lebanon, controlled by both Israeli military and South Lebanon Army militia. They may be public buildings commandeered by security forces, or their precise location may not even be known. In Sudan, people are well aware that detainees may be spirited away to secret 'ghost houses' for torture sessions, like the victim shown in Figure 5.3. The dread of being taken there adds to the mental anguish of detainees and their relatives. What happens inside hardly bears thinking about.

Beating the opposition

The immediate fear of anyone held in custody, whether by agents of the state, criminal gangs or guerrilla forces, is that they may be ill-treated or killed. It is a natural fear when removed from family, friends and familiar surroundings.

Probably the most frequent breach of human rights reported to AI is the beating of prisoners from the earliest moment of arrest or incarceration. Physical assault may begin with manhandling during arrest or abduction. Violence inflicted on detainees at the point of arrest warns

Figure 5.3. Sudan: after six weeks in custody, civil servant and former soldier Camillo Odongi Loyuk died handcuffed to the bars of a window in a Khartoum 'ghost house' on 1 August 1992.

those who witness it not to intervene. When Han Dongfang, a former prisoner of conscience in China, answered a summons to attend the Dongcheng District People's Court in Beijing at 8 a.m. on 14 May 1992 to 'discuss' a housing order, he was subjected to insults from the judge,

Zhong Junming, in the course of an argument and decided to leave. He was seized and beaten by court officials. He was pushed to the floor, his hands cuffed behind his back, trodden upon and prodded with electric batons and then taken to a room where the beatings continued until 12 o'clock. By then he had difficulty breathing, a high fever, pains in his chest and abdomen, dropsy in many parts of his head and body, and bleeding under the skin. A medical examination revealed that his lungs had filled with fluid with a relapse of the tuberculosis he had contracted during an earlier 22-month imprisonment. The court denied his version of events, claiming that Han had 'tried to injure himself to create disturbance' by beating his own head against a desk.

An apparently innocent visit to court may seem the least likely circumstance in which to receive an 'official' beating. The more usual experience of such violence, according to reports received by AI from all over the world, is at demonstrations or when first arrested. In Romania, where ill-treatment of Roma appears to be widespread, police entered the house of the Laca family in December 1993 and attacked several family members while officially investigating complaints laid against Mircea, the 19-year-old son of the household. His mother, Elena, was hit in the face and her blouse was torn; her daughter-in-law was also beaten, as was a 12-year-old boy. Mircea was then handcuffed and beaten. His mother described the scene: 'He was placed between two wooden benches and the officers continued to beat him by hitting the top bench.' She said that he was beaten on the soles of his feet with truncheons and one of the officers shouted, 'We will kill you as well as all the other gypsies.' Mircea was taken to the police station but released without charge.

Often beatings are conducted while prisoners are blindfolded. Covering the eyes has little to do with preventing prisoners from identifying their persecutors; it is more to do with disorienting the victims, and reducing their capacity to brace themselves against what is to come. As one victim explained, 'the worst thing about being blindfolded is that you can't anticipate the next slap or kick and prepare yourself for it, it just comes from anywhere out of the dark'.

During initial interrogation and later, attacks with fists, boots, knees and blunt instruments, including pistols and rifle butts, batons, broom handles, chair-legs, rubber hoses, electric cable and makeshift or ready-made whips and scourges, have been reported almost everywhere that ill-treatment occurs. Beatings have also been conducted with barbed wire.

In Pakistan sticks and leather whips are often used, but special weapons have also been devised. The *chittar* is a form of truncheon with a piece of car tyre or leather nailed to a wooden handle. Prisoners are beaten with it on the back, the buttocks, the genitals and the soles of the feet.

Sometimes prisoners have had their feet thrust through the bottom of an upturned string bed to receive this beating. One reported that a police officer would sit on his back and pull his feet up so two others could hit them.

Among other techniques recorded in Nepal are beatings with *sisnu*, a plant that causes painful swellings on the skin, while in Myanmar (Burma) prisoners have reported beatings conducted after their bodies had been padded out with folded rice bags to reduce the likelihood of external evidence of beatings but affording no protection against internal injuries. A student held by Special Branch officers in Mandalay in 1987 described the beating he and a friend received:

> '*a team came in, stripped us of all our clothes . . . tied up our hands with handcuffs and hung us up to the ceiling with a rope. . . . They interrogated me again and asked the same questions, to which I gave the same answers. So they whipped me with a car's fan belt. . . . Altogether I may have been given 70 or 80 lashes. . . . after a while I lost consciousness completely. They "treated" my wounds the same way they treated my friend's. . . . They took him down, poured salt and curry powder on his back . . . and then urinated on his back.*'

In August 1992 security forces (Asayish) in Iraqi Kurdistan arrested 13 Kurdish political activists after opening fire on a demonstration in Arbil. The injured mother of a young girl shot dead in the incident was taken into the Asayish headquarters: 'They tortured me for about one and a half hours in one of the offices. They beat me on the bullet wound and on my back with a hosepipe.'

Another woman described her ordeal:

> '*They blindfolded me and tied my hands and feet. They subjected me to falaka (beatings on the soles of the feet) and hit me on the back. Then they suspended me from a wooden bar fixed onto a wall by my hands, which were tied behind my back. My right shoulder became dislocated. . . . They beat me first with a hosepipe, then with a belt, on my legs and other parts of my body. Afterwards they applied electricity to my wrists. . . . They also suspended me from the ceiling with a rope tied to my hands and made me revolve.*'

Beatings with lengths of wood, iron bars, bottles, rocks and electric cables have been reported from Indonesia where, in January 1993, a mother and father and their 9-year-old son, who was suspected of stealing a wallet, were detained and beaten by police in Indramayu, West Java. The mother was strung up by her feet and her hair pulled as the beatings continued. Her son was forced to beat her. She lost consciousness and remained in a coma for three days. The boy was then forced to watch his father being beaten, kicked and punched to death.

In China a pregnant young Tibetan woman, Damchoe Pemo, was forced to stand for 12 hours and repeatedly beaten with electric batons after her arrest on 20 May 1993. She miscarried a week later.

On 3 December 1991 a woman who works with the hard of hearing received rough treatment from a soldier in Marchand Dessalines, Artibonite Department, Haiti, after a complaint that she had stopped a man cutting down a tree in her mother's garden. He took her to his commanding officer and alleged she was a *lavalassiene*, a supporter of the deposed President Aristide. 'Beat her,' came the order.

> *'I was astonished. I didn't think they were going to beat me. I was really scared. There were three soldiers. I was beaten with a* rigoise *[a leather lash] on my face, on my head. The* rigoise *cut my back. . . . When they were beating me I tried to stop the blow, and they broke my arm. . . . So they beat me with a* rigoise *and with a big wooden stick and another soldier beat me with his hands. When they were tired they left and then another came, and the one who had arrested me came with his* rigoise *and beat me a lot . . .'*

She was then locked in a cell, and after being taken before a tribunal spent a night in hospital before being returned to the barracks. Four months later her arm was still not mended.

Indiscriminate beatings always carry with them the risk of death, since those handing out the punishment can have little knowledge of the physical or medical condition of their victim. Nazir Masih, a Christian and father of seven children, from Faisalabad, Punjab Province in Pakistan, was beaten to death for refusing to supply police officers with alcohol. He was arrested early in the morning of 21 May 1993, and five policemen were seen beating him at 2 p.m. that afternoon. By 7 p.m. he had died.

Torture and ill-treatment by the security forces is widespread in Kenya. It is routinely employed to obtain a confession and usually happens shortly after arrest. It is frequently very brutal, usually consisting of beatings with sticks, fists, handles of hoes or gun butts. Serious injuries often result, but medical treatment is refused, and doctors who treat torture victims are harassed by police and prison officers. Investigations into allegations of torture by police are rare – prosecutions rarer still – and many police officers appear to act with impunity. AI has reports of some prisoners being taken into the forest at night, suspended from trees and then beaten, or having their fingernails and toenails pulled out. In December 1994 four young men were permanently disabled by Special

Branch officers who tied them to trees in Dundori Forest, near Nakuru, and beat them. Despite their injuries they were not taken to hospital for six days. Two days later one of the four had his arm amputated after it became gangrenous.

Beatings are not confined to the early days of imprisonment, though the first beatings are often the most severe. Throughout long periods of imprisonment, captives held in the late 1970s and early 1980s at African National Congress (ANC) military and prison camps in Angola, Tanzania, Uganda and Zambia were regularly subjected to punishment beatings. They were dubbed 'corrective measures' in Quatro Camp in Angola, where prisoners of the ANC were held between 1984 and 1988.

For some years AI has been receiving reports from all over Portugal of regular ill-treatment of prisoners by members of the country's various police forces and prison staff. In December 1992 an official inquiry was opened into 32 complaints laid against officers of the Judiciary Police, all but one in the Lisbon area during the previous two years. At the time the inquiry did not include the case of Orlanda Correia, a French citizen of Portuguese parentage, interrogated by police while in prison in September 1992. When he refused to co-operate because neither a lawyer nor an interpreter was present, he was verbally and physically assaulted, a pistol was pushed into his mouth and he was tied spread-eagled against railings. That afternoon he was admitted to the prison hospital unconscious.

An appeal to the international community from political prisoners at Hanyang Prison in the Hubei Province of China dated March 1993 described how their protests had been sparked off by a series of beatings in the prison.

> 'One evening in December [1990], Ye Youwen was passing by the iron gate of the brigade camp and was ordered by the guard to stop. He was slow to react, being very short-sighted, but a guard considered that he was being deliberately offensive. After Ye opened the gate the guard beat him repeatedly with an electric baton . . . until Ye collapsed . . .'

Prisoners demanded medical treatment for the injured man, and entrusted one of their number, Pan Huijia, to draft a letter of petition:

> 'The prison authorities pretended to be sympathetic and offered Ye medical treatment but in fact locked him up in isolation. . . . Pan Huijia . . . was put in solitary confinement . . . for a month. . . . While he was there the prison officer who had beaten Ye Youwen, named Wei, broke into his cell and inflicted a brutal beating on Pan; the beating was so fierce that he broke a leather belt in two.'

Systematic and insidious abuse of prisoners held in prisons in Russia has been common for many years, both before and since the breakup of the Soviet Union. Describing conditions in two Moscow investigation–isolation prisons he visited in July 1994, the United Nations Special Rapporteur on Torture commented: 'The senses of smell, touch, taste and sight are repulsively assailed. The conditions are cruel, inhuman and degrading; they are torturous.' Many Chechen and Ingush people detained by Russian security forces during the conflict in the Chechen Republic have alleged brutal treatment while in custody. Chingizkhan Uveysovich Amirkhanov was arrested, assaulted and robbed in Grozny by drunken Russian police officers in January 1995. He was still suffering from the injuries he received during a week-long detention when he met with AI delegates two months later. He had been handcuffed to a tree and the police were ready to shoot him but an officer intervened, released him and pushed him to the ground. He was then handcuffed again and taken away with others in a truck. They were made to lie on the floor with a policeman sitting on each of them for the whole of the seven-hour journey. If they moved they were beaten with truncheons. On arrival at Mozdok they were again beaten, then stripped and loaded into railway carriages:

> 'They told us, "Today we are going to shoot you." They were all masked, and without identification. We were moved to small rooms. With me were two other Ingush, two Chechens and three Russians. They took us out one by one for interrogation. There they were also masked. They undressed me and tied my hand and foot. One sat in front of me and asked, "Are you a fighter?" I replied that I was not; he hit me on the knee with a truncheon and asked again, "Are you a fighter?" And then he calmly said: "With each blow 5 millimetres of tissue is stripped off. Thus the bone will be reached. Think about how your legs will rot." I asked what I had to do. "Confess that you are a prisoner of war and you'll get 15 years; confess that you are a criminal and we'll shoot you." And so they continued to beat me. They beat me all night. Competently. As soon as they saw that I was losing consciousness they poured water on me. You don't want to, but you come round.'

Another Ingush arrested in Grozny and taken to Mozdok at about the same time also alleged ferocious beatings. At least three of the beaten detainees died, allegedly of suffocation after being crammed into a car for the journey. And yet another, airlifted to Mozdok by helicopter, told of assaults that included the setting of Alsatian dogs on injured detainees.

Such beatings are routine throughout the world regardless of the age, sex or alleged offence of the detainee. In Haiti, when Roosevelt Charles tried to avoid arrest on 13 February 1992, he was stoned by soldiers, then beaten daily while in custody, receiving 250 blows with sticks just before his release eight days later. His wounds became infected and he had to be flown out of the country for skin grafts. He was co-ordinator of the National Progressive Revolutionary Party of Haiti, where children as young as seven years old have been beaten by soldiers.

Bludgeoning people into submission is brutish and cowardly. There can be no legitimate excuse for such ruthless behaviour, especially when it is inflicted on a child.

Suffer the children . . .

It is hard to imagine how anyone could torture a child. Every time the courts or the media turn the spotlight upon the case of a child who has died or been scarred physically or mentally at the hands of a parent or guardian we are forced to confront the unpleasant reality that it happens in our midst, in domestic situations, and often because of the perpetrator's inadequacy or history of childhood trauma. Torturing children for political reasons is even harder to stomach or explain, but AI regularly receives evidence that children are being tortured, killed or imprisoned by governments, military forces and the police throughout the world.

The General Assembly of the United Nations adopted the Convention on the Rights of the Child, which came into effect on 2 September 1990. By April 1995 it had become the most widely ratified international human rights treaty ever, with 172 official states party to its terms, and another nine indicating their support by becoming signatories. Twelve others had not formally recognized the Convention: Andorra, Brunei, Darussalam, Kiribati, Oman, the Republic of Palau, Saudi Arabia, Singapore, the Solomon Islands, Somalia, Tonga, Tuvala and the United Arab Emirates. Yet from the evidence of widespread ill-treatment of young people collected by AI it would seem that children have much to fear from governments that pay lip service to the terms of the Convention, which are quite specific about what they should expect from agents of the state.

Children are at their most vulnerable in civil wars, where civilians are in the front line and it is difficult to tell who is friend or foe. However, there is plenty to suggest that children are deliberately targeted. A slogan broadcast in 1994 on Radio Télévision Libre des Mille Collines, a local radio station in Kigali, perhaps best sums up the attitude of those willing to inflict violence upon young children: 'To destroy large rats you must kill them when they are small.' That year tens of thousands of Tutsi children were massacred by Hutu militia in Rwanda.

Both the security forces in Peru and the insurrectionary Communist Party of Peru (Shining Path) have been guilty of killing or effecting the 'disappearance' of children, and media coverage of the collapse of the Soviet Union, the plight of the Kurds in Iraq and the internecine strife in Bosnia-Herzegovina has provided a constant reminder to the world of the traumas suffered by children when adults go to war.

In the political chaos that has followed the Soviet withdrawal from Afghanistan, where the government, rival *mujahideen* groups and, since late 1994, *taleban* (religious students) have been fighting for control, children have suffered as much as their parents. A woman who subsequently fled to Pakistan described to AI a not untypical incident that occurred during heavy fighting in the Bibi Mahroo district of Kabul early in 1994:

> *'My sister-in-law had two young children and we were worried about what might happen to them. One day we noticed that they were missing. They had gone to the corner shop and had not returned. We searched everywhere and could not find them. Then we discovered their bodies in a ruined building. Their heads were battered, their faces swollen. We brought the bodies home and buried them there.'*

Kurdish children in Turkey have suffered at the hands of both government forces and armed members of the Kurdish Workers Party (PKK). In March 1992, in the aftermath of disturbances during the Kurdish New Year, a teenage girl, 16-year-old Biseng Anik, was killed in police custody. Her mutilated body bore the marks of torture, yet officials claimed she had committed suicide after finding a rifle in her cell.

There have been many reports of almost casual killings of young children in army operations throughout Myanmar (Burma), and of the torture of youngsters. In March 1988 a 15-year-old boy was taken into custody from Yangon (Rangoon) General Hospital while suffering from severe burns caused when a car was set on fire during a student demonstration. He was admitted to the prison hospital the next day, where it was found that every bone in his arms and hands and his legs from knees to toes had been systematically broken. He died 17 days later.

There would seem to be little purpose other than sadism to subject a child to such agony, but AI has evidence that children are sometimes tortured or threatened with torture as a means of persuading a relative to co-operate with security forces. In September 1992 Song Hae-suk, the wife of a political detainee in South Korea, was arrested, beaten, shown pictures of torture and threatened with sexual torture in the presence of her three-year-old son to coerce her into signing an espionage 'confession'. Similar threats to children have been reported from Venezuela.

In Bangladesh some 50,000 children were estimated to be earning a living on the streets of Dhaka alone in 1993, surviving through odd jobs, prostitution or scavenging on the city's rubbish dumps. The police regularly apprehend and abuse these youngsters, extracting bribes and beating them. Some are taken to vagrants' homes; others imprisoned on petty charges. Once in custody many of these children are subjected to torture, shackling and sexual assault by prison staff and other prisoners. Like thousands of street children in Brazil and Colombia who have been ill-treated or killed, they are victims because of their poverty.

Reports emerging from China in 1995 indicated that among the hundreds of political prisoners and prisoners of conscience in Tibet, mostly Buddhist monks and nuns, were at least 45 who were under the age of 18 at the time of their arrest. The two youngest, aged 12, were sentenced to between two and six years' imprisonment.

In China juveniles can be committed to labour camps by administrative order rather than being tried. Despite the provisions of Article 49 of the Chinese Constitution, which forbids maltreatment of children, and Article 52 of the Law on the Protection of Minors, which makes it a criminal offence for agents of the legal system to inflict corporal punishment or otherwise ill-treat children in their custody, some of these youngsters were also subjected to beatings, electric shocks, solitary confinement, and deprivation of sleep, food and drink.

In 1987 a 13-year-old boy held at Lhasa police station was beaten on arrival, then hit with an iron rod. Electric shocks were applied to his torso. He was ordered to strip to his underpants, then kicked in the mouth, and an electric baton put in his mouth. His hands were cuffed behind his back and bottles stuck inside his elbows. He received no food or water during his interrogation, and was kept for a day and a night alone in a cell. He was released a few days later.

From Lhasa police station many detainees are sent to Gutsa Detention Centre, where a 16-year-old boy was among those forced to balance upside down against a wall for an hour on their arrival in September 1990. He was later slapped in the face and kicked during interrogation and kept alone in a cell for six months. Sentenced to three years' imprisonment, he was injured while working in a stone quarry with adult prisoners and then had his arm broken with a wooden baton for trying to smuggle a letter out of the prison for somebody else.

A 12-year-old girl, detained for four months at Sangyip Detention Centre near Lhasa after a demonstration in 1990, was kicked on the head and body and given shocks with an electric baton while she lay on the ground. She temporarily lost the use of her left leg and needed hospital treatment. She was later forced to shovel excrement from waste pits onto lorries with other women detainees and suffered eye inflammation from the noxious gases.

Arrested for singing nationalist songs, five teenagers, including a 13-year-old, were beaten and kicked as they were being taken to Lhasa police station in December 1993. Forced to strip to their underwear, they were beaten and kicked all night and the following day. Their assailants used whips made from electricity wire. When the youths collapsed, their interrogators stepped on them. They were released after three days.

Even when arrested by the civil police under due process of law, young people cannot be sure of humane treatment. Karim Zada, a 15-year-old suspected of theft, was held for 15 days in Karachi, Pakistan, because he would not confess. To obtain a confession police described the tortures they would inflict upon him:

> 'They said they would close my penis and give me a lot of water to drink. It can't come out and they said I would burst. They also threatened to torture me by spreading my legs very wide. They said the veins start bleeding. Then I said I had committed the crime . . .'

Police in India have been responsible for appalling ill-treatment of young children picked up on suspicion of petty offences. Four teenage girls, members of a nomadic tribe, were tortured by Maharashta police in 1989 after being charged with 'moving about under suspicious circumstances'. In the same year 11 children from the Delhi slums were detained on suspicion of theft. They included two 10-year-old girls and a six-year-old boy. A girl of 13 was stripped and beaten, a 12-year-old boy was subjected to electric shocks and beaten with a leather belt; and another child was stripped, hung upside down from the ceiling and beaten unconscious.

In February 1990, 12-year-old Sabina Yasmeen was arrested on trumped-up charges and tortured by police at a Balgarth police station in West Bengal: 'Four policemen pulled me by my hair while another hit me with a *lathi* . . . one of them tried to urinate in my mouth.'

Between August 1991 and April 1992 eight young men from the largely Catholic nationalist community of Ballymurphy, Belfast (in Northern Ireland, part of the UK) were arrested by the Royal Ulster Constabulary following two separate incidents in which a number of police officers and civilians were injured by a grenade and coffee-jar bombs. Seven of them were teenagers at the time of their arrest. All eight alleged that they were coerced by ill-treatment to make incriminating statements while in custody and without the benefit of a lawyer.

Ethnic Albanian families in former Yugoslavia have reported the systematic use of violence by the police when homes were being searched for arms on a daily basis during 1993–4. The beating of adults during these raids appears to have been commonplace, but on a number of occasions elderly people and young children have also been assaulted. On

31 January 1994, 10-year-old Labinot Hoti was picked up in a police car and beaten. A knife was allegedly held at his throat and he was ordered to tell the officers where weapons were hidden in the village of Josanica (Klina). On 21 February eight secondary school students were reportedly beaten up by police while returning from private lessons in Runik, near Srbica. And on 24 March a young girl, Malësore Gashi, was beaten by police in Smira (Vitina) when they turned up to search the family house while her parents were absent.

Adrian Curri, an 18-year-old student from Gornji Streoci, near Pec, was taken in April 1994 from a school bus by police, with two others.

> '[T]hey asked me for my identity card. I gave it to them, and then one of the officers suddenly grabbed me by the hair and pulled me out of the bus. They handcuffed me and put me in their car. They took all three of us to the police station. They led us inside and separated us. They took me into a room and then the beating and torture began.
>
> 'Next they tied me to a radiator and three police officers sat on me; one of them pulled out a knife and after he had pulled up my shirt he cut a cross [on my chest] with the Cyrillic 'S'. After two hours they put me in a car and brought me back to the bus stop in Pec . . .' (Figure 5.4)

Children sentenced to custodial sentences should at least expect to be protected from further abuse, but often the conditions they must endure are at least as bad as those imposed on adults. In 1992 AI highlighted the case of Nazrul Islam, released from prison in Bangladesh during October of that year. As a 12-year-old boy he had been sentenced to seven years' imprisonment on a robbery charge but remained in Satkhira prison for 12 years. For 11 of those years he had been shackled with leg-irons.

On 30 March 1993, when young offenders in Brazil incarcerated at the Tatuapé Juvenile Detention Centre, São Paulo, protested about the harsh and overcrowded conditions, the riot was quashed by staff aided by military police and a private security firm. An inspection soon after discovered that 75 of the 113 youths involved had injuries sustained through beatings, and six required hospital treatment.

The alternative to custody may still be corporal punishment for some young people. The law in Trinidad and Tobago allows children under 16 to receive up to six strokes from a tamarind rod, birch or other form of switch for some offences. In April 1993 an 11-year-old boy found carrying cocaine received 20 lashes with a leather belt, more than three times the legal maximum.

AI has received many reports of the sexual abuse of children, including the abduction of young people specifically for sexual purposes. At around

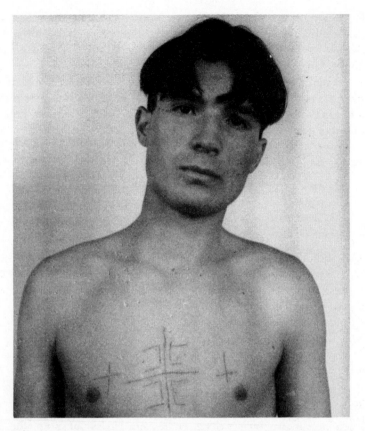

Figure 5.4. Former Yugoslavia: ethnic Albanian student Adrian Curri from Gornji Sreoci bears the Cyrillic emblems of the Serbian motto 'Only Unity Saves the Serb' cut into his chest after police took him off a bus.

midnight on 28 July 1993 Mohammed Shawkat, a 13-year-old who sometimes worked as a market porter in the Bangladesh capital, Dhaka, was woken from his makeshift bed on the veranda of a residential building by two police constables. They told him to follow them and took him to a nearby field. He was ordered to strip and the two men sexually assaulted him. Mohammed later reported:

> 'I shouted loudly when the dark constable forcibly pushed his penis in my rectum. After half an hour I was brought to Azimapur police substation outpost where the nice-looking constable began to sexually assault me a second time and I fainted when the constable passed his penis completely into my rectum and afterwards I became senseless.'

He was taken to Dhaka Medical College Hospital and his rape was reported by the press. The two police officers were suspended but no charges brought against them. By 1 August Mohammed had 'disappeared' from hospital.

Abduction and rape is prevalent in guerrilla wars, where male soldiers are constantly on the move. One woman in Afghanistan reported what happened to her 13-year-old niece when Party of Islam (Hezb-e Islami) guards came to the family home towards the end of 1993:

> 'They said their commander wanted her. They took her away. She was resisting and screaming but they dragged her away. We were frightened that if we did anything we would all be killed. Several months later the commander was killed during fighting and the girl was able to come back to her father's house. Abducting girls has been very common in recent years. They will kill any girl who does not go with them.'

Many other young girls suffered similar fates and simply 'disappeared'. Women especially are at risk of sexual assault when the rule of law breaks down, and in recent years the systematic use of rape has become more widely recognized as a weapon of terror.

Sexual violence

Sex is a potent weapon in power relationships, and rape is the most degrading expression of the contempt of one human being towards another. Since conflict erupted in former Yugoslavia, media coverage has provided almost daily reminders that systematic rape is also a weapon of political terror.

One 17-year-old Muslim girl from Višegrad was taken to the Vilina Vlas Hotel in the town in June 1992 together with her sister and a friend. There she stated that Serbian paramilitaries raped her while she listened to screams and then the sound of her sister's voice outside the room. Her sister and friend have never been seen again. Other women were reportedly raped by Serbian paramilitaries in the town; some were taken to the Vilina Vlas Hotel, never to be seen again. Reports or rumours of rape were used as excuses for acts of retribution. In the same month a 37-year-old Serbian woman in Novigrad, northern Bosnia, reported that she and three other Serbian women were abducted and raped by seven uniformed Croatian men, including neighbours, who justified their actions by claiming that Serbs had raped 150 women in the area.

In 1993 Serbian militia were reported by a spokesman for the United Nations Commission for Refugees to have been responsible for the rape of two 65-year-old Muslim women and an attack on the home of an elderly Muslim couple after which the 80-year-old woman was left stripped naked. These actions were part of a terror campaign to force Muslims and Croats to leave the town of Banja Luka.

Croatian Defence Council (HVO) forces also stand accused of using strip-searching and rape in their efforts to drive Muslim women from Vitez, Mostar and Capljina. On 17 November 1993 the UN Special Rapporteur on Human Rights in the former Yugoslavia recorded that 'at least 100 women were reported to have been raped by Bosnian Croat (HVO) soldiers between April and October 1993'. The rape and sexual humiliation of women and young girls has continued despite the presence of UN forces in the region.

In Angola, troops of both parties in the civil war have raped women, most often women from their own side from whom they have demanded sexual favours, but rape is also one of the human rights abuses carried out after the occupation of enemy territory. Similar reports of organized sexual assault have emerged from Djibouti and Haiti.

Kurdish women in south-east Turkey and in northen Iraq have also been abused by government forces. In the late 1980s a Kurdish woman member of the Iraqi Communist Party (Pesh Merga) was repeatedly raped in jail:

> 'No matter how much I'd heard about it, nothing prepared me for the actual experience. It lives on inside me. I still bleed a lot. It was done not just by one man, but by a group of them. They stifled my screams and protests. I had to give in. And it was a side-show; lots of people came to watch.'

Guarina Celso and Raquel Gorpido, two women accused of belonging to an opposition paramilitary group in the Philippines, were arrested by government troops and local militia on 13 July 1989 in northern Samar. They were bound and beaten, and their trousers were cut from their bodies and stuffed into their mouths. They were then raped by more than half the 50 soldiers who arrested them. A senior officer who also took part in the rape sliced their ears with a hunting knife. The following day he cut off their external sexual organs before the two women were stabbed to death and buried near a river.

Since the annexation of East Timor by Indonesia, AI has received many reports of sexual molestation and rape of East Timorese women. One young woman told how, on the day after she was admitted to a military hospital at Dili with five gunshot wounds received during the 1991 Santa Cruz massacre, two soldiers cut off her clothes and molested her. While she was being interrogated during her recuperation another soldier threatened to sleep with her. That night he came to the ward she shared with another woman while she was asleep and molested her. Describing her ordeal, she said: 'If men are hurt they can recover and forget what happened, but for women, if they are raped or tortured, they cannot forget. Their life is destroyed for ever.'

Sexual atrocities committed by drunken government soldiers in Myanmar (Burma) include the rape of a three-year-old girl and an eight-year-old girl in Kayin State during 1991. And in 1992 a Christian woman forced to dig trenches and latrines at an army camp in Kayin State was ordered into an officer's room with her arms tied behind her back:

'He took out a knife and held it against my skin on my throat and threatened to kill me – I said I'd rather he did, and kept on praying. He cut my arm and drew blood, then he drew the knife down my chest and stomach, leaving a thin line of blood. Then he got his penis out. I was still struggling, and I managed to hit him in the testicles, but that just got him madder and finally he raped me. He was very rough; he is a big man. He raped me three times, though I was bleeding. I kept on praying and hoping he would stop. I was so ashamed.'

Muslim women in the same region reported similar treatment when pressed into service as porters by Government troops in 1993.

A survivor of the April 1992 massacre at Bulohawo in Somalia carried out by General Aideed's faction of the United Somali Congress party was able to describe atrocious mutilations carried out by the soldiers: 'I saw people with their tongues cut out or their arms or legs cut off, left to die. Women were gang-raped and bayoneted in the vagina. Pregnant women had their stomachs slit open.'

On 7 June 1992 in Peru, Froily Mori Vela, a 14-year-old girl, was forcibly removed from her parents by a group of six soldiers led by a lieutenant from the Bellavista provincial barracks in the Nueva Lima district. The soldiers had been searching the family house in the hamlet of La Unión. She said: 'They took me to the far end of the vegetable garden, where one after another they raped me, starting with the lieutenant.'

Soldiers from a counter-insurgency brigade in Colombia broke into a house in Sabaneta, Santander Department, during November 1992. While her husband was being beaten, Sonebia Pinzón was taken outside and raped in front of her three-year-old son. She could hear her two-year-old daughter Marcela screaming inside. The toddler was found semi-conscious and bleeding: she too had been raped. In October 1993 six young women were raped by government soldiers in the village of Alto de la Loma, Valle de Cauca Department, before being forced to don military-style uniforms. They were then executed with seven other villagers.

Indigenous peoples are especially at risk from persecution. Two pregnant peasant women were among a group of 15 members of the Irapuato Popular Settlement Union detained without warrants by the police in Mexico in January 1990. Both were beaten on the stomach and one later miscarried. Another woman was thrown out into the street partially dressed. The detained men were threatened that the women would be raped. And in the Chiapas region, on 4 June 1994, three young Tzeltal women, sisters aged 16, 18 and 20, were raped by about 10 soldiers after being stopped at a road-block while on their way home from market.

Unaccompanied women and girls who try to escape the risks of remaining in war zones have found themselves even more vulnerable as refugees. In the huge refugee camps that spring up near trouble spots or famine areas the threat of rape is ever-present. Sexual favours may be demanded by officials or male refugees in return for food or documentation. Hundreds of Somali women have been raped in the refugee camps of Kenya.

An Ethiopian woman described a typical experience in the 1980s when she sought refuge in a neighbouring country:

> 'I was five months pregnant . . . we were stopped by two men who asked us where we were going. When we explained, one pulled me aside and said: "No safe passage before sex!". . . he forced me down, kicked me in the stomach and raped me in front of my [two] children. He knew I was pregnant, but that made no difference to him.'

Rules, regulations and conventions are easily abandoned in wartime and during mass displacement, but laws in some countries positively encourage violence against women and men just because of their gender or sexual orientation. In Iran women have allegedly been sentenced to flogging for not conforming to the dress codes laid down by the Islamic Republic, and women risk 100 lashes if convicted of *mosaheqeh* (lesbianism) on the evidence of 'four righteous men'. Four convictions can result in the death penalty.

In July 1992 Shamin, a 21-year-old mother of two children, was kidnapped and raped by three men in north Nazimabad, Karachi, Pakistan. When her mother reported the crime, Shamin was arrested and threatened with a charge relating to the sexual offences of adultery, sexual intercourse between unmarried partners and rape, unless she could pay a bribe. Under the Islamic *Zina* Ordinance of 1979 it is difficult for a woman to substantiate an allegation of rape. By reporting the offence she lays herself open to the charge of illicit sexual intercourse, an offence punishable with death by stoning. In this case the woman could not raise the money demanded for her release. She was held at the police station where three men, including two police officers, repeatedly raped her.

Village elders in Bangladesh, meeting as the traditional arbitration panel (*salish*), exceeded their authorized powers by sentencing a 16-year-old girl from Kalikapur, Satkira District, to a public flogging for fornication with a Hindu boy from a nearby village. When she died shortly after being tied to a bamboo pole and given 101 lashes with a broom, police filed charges against *salish* members for 'abetment to suicide'.

Quite apart from laws that discriminate against women, the social stigma attached to rape also makes it difficult for women to report the offence or to continue to live in the community. A 23-year-old woman was raped by two or three soldiers every night for three months while in detention in an army camp in her native Bhutan during 1990. She eventually made her way to a refugee camp in Nepal, where she told AI:

> '*On release I went home where I stayed for one month until I realized I was pregnant. I was so ashamed that I couldn't face the other villagers so . . . I left my children with my mother-in-law. I went into the jungle, hoping I would die there. . . . As a result of the rape, I had twins, one of which died . . .*'

Police are expected to honour the trust that people have in the law, but their unique powers of arrest and interrogation are frequently abused. The humiliation of women detainees has distinctly sexual connotations, not least because invariably the perpetrators are men. Stripping women in public and conducting intimate strip searches are prevalent methods of humiliation used in many countries, sometimes on the flimsiest of pretexts.

Women among 33 people arrested in Greece on 2 November 1991 for putting up political posters in Athens were subjected to abusive treatment at the headquarters of the Security Police. Two women, including one who was pregnant, were grabbed by the hair and had their heads banged against a wall while officers called them 'whore' and 'tramp'. Another was spat at by officers, who made sexually abusive comments. The women described the humiliation that followed:

> '*[we] were ordered to get completely undressed so [the police officers] could carry out body searches. These were carried out under conditions which were offensive, crude, irregular and humiliating for us. They left the doors open and we were naked in full view of policemen who were wandering about outside . . . who made comments of a sexist nature such as "Look at them – they're like sexually frustrated bitches."*'

Women suspected of membership of the Basque separatist group ETA have been forced to strip and suffer sexual insults and humiliation while under interrogation by police in Spain.

In early 1992, during a military operation against poaching in the Salonga National Park, Zaire, over a dozen young teenage schoolgirls were raped by soldiers. Gendarmes forced a man to rape his 18-year-old daughter at gunpoint in front of other detainees, and married women were repeatedly raped in front of their husbands.

On 17 October 1992 a 14-year-old girl, Lau, was allegedly raped by three police officers in Tando Ghulam Haider, Hyderabad district, Sindh Province, Pakistan. She was among eight members of the Bheel tribe arrested and beaten by police as they returned from a festival.

For many years AI has been receiving evidence of rape by security forces in India, particularly of migrant women, and tribal women in rural communities. Among incidents claimed in 1993 were the multiple rape of an 11-year-old Bangladeshi girl at Seemapuri police station, Delhi, in June, and the gang rape of up to 20 women, some assaulted in front of their children, during a police investigation of a land dispute in the Jagasingpur district of Orissa, in October. A 20-year-old woman suffered gang rape by six Punjabi police commandos at Garepalli in the Karimnagar district on 11 November 1994, and a mother and daughter reported multiple rape at gunpoint by 12 police officers on election duty in Siwan, Bihar, on 18 February 1995.

In May 1993 a man and a woman in East Timor (annexed by Indonesia), suspected of having illicit sexual relations, were beaten and forced to re-enact the 'crime' twice on the floor of the police interrogation room.

In July 1993 a French woman of Tunisian origin, detained on crossing the Franco-Italian border without identity papers, was subjected to racist abuse, stripped, body searched and raped by border police in Italy and then subjected to a further sexual assault and racist abuse by a border police officer in France.

Two young Catholic activists involved in anti-nuclear, anti-slavery and human rights work, Kim Un-ju and her brother Kim Sam-sok, were arrested by the security forces in South Korea in September 1993 and forced to make confessions implicating them in a North Korean spy network. Kim Un-ju was deprived of sleep, forced to do repeated physical exercises, slapped, shaken, insulted and threatened with sexual assault. Her brother was beaten and sexually assaulted. He bit his thumb in an attempt to prevent his thumbprint being put to his 'confession'. Kim Sam-sok was imprisoned for seven years (reduced on appeal to four years); his sister received a suspended three-year sentence.

On 6 November 1994 Cecilia Silva Godoy, a 43-year-old housewife from Temuco in Chile, was reportedly beaten and stripped by police when she went to the station to complain about noisy neighbours.

Once in custody women may find that their captors expect them to provide sexual favours. One example of the way that women prisoners are used for the gratification of their captors was described by a 17-year-old girl in Ethiopia who was a virgin on her arrest in 1993:

'I was taken with a group of prisoners to the airforce officers' club . . . I was taken at gunpoint to a dark room inside the prison where some man I could not identify raped me violently. I became pregnant . . . and gave birth . . . to a child whose father I did not know.'

AI reported in 1992 on sexual abuse of prisoners held by the ANC in Angola, Zambia and Zimbabwe between 1984 and 1988. One woman held in Quatro Camp in Angola was severely beaten for refusing to sleep with guards, one of whom then masturbated over her. The testicles of one male prisoner were mutilated with pliers.

In 1992, 70 women prisoners at the Georgia Women's Correctional Institution in the USA filed affidavits alleging gross sexual abuse by prison staff over a period of years. At least 12 prison officials were charged, several were dismissed, and state officials resigned when it was revealed that a regime of terror had developed inside the jail involving rape, sexual abuse, prostitution, coerced abortions, and the supplying of sex in return for favours.

In November of the same year, the army in Pakistan uncovered a similar scandal at a private rural jail in which bonded labourers were held by a rich landlord in the Hyderabad district. Beatings and gang rapes by the landlord and his watchmen were common. Ghulam Hussain Khokhar used rape as a punishment as well as for his own perverse gratification. When he suspected a woman of stealing a watch he ordered her own father to rape her. When the man refused, two of the landlord's servants were told to carry out the assault instead. One woman said: 'They would chain our men at night and take our girls and rape them.' A male inmate added: 'at times they didn't even bother to take them to their bunkers; they raped them right in front of us.'

Gay men, transvestites and transsexuals also face discrimination and risk assault and murder in many countries solely on the basis of their sexual orientation. AI has highlighted a series of at least 11 killings of gay men between June 1991 and February 1993 in the state of Chiapas, Mexico, as one example of an apparently systematic campaign designed to terrorize the gay community. Five men subsequently arrested in connection with the murders were all released when it became clear that their 'confessions' had been extracted from them under torture.

In some countries homosexuality is a capital offence. Under *shari'a* jurisprudence in Iran the punishment (*shageh*) may involve those convicted being cut in two halves lengthwise, thrown off a cliff, or stoned to death. In Romania, where sexual acts between persons of the same sex remain an offence punishable by up to five years' imprisonment, there have been many instances of ill-treatment of gay men while under arrest.

In a number of countries, including Argentina, Bolivia, Chile, East Timor, Kenya and Mexico, there have been frequent reports of beatings directed specifically at the genitals and threats of sexual assault.

In Pakistan, police officers conducting torture have deliberately set out to damage male genitals, applying pressure on them with heavy wooden or metal rollers while the victim is held down, crushing blood vessels and muscles.

Both men and women have been subjected to violent forms of sexual humiliation in Kenya. Men have been tortured by having their genitals pricked with large pins or tied with string and pulled. Women have had objects inserted into their vaginas.

Male rape is not uncommon. In November 1992 a 14-year-old boy was beaten and raped by a police officer at Meldsi near Shahdadpur in the Sanghar district of Sindh Province, one of several such incidents reported to AI.

Mehmet Hayrettin Arat, a Turkish Kurd arrested on drugs-related charges in Greece in 1991, was allegedly subjected to 17 hours of torture including a mock execution with sexual overtones. A plastic bag was placed over his head seven times, and water thrown over him as he lost consciousness. His interrogators played 'Russian roulette' four times by placing in his mouth a gun with a single bullet, spinning the cylinder and pulling the trigger. Then the man's jeans and underpants were cut off with scissors. An officer put on a glove and inserted his finger into the man's anus saying, 'I'll make a faggot of you.'

Sexual abuse by interrogators in Egypt has included the insertion of fingers, sticks and other implements into the rectum of their prisoners.

Isidro Albuquerque Rodrigues, arrested by police in Alcântara, Portugal, on 26 June 1990 on suspicion of assault, robbery and being an accessory to murder, was stripped naked, handcuffed and beaten by police. He claimed that a shampoo bottle was forced into his anus and he was whipped with a flexible metal hose-pipe. Medical evidence supported his allegation.

In India, chilli powder is rubbed into the genitals and other sensitive parts of the body, including deliberate incisions cut into people's flesh. Many other methods of torture are routine. Shopkeeper Manzoor Ahmed Naikoo recorded the abuse of his torturers in 1991:

'After tying me down, they removed my pyjamas. They tied cloth to my penis and set it on fire. . . . Then they laid me face down. One man stood

on my back. Another brought a rod and inserted it deep into my rectum.
He kept thrusting it forward and back.'

Leroy Neil, a Jamaican arrested in the Netherlands Antilles, collapsed
and died of peritonitis while under interrogation in February 1991. Police
continued with an interview although he was visibly ill and was receiving
medical treatment. He had alleged that a truncheon had been inserted
into his anus, and the pathologist who conducted the autopsy confirmed
that his fatal condition might well have been caused by this assault.

In Turkey, sexual molestation by police officers and damage to their
victims' genitals is common. In 1992 Kadir Kurt was one of four men
tortured to death. He died on 19 April after he and his brother had been
subjected to a night of torture. Davut Kurt reported: 'They tortured my
brother next to me. They inserted a truncheon into his anus.' The
following month Ismail Yilmaz was beaten, subjected to *falaka* (beating of
the soles of the feet) and electric shocks to his penis, and raped with a
police truncheon before being released without charge.

Not content with inflicting pain and submission through beatings, or
effecting psychological trauma by simply cutting people off from the
outside world, many torturers seem intent upon the total humiliation of
their victims. Sexual abuse reveals much about the alienation of the
torturer. Rape, mutilation and the emasculation of male detainees suggest
a personal need to dominate and degrade as well as symbolizing the
power of life and death held by torturers. It is not as if they are short of
other techniques and tools with which to crush the body and spirit of
their captors. What is both intriguing and sickening is that the
perpetrators concoct 'pet names' for the obscenities their victims are
forced to endure.

Naming the unspeakable

Mass media coverage of the Vietnam War introduced the world to what
might be termed 'the gook syndrome', 'gook' being a derogatory term
used by the American soldiers to describe their opponents. By defining
the enemy as objects, or at least subhuman, it is easier to order their
destruction and to persuade those who must do the killing that their
actions are not subject to the moral constraints that rule out murder or
torture as acceptable human behaviour. Throughout Western European
history, terms such as 'heathens', 'infidels' and 'savages' have been used in
the justification of imperialist conquest. Whole societies have been characterized as 'non-people' or *Untermenschen* solely on the basis of skin
colour and cultural differences. All racial minorities have suffered in this
way.

Similar techniques are used by those who train torturers in order to desensitize trainees to the humanity of the people they are paid to hurt. Perhaps as a measure of their alienation, or perhaps to protect themselves from the unspeakable nature of their actions, torturers everywhere have invented 'nicknames' to describe the punishments they administer. The precise nature of the ill-treatment they mete out is obscured by an extraordinary range of euphemisms, some of which are common to several countries.

In pre-1989 Romania, detainees were strung up by the legs, with the hands tied, and beaten all over before being lowered to allow the soles of the feet to be beaten, in a technique called *rotisor*. This technique has not been reported in the past five years.

Variations on the term and the technique occur in many different countries. In Tunisia it is known as the *poulet rôti* (chicken on a spit). The 'chicken' position (*kukhura*) in Nepal involves even more contortions. The victim's hands are loosely tied behind the back then pushed under the thighs and the head is forced down under the rope that ties the hands together. In Mexico the victim is suspended by the feet, knees, wrists or arms from a pole known as the *pollo rostizado* or parrot's perch. The Sri Lankan variant is known as *dharma chakra*, 'the wheel of Buddha's teaching'.

In Myanmar (Burma) a similar punishment is known as 'the helicopter'. The victims are suspended by their wrists or ankles, or in a sack, from a rotating ceiling fan or fixture and spun around while they are beaten. Detainees in India have been beaten while held in the 'aeroplane', with their arms bound to a pole resting on their shoulders. And when 'the plane takes off' in Sudan, 'the prisoner's elbows are tied to his knees and a wooden pole is pushed through the gap. He is left hanging for days. They give him drops of water and keep flogging him.'

In Syria detainees are subjected to 'the German chair' (*al-Kursi al-Almani*), a metal contraption with a movable backrest. Victims are strapped in and the back of the chair is let down, causing acute extension of the spine and severe pressure on the neck and limbs. This can constrict breathing to the point of asphyxiation and result in loss of consciousness and fracturing of the vertebrae.

A favoured position for beating prisoners in Bolivia involves a contortion known as 'the pig' (*chancho*). The prisoner is made to stand with hands cuffed behind the back, and then bent over backwards so that the head is on the ground and pushed against a wall. The beatings may then continue for hours on end.

'The bell' (*la campana*) leaves no physical sign. The victim's head is inserted into a metal container which is beaten repeatedly. The noise and vibration are devastating.

Figure 5.5. Chad: an MPS soldier stands guard outside the military barracks which houses the detention centre known as the 'Camp des Martyrs'.

Serious permanent damage including loss of hearing can result from the 'telephone' (*teléfono*) torture used in Chile and Mexico among others, involving incessant blows to the ears. In a similar torture, 'the twin slap' (*calotte marassa*), employed in Haiti, victims were slapped simultaneously on both ears, usually from behind. And in the version used at ANC prison camps in Angola, prisoners were required to puff up their cheeks before guards slapped them in the face. Known as *pompa,* it ruptures the eardrums and can lead to ear infections.

The secret police in Chad (Figure 5.5) devised many hideous tortures for their opponents. The *supplice des baguettes* (or 'French bread' torture) involved tying a cord round the head and then twisting it with two sticks, causing severe pain and eventually haemorrhages from the nose, and loss of consciousness. The 'black diet' (*diète noire*) simply meant starving the prisoner to death.

Although torture was virtually eradicated in Algeria between 1989 and 1991, it has returned with a vengeance in recent years. The most common form of torture used by the security forces is the 'cloth' (*chiffon*) which can take different forms. A piece of cloth is packed into the mouth of the detainee, who is then tied to a bench or suspended from a bar.

Large quantities of liquid, including dirty water mixed with detergent or other chemicals, is then poured onto the cloth. A medical doctor, Noureddine Lamdjadani, received this treatment when he answered a summons to attend a police station in Algiers on 17 May 1994. First he was blindfolded, undressed and handcuffed. While the *chiffon* was being administered by one police officer, another forced his hands apart with a stick and others used sticks to beat his head and feet. The process was repeated many times over a period of 57 days.

In Myanmar (Burma), detainees are said to be 'having a bath' when their tormentors force them to sit in a plastic bag while they are whipped with electric cables. The bag is removed and they are drenched with water, then the bag is replaced and the beating continues.

Several countries apply another water torture known as 'wet submarine', where the victim's head is repeatedly submerged in water, with the possibility of asphyxiation and drowning. Sometimes the victim's face is pushed into a lavatory bowl filled with faeces, chilli powder, chlorine or other chemicals. There are reports of such irritants being rubbed into raw wounds.

A similar term and technique is used in Bolivia (*submarino*) and in Mexico (*submarino húmedo*, also known as *el pozole* or *pozoleado*), where the *Tehuacanazo* or 'mineral water torture' takes its name from a popular brand of carbonated mineral water, Tehuacán. The fizzy liquid, sometimes mixed with chilli powder, is forced up the victim's nostrils. Alternatively tap water is squirted up the nostrils through a hose. Detainees may risk suffocation in the 'dry submarine' (*submarino seco*, or *la bolsita*, 'the bag'), when a plastic bag is pulled over the head and tied at the neck.

These horrendous techniques are not confined to the interrogation cell. To prevent the police from harming his wife and friends, a senior Mexican lawyer, Antonio Partida Valdovinos, former President of the Tepic Bar Association and former Vice-President of the National Federation of Bar Associations, confessed to drug offences in November 1989 after a raid on his friend's house:

> 'It was like a nightmare. They arrived at three in the morning at my friend's house and after searching the house, and assaulting my wife, my friend's wife and our children, they accused us of being drug traffickers. In front of his children, they placed a plastic bag on my friend's head. The way he started to suffocate was like a horror film. . . . He was purple and the plastic bag was almost stuck to his face. His children were crying. His wife tried to stop them torturing him, but they pushed her away, hitting her. They put my hands behind my back and covered me with a blanket

and started beating me. We couldn't believe it. . . . They insulted our wives. They also beat them as if they were men.'

Mexican torturers also make frequent use of 'the buzzer' (*la chicharra*), an electric prod attached to the eyes, gums, tongue, nipples and genitals of their victims. They also force parts of the body into light fittings, or connect victims to the main supply via cables fixed to their feet and hands.

In China, a guard at the Mian County Detention Centre, Shaanxi Province, is reported to have boasted about knowing 39 different ways to shackle a prisoner. One such punishment, which causes pain and humiliation to two prisoners at once, is called 'bending three wheels' (*piansanlun*). The wrists of one are secured to the ankles of another, forcing one to squat and shuffle along behind the other. There is no respite for sleep, eating or use of the toilet, sometimes for days on end. Another form of shackling is known as 'Su Qin carries a sword on his back' (*Su Qin bei jian*), a reference to traditional methods of carrying a weapon. In fact it describes a painful form of shackling that incapacitates the prisoner. One arm is pulled over the shoulder and handcuffed to the other arm which has been twisted behind the back. The prisoner is unable to do anything without help. Prisoners subjected to 'chain shackling' (*liankao*), less euphemistic but no less obscure, have their hands and feet secured together in a variety of ways. The most contorting is when the hands and feet are shackled together behind the back.

A particularly vicious form of torture inflicted upon two prisoners at the same time is known as 'the old ox ploughing the land' (*laoniu gendi*). AI received a report about its use during the winter of 1989–90. As punishment for their involvement in a fight two men were handcuffed together back to back and secured to a rope pulled by other prisoners. The guards beat the 'oxen' with sticks and batons to make them run fast dragging the two men across rough concrete. The man facing forwards was forced to crawl while Xie Baoquan, the man he was tethered to, scraped along the ground on his back. This continued until the area was covered in blood. Xie Baoquan received no medical treatment and his cell mates had to scrape pus and congealed blood from his wounds as his raw back suppurated throughout the winter, filling the room with the smell of rotting flesh.

Among many other terms used to describe excruciating practices in China are *dian ji* (electrical assault), *gui bian* (down on knees whipping), *liao quan jiao* (martial arts practice), *jiaxin mian bao* (the sandwich filling) and *zuo feiji* (jetplane ride).

Detainees in Myanmar (Burma) have been subjected to 'the iron road'.

The skin is slowly stripped from their shinbones by repeated scraping with bamboo rods, bottles and iron bars. 'Motorcyle riding' is the term used to describe prolonged squatting as if driving a motorbike.

In the Morris Seabelo Rehabilitation Centre (also known as Quatro, or Camp 32), near Quibaxe in northern Angola, prisoners of the ANC were made to sit on or crawl through red ants' nests. They were also forced to crawl through patches of bush known as 'napalm' because the plant caused itching and stinging. Sometimes the leaves would be rubbed into the prisoners' skins. Alternatively they might be subjected to the 'gas mask', when the skin of a pawpaw (papaya) fruit was rubbed into their faces until they could not breathe. And they were taunted with offers of 'coffee' or 'guava', meaning they could choose whether they would be beaten with sticks from the coffee plants or guava trees that surrounded the camp.

Prisoners were made to dig deep pits and then told to try to climb out of them while they were pelted with stones. Prisoners at a camp in Zambia were also made to endure this 'game', dubbed 'slaughter' by the guards, who delighted in playing it during the rainy season. The prisoners themselves were forced to adopt humiliating pseudonyms while in custody: Muzorewa (after the Black clergyman Prime Minister of short-lived Zimbabwe-Rhodesia); Dolinchek (a mercenary employed by the South African government during apartheid); *porco* (pig); *macao* (monkey); and *lerete* (testicles).

No doubt the hundreds of thousands who have suffered at the hands of the world's torturers have devised their own angry vocabulary of protest. Certainly inmates of St Catherine's District Prison, Jamaica, had a nickname for one group of warders who meted out vicious treatment. They were known simply but eloquently as the 'Viper Squad'.

The final solution
Interrogators may not intend to kill their victims in the torture chamber, but hundreds, perhaps thousands, of people do die each year under interrogation. On occasion the death of a detainee may be regarded by the captor as a failure. But at best it may be treated as an inconvenience.

AI has publicized details of hundreds of deaths in custody, some reportedly as a result of torture, which have emerged from different parts of India. Between 1990 and 1994 over 700 were recorded in the state of Jammu and Kashmir, where the government faces continued violent political opposition. In some cases mutilated corpses have been dumped by the roadside or in rivers. Some bodies were simply returned to relatives. In recent years the government has claimed that those killed were caught in crossfire or died in encounters between security forces and militants.

Clearly the impunity that allows torture in the first place also acknowledges that murder is permissible. If it cannot be turned to the advantage of the perpetrator by displaying the tortured body as a warning to others, corpses can be destroyed or secretly buried.

Some regimes prefer the bodies of their dead opponents not to be found, and the tragedy of the 'disappeared' lives on in the anguish of their relatives. Mass graves are often hidden away from centres of population and may not be discovered until those who supervised the interments reveal their location. A former police officer in El Salvador revealed that prisoners were sometimes buried alive:

> 'My superior told us: "I have a good place for this man." He was talking about a dry well located near a crossroads [near] Las Placitas in San Miguel. There was a fence and a wire gate surrounding the well. . . . [The victim] had his arms tied behind him and he was blindfolded. He was taken inside the gate, and he was thrown down the well alive. He fell to his death, because the well was very deep. My superior told me there were more than 15 dead bodies at the bottom of the well.'

The lack of care about whether someone lives or dies has a bearing upon the living conditions they are expected to endure. Unhealthy and overcrowded prisons and lack of medical attention increase the likelihood of premature death. A series of such incidents were recorded in Cuba during 1992. Several prisoners were reported to have died from beatings in Cuban prisons in 1992. They included one young escapee who died three days after giving himself up to the Havana police. His body was reportedly covered in wounds and bruises and his wrists fractured, showing marks of handcuffs. The authorities claimed that he had caused his own death by throwing himself against the walls and bars of his cell and that he had been given appropriate medical attention. No independent autopsy was carried out.

When 40 injured opposition supporters were crammed into a cell designed to hold five it was not surprising that there were fatalities. It happened on 27 August 1993 at the Blitta gendarmerie in Togo. All 40 had been arrested and beaten by members of the Public Security Force (FSP '93) in disturbances after irregularities in the presidential elections. At least 21 died in the cell or in hospital in Sokodé. The authorities claimed that the detainees had been given poisoned food by members of their own political party, though there was no examination of the bodies to verify this. On 27 August a relative of one of the detainees, Kokou Okessou Mbooura, was arrested in Blitta and charged with attempting to administer a poison.

During the same year AI discovered that prisoners were being poisoned with strychnine in Ndjamena's detention centres, and at Bitkine, in eastern Chad, 93 prisoners died after being fed poisoned millet.

Prison authorities often claim that unexpected deaths while in custody are the result of suicide, offering fear or shame and despair at betraying their cause as the motive. There were two such incidents in Pakistan during 1992. Medical student Mujib Aijaz Jatoi was alleged to have hanged himself in a toilet the day after he was arrested by Sindh police in August and handed over to the army. The head, chest, legs and testicles of his corpse bore the marks of torture, and nails from four fingers had been pulled out.

Noor Muhammad Qureshi, a young merchant, was arrested in December by police from Pinyari station in Hyderabad district. They were seen beating him and taking him away in their van. Two hours later his bruised body was found lying half in the water of a nearby canal. One of his arms had been broken. Police claimed he had leapt from the van and drowned in the canal.

For those incarcerated in appalling conditions, deprived of sleep, food and company, beaten and abused regularly, death may be something they wish for as a release from the torment. Some are indeed driven to take their own lives. And suicide is not uncommon among former detainees who continue to suffer pain and mental anguish long after they have been released.

However, the determination to resist has led some to risk their lives through hunger strikes. Alfredo Díaz Ortiz, aged 67, died in the Lenin Provincial Hospital, Holguín, Cuba, on 30 May 1992 after refusing food in protest at his treatment by the state security forces. He had been arrested four months earlier and accused of enemy propaganda though no compromising documents had been found at his home. His interrogators played him taped recordings of his son and daughter-in-law to make him believe they too were in custody.

The threat of summary execution is often used to instil terror in detainees. In July 1990 police arrested Sehmus Ukus, a Turkish Kurd, in Greece. He claimed to have been taken to high ground, stripped and hung from a tree. When he was taken down the police officers cuffed his hands behind his back and tied his legs together, then burned the soles of his feet and his genitals with a cigarette lighter before beating him with sticks. When he asked them either to stop or to kill him, they said, 'You are going to die slowly.' Their wretched captive began to beat his head against the tree. He was then taken to the police station where the beatings continued the next day, and pens were put between his fingers which were then crushed together, but he was not killed. When a senior police officer asked why they were beating him, they replied, 'He is a Turk.'

All around the world survivors have reported the use of mock executions as part of the psychological warfare directed against prisoners and their families. Events leading to the death under torture in Mexico of Ricardo López at the North Preventive Detention Centre, Mexico City, exemplifies the way in which death and the threat of death are regarded as legitimate weapons when accountability is not at stake. The 19-year-old young man was arrested on 22 March 1990 and charged with kidnapping a young child. He was held incommunicado and allegedly 'confessed'. Five days later his mother, aunt and uncle were detained and beaten for 48 hours. After he had been formally charged, his mother, Guadalupe López, visited him and saw that he had been severely beaten and his left hand damaged. She told prison wardens she would make an official complaint and was then visited by police officers, who threatened her with death if she proceeded. She moved house. In May her son wrote protesting his innocence and said the confession had been induced by torture. He was not at the prison when she next visited him, and on 22 June she was abducted by armed police. Her badly injured son was in the vehicle that took her away. They were handcuffed and blindfolded and taken to a house where the blindfolds were removed, and they were stripped and handcuffed to a pipe in the bathroom. Guadalupe says that her son was semi-conscious. There were open wounds on his body, which bore the marks of cigarette burns, and his foot was broken. Over the next two days they were pushed into water tanks connected to the electricity supply, had their heads submerged in a toilet containing excrement, and were beaten, burned with cigarettes and subjected to mock executions. They received no food or drink. It is one of the few cases where one of the torturers was a woman, a police informer (*madrina*). On 24 June Ricardo was so badly hurt that he barely reacted when two of his toenails were pulled out. Both were then taken by car to near their original family home and Guadalupe was dumped in the street. She spent three days unconscious in hospital. Her son died in detention that night. His body was dressed to make it appear that he had committed suicide. When it was later located at the mortuary, his death certificate recorded 'asphyxiation due to strangling following multiple trauma'.

Mock executions are often staged to intimidate prisoners. Yusuf Jakhrani, a leading National Democratic Party politician in Sindh Province, Pakistan, and a former political prisoner, was arrested at his home in Kandhkot in the early hours of 6 June 1992 with a friend, Dodo Khan Nandwani. They were tortured for five days. On 12 June, an Islamic holiday, they received the conventional feast-day greeting '*Eid mubaruk*' from their guards before Yusuf was taken out and beaten. The two men were then thrown into a van. Dodo Khan Nandwani was blindfolded.

After his release without charge the following month he told AI:

'The soldiers said now they would kill us . . . even in the van they kept beating us. . . . Yusuf was hit with a gun. I could hear that. He was moaning. . . . After a while the van stopped. An army officer came to the back and said, "Yusuf is finished." They shifted me to another vehicle and the soldiers said they would finish me too, like they had killed Yusuf . . .

'I must have fainted for when I came to I found myself in the army hospital in Pano Aqil. . . . After some hours the army people took me again away in a van. On the way they stopped the car and made me stand against a wall. They said they were going to kill me and made me recite the Holy Koran. Then they fired in the air to frighten me.'

During one incident in Ecuador soldiers selected passengers for interrogation from a boat on the Putumayo River in December 1993. One of two men handcuffed and blindfolded and taken to a military base, Reineiro Jurado explained what happened:

'I had a water bag put over my head, then they sprayed me. . . . They injected my right shoulder after which I could not move my arms. They said they would kill me at 4 p.m. When the time came I was hung again and asked about the guerrillas.

'I was tortured from 4 to 7 p.m. My friend was also beaten. . . . After saying to me, "Let's go, because the time has arrived for you to die," they grabbed me by the arms and pulled me down a road. I heard the sound of the river and thought we had arrived at the jetty. There they said, "Throw him into the deep part." They uncocked their firearms and started up the engine of the boat. I was very frightened. I thought my time had come. I felt them throw me out of the boat, but I landed on the ground. Then they told me to take off the blindfold – it was then I realized I was on the jetty at Puerto Ospina.'

In 1993 student Benevides Correia Barros, who had been collecting photographic evidence of Indonesian occupation in East Timor, was apprehended by the security forces twice in a fortnight. He was with a friend on the second occasion:

'They ordered us to lie down on the side of the road, tied our hands up, and one of them threatened to execute us there and then. . . . They frogmarched us to a small hut . . . stripped us naked and started beating us for about an hour, hitting our heads, chests, genitals, kidneys, thighs and knees. Soon our noses, mouths and ears were bleeding . . .'

The two men were taken to an interrogation centre and beaten for five hours before being separated. Benevides was driven away by car: 'I was pushed out of the car still handcuffed, ordered to kneel down and start praying in preparation for being executed. This happened three times.'

A young seminarian, Salvador Sarmento, experienced a similar threat during a violent interrogation in January 1994:

> 'As they beat and kicked me I said, "Please just kill me rather than torturing me like this. In the name of truth I am prepared to die." Then they said, "If you really want to die we can easily arrange for your corpse to disappear."'

> 'Then they ordered me to pray, and so I prayed: "Oh God, please receive my soul and forgive them for what they do." As I prayed one of them said, "Let's just shoot him and throw his body in the sea." When I had finished praying they did not shoot, but they threatened me twice more with a pistol.'

AI reports from the United Kingdom about 'punishment shootings' by both Republican and Loyalist paramilitaries in Northern Ireland indicate that victims are threatened with death unless they desist from 'anti-social behaviour' or leave the province. Alleged informers have been summarily executed; young people involved in burglary, drug-dealing and 'joy-riding' have been 'kneecapped' (shot in the leg), severely beaten and warned that worse may be to come. In January 1992 the mother of 18-year-old Danny Morris claimed that he was held down and beaten by eight Irish Republican Army (IRA) men, who tried to hammer a chisel into his legs. He was treated for a broken leg and arm, and ordered to leave Northern Ireland within 48 hours of leaving hospital. In November 1992 Donna Wilson, whose noisy parties had been complained about by neighbours, was beaten to death by up to ten alleged members of a Loyalist 'punishment squad' using baseball bats and pickaxe handles. And in December 1992 John Collett was shot in the legs by the IRA. Both his legs had to be amputated and he later died from his injuries.

During a clampdown on 'mafia-criminal structures, pillagers and marauders' announced in Tadzhikistan in December 1992 it was made clear that 'measures up to and including execution on the spot' would be applied. They were. But among the bodies that subsequently turned up at the Dushanbe city morgue were some that had clearly been tortured before being killed. Fingernails had been pulled out, limbs had been broken, ears cut off, faces slashed across the eyes, throats cut. Some had been partially skinned alive, and others burned to death.

Harjinder Kaur's neighbours in Latala village, Punjab, India, were told to give her cause of death as 'buffalo blows' after she and members of her family had been tied up by police and beaten at their home on 11 August 1992. Her husband, sister and brother-in-law were taken away by police; she was left to die.

Death is no less final for being 'accidental'. Omasese Lumumba fled his homeland after harassment and 18 months of political imprisonment following the assassination of his uncle Patrice Lumumba, first prime minister of what is now Zaire, in 1961. Omasese had spent 10 years in Switzerland before coming to the UK. A month later he died in the custody of prison staff at Pentonville Prison in London on 8 October 1991. For weeks he was held largely in isolation, locked up for 20 hours a day, and showed understandable signs of depression and anxiety. When he finally refused to co-operate he was 'restrained' by at least six prison staff. They attempted to strip him while he struggled (a woman officer even cut off some of his clothes with scissors), and a doctor was called to give him a tranquillizing injection. When the doctor arrived Omasese was dead, still held down by at least five prison officers.

His was not the only such death linked to Britain's immigration policies. Joy Gardner was physically restrained, bound, and gagged with adhesive tape when she resisted arrest by police and immigration officials in July 1993. She collapsed into a coma and died four days later.

Reprisals and the threat of reprisals are a form of ill-treatment most often carried out during wars. Among many such incidents reported from Iraqi Kurdistan was the killing of 19 Kurdistan Democratic Party members captured by the rival Patriotic Union of Kurdistan in May 1994:

> 'That evening they brought out five of the detainees, drove them to Gurdi Husni and executed them. Then five others, and then the rest, in groups.
> . . . Some of them had their hands cut off and the eyes of others had been gouged out . . .'

Even when hostilities are officially at an end the risk of death and torture lingers as both victors and vanquished adjust to their status. In the aftermath of the Gulf War many hundreds of Sunni Islamic opponents of the government, Shi'a Muslims and Christians have been arrested, harassed and tortured in Saudi Arabia. Such ill-treatment was not unknown before that war increased tension in the region. Forty-year-old Zahra' Habib Mansur al-Nasser (Figure 5.6) was detained and allegedly tortured at a check-point on the Jordanian border after returning from a holy Shi'a place of worship. Her body was handed back to her family after she had spent three days at the Hudaitha check-point detention centre. And in January 1991 members of the Riyadh International Charismatic Fellowship were arrested for the second time in four months.

Figure 5.6. Saudi Arabia: Zahra' Habib Mansur al-Nasser, a 40-year-old housewife from Awjem, Eastern Province, died in the custody of border police on her way back from visiting a Shi'a shrine at Sayyida Zainab, Syria, in July 1989.

On the first occasion three Filipino nationals were held and reportedly flogged, on the latter five more Philippine Christians were arrested and sentenced to a year's imprisonment and 150 lashes. They were released in an amnesty later in the year, but in 1992 their pastor, Oswaldo Magdangal, was arrested. There were reports that he was beaten and, with another man, was due to be beheaded. Instead the two men were deported to the Philippines.

Tens of people have died in custody in Tunisia in the past few years. Among them was Faisal Barakat, a 25-year-old mathematics and physics student at Tunis University, a member of al-Nahda, an unauthorized Islamist party, and of the Union Générale Tunisienne des Étudiants

(UGTE). Following his arrest on 8 October 1991, he was tortured while detained incommunicado in Nabeul police station and died. The autopsy report states that he bore bruises on the soles of the feet and elsewhere. However, the Tunisian authorities maintained that he was never arrested and that he died in a road accident.

In South Africa under apartheid, brutality, torture and extrajudicial execution intended to intimidate whole communities, by the police, security forces and paramilitary groups, were widespread. After the first successful non-racial elections in April 1994, the new government signed a number of human rights treaties and began reviewing the interim constitution which guarantees certain 'fundamental human rights', including the right not to be tortured. Political violence subsided after this except in Natal. In August 1994 visiting Dutch police discovered torture equipment in a police station, precipitating an independent investigation. In a few cases, perpetrators have been brought to justice.

Death may be sudden or long-drawn-out. Judicial killings, the 'death penalty', may involve unnecessary cruelty both in the execution and in the legal process. Lengthy delays in carrying out the sentence mean that many of those condemned to death live for years in a state of limbo torn between the knowledge that they are to die and the hope that they may win a reprieve. Death row is a torture chamber in which no one need lift a finger to hurt the inmates. And because they are 'about to die', conditions are often appalling.

Judicial executions in the USA may take a variety of forms: the 'electric chair', the gas chamber, hanging, the firing squad, and the administration of lethal injections. Elsewhere in the world the 'final solution' may also involve decapitation, crucifixion or stoning to death. In many countries public executions are still common.

Judicial execution is nothing less than state-sanctioned murder. It is the language of terror and the ultimate sanction of the torturer. They do not have to take place in public, nor do the bodies have to be displayed. It is the final form of retributive punishment and has little meaning unless the 'message' gets across to the rest of the population. Where the death penalty exists the sentence and the execution are generally well publicized. In countries where the state does not need to rely upon subterfuge and 'disappearances' it is a reminder of the ultimate authority that those in power wield over the population. That gives it the hallmark of torture.

CHAPTER 6

The Torturers

Felicity de Zulueta

A man from Tunisia describes how he was tortured: two men beat him with pipes and sticks and then they forced him to walk even though he could hardly stand up. As he started to lose consciousness, his torturers revived him with ether and then pulled him by his genitals. They tore the skin from his nails and from in between his toes and his fingers, and they burnt his sensitive parts by simmering alcohol and then lighting it. He still has the scars today. They then forced him to sit on a bottle and both his torturers pushed down on him till he fainted. They tore out his moustache with their hands. These men then put sticks in their victim's ears and twisted them against the eardrum until he fainted. Their victim continues describing his torments: how he was made to stare at a very bright light for hours, kneeling on the floor holding a chair with his hands high above him while his torturers beat him. His worst experience, however, was after having fainted when he was beginning to regain consciousness: he found that he was chained by his hands and feet, on one side to the bars of a window and on the other side to an iron bed; one of his torturers unzipped his trouser and pulled out his penis. He then urinated into his victim's mouth. At this point, the Tunisian man who is giving this terrible account stops, visibly distressed, and says, 'I can't bear it . . . I'm sorry.' When asked why he did not co-operate under all this pressure, this brave man answered that he wanted to preserve his dignity. He could not admit that people can be forced against their will. To admit it 'is to feel humiliated in the very depth of my being' (Bloomstein, 1990).

Listening to this account is harrowing. How can any human do these terrible things to another? One could easily believe that what we find out is taking place in the torture cells all round the world is the grossest form of inhumanity that exists. Those who inflict such pain and suffering must surely be evil perverts. No ordinary person could be so vicious. And yet those who have carried out these terrible deeds, those who have maimed and raped, tortured and killed, will tell us that anyone can become a torturer. Do we believe them?

The only way to answer the question is to attempt to understand how an individual becomes a torturer and what psycho-social conditions encourage and produce torture. When General Massu, commander of the French army during the Algerian War of Independence, was asked what would make a good 'interrogator', his reply was that such an individual should be intelligent and detached. He must not show hate or passion but 'icy coldness' (Bloomstein, 1990).

What the General could not have known is that around 1974 a laboratory investigation was to be set up which goes far to helping us understand what sort of individual has the propensity to become a torturer.

The potential torturers among us

When Stanley Milgram and his team set up their experiment in the Interaction Laboratory of Yale University, their aim was to study human obedience. All their subjects enrolled in the project after responding to an advertisement to participate in 'a study on memory'. They were given an introductory talk by the experimenter on theories of learning during which they were told that 'people learn things correctly whenever they get punished for making a mistake. A common application of this theory would be when parents spank a child . . .' (Milgram, 1974, p. 18).

The volunteer was unaware that both the learner strapped in his electric chair in another room and the experimenter were acting. Nor did he know that no real electric shocks were being administered. The volunteer was seated in front of an instrument panel which consisted of level switches set in a line. Each switch had a labelled voltage designation ranging from 15 to 450 volts. The last four switches of this shock generator were also marked 'Danger: severe shock'.

The volunteer was given orders to move one level higher on the shock generator each time the learner in the electric chair gave a wrong answer. The latter started to scream and plead as the shocks appeared to become more painful. Though many learners protested verbally at having to continue, they obeyed instructions and, once the experimenter agreed to take responsibility, 26 out of 40 continued administering even greater shocks until the maximum voltage was reached. This happened even though the learner went quiet and the volunteer expressed a fear that he might have died. One of the volunteers, Mr Prozi, turned to the experimenter at this point and said: 'What if he is dead in there?' He gestured towards the room with the electric chair. 'I mean he told me he can't stand the shock, sir. I don't mean to be rude but I think you should look in on him' (Milgram, 1974, pp. 73–7). As Milgram says, 'the subject's objections strike us as inordinately weak. . . . He thinks he is killing someone and yet he uses the language of the tea table' (Milgram, 1974, p. 77).

It is important to note that it was crucial for this man that the experimenter should accept responsibility for what might happen if the volunteer continued to obey. The other important observation to make is that, having passed on all responsibility to the experimenter in the white coat, Mr Prozi's language changed and became that of an obedient child, both courteous and respectful. Though some volunteers like Mr Prozi obeyed instructions to the point of potentially killing their victim after apparently inflicting considerable pain, they were not as 'icy cold' as General Massu would have wished. However, such detached individuals did find their way into Milgram's project. One was Mr Batta, a 37-year-old welder. He had his victim sitting by his side in the room, a factor which normally greatly reduced the number of subjects able to give maximum shocks. However, it had no such effect on Mr Batta, who, when his victim refused to put his hand on the plate after the 150-volt level, simply forced the man's hand down on the plate. He ignored all the learner's pleas for mercy. Milgram wrote as follows: 'What is extraordinary is his apparent total indifference to the learner: he hardly takes cognizance of him as a human being. Meanwhile, he relates to the experimenter in a submissive and courteous fashion' (Milgram, 1974, p. 46). As Mr Batta increases the power of his shocks and subdues his screaming victim, his face remains cold and impassive. When interviewed at the end of the experiment, he said that he never felt nervous but he became 'disgusted' when the learner wouldn't co-operate. Clearly, for Mr Batta, the learner was not a human being in pain; he was simply a threat to the smooth running of the experiment.

We now have evidence as to the conditions under which children can become like Mr Batta. Their early experiences are not so different from those encountered in the torture chambers around the world and re-created by Milgram's subjects. However, before we look at the childhood development of people like Mr Prozi or Mr Batta, let us look at another of Milgram's subjects, one of the 14 original male subjects who did not obey orders to the end. Mr Rensaaler had emigrated from the Netherlands after the Second World War. He obeyed the instructor until he reached the level of 255 volts, when he stopped. The experimenter told the subject to continue and added that he had no choice. Mr Rensaaler replied:

'I do have a choice. (Incredulous and indignant) Why don't I have a choice? I came here on my own free will. I thought I could help in a research project. But if I have to hurt somebody to do that . . . I can't continue. I am very sorry. I think I have gone too far already, probably.'

Unlike people like Mr Prozi or Mr Batta, this subject refused to assign any responsibility to the learner or the experimenter. When looking back at the experiment he wished he had stopped when the learner first complained, but:

> 'I turned round and looked at you. I guess it's a matter of . . . authority, if you want to call it that: my being impressed by the thing and going on although I didn't want to. Say if you are working in the army, and your superior tells you to do it. That sort of thing, you know what I mean?'

(Milgram, 1974, pp. 51–2)

These three subjects represent three different levels of obedience, and what we can see is that high levels of obedience to authority figures are associated with high levels of violence towards the 'learner', a strong tendency to dehumanize the victim and a relinquishing of personal responsibility which is associated with the subject showing a childlike attitude to people in authority. Both men and women participated in this act of obedience to authority.

To explain his findings, Milgram suggested that human beings are born with a potential for obedience which, under certain conditions, can produce the 'obedient' man, a man who could function in a hierarchical structure.

What Milgram was not aware of was the immense potential for violence and obedience which exists in the general population. As we shall see later, people are not born to kill or torment, as some would have us believe, but certain individuals are brought up in such a way that they develop the capacity to torture and destroy under orders. As a result, Milgram's prediction remains depressingly valid:

> The kind of character produced in American democratic society cannot be counted on to insulate its citizens from brutality and inhumane treatment at the direction of a malevolent authority. A substantial proportion of people do what they are told to do, irrespective of the content of the act and without limitations of conscience, so long as they perceive that the command comes from a legitimate authority.

(Milgram, 1974, p.189)

Before we move on to an understanding of how people can become torturers, it is worth spending some time looking at another research study which replicated Milgram's findings. Zimbardo chose a group of volunteer students to study what people can do when given legitimate power over another (Sabini and Silver, 1982). He simulated a prison environment with students arbitrarily assigned to either prisoner or warder roles. As it turned out, the reaction of both groups of subjects was so extreme that the experiment had to be stopped after only six days instead of the planned two weeks.

Unlike the volunteers in Milgram's study, the students participating in Zimbardo's experiment were highly selected; they had filled in a questionnaire and were interviewed. Only the most mature, stable and least involved in antisocial behaviour were selected to participate in the study.

The original findings were as follows: the guards were characterized as falling into three groups. There were the tough but fair guards who kept within prison rules. There was another group who were especially 'good' according to the prisoners: they carried out favours for them and never punished them. And finally, about a third of the guards were extremely hostile and despotic: they invented new ways of degrading and humiliating the prisoners and appeared to enjoy the power they had when they got into their uniform and wielded their sticks. Unlike the 'good' guards, these hostile guards did not appear to be able to empathize with their charges: on the contrary, they seemed to get satisfaction from the pain and distress they caused the prisoners, whom they did not perceive as human beings.

The findings drawn from both Milgram's and Zimbardo's experiments show that, under conditions where abuse is made legitimate, a certain proportion of people can become violent and destructive towards others. How can these findings be explained? Recent research in the field of child development is beginning to provide us with some understanding as to how we can be made to become potential torturers given the right social conditions.

The making of potential torturers

The pale, white-haired man before me spoke quietly and without emotion. He was describing the last moments of his daughter's life. He had killed her when she was two and a half years old.

Originally she had been looked after by her grandparents while her parents set up home in England. Her mother had apparently hated her from the moment she was born but when this infant joined her parents, both father and mother began tormenting her. She was regularly starved and beaten as a baby and a toddler. Mr Brown described how this pale little girl would be found wandering outside in the freezing weather. She was so cold her feet would get stuck to the ice. Her father would then attempt to warm them up by burning them with lighted cigarettes and burning coals. She ended up being taken to a hospital casualty department with her feet covered with blisters.

On the day of the fatal 'incident', this 'little waif', as he described her, had been locked up in her room all day without having been cleaned or fed. On his return from work, his wife told him to go upstairs and clean 'the thing'. He found his child in a mess of faeces and urine and proceded to clean her up. He then brought her downstairs into the sitting room and then attempted to get her to talk to him but the little girl just stood in silence looking pale and distressed. He desperately wanted her to speak, to make him feel better about her. He recalls going up to her and shaking her. Nothing else . . . The next morning she was found dead in bed.

Throughout this painful account, Mr Brown remained emotionally detached, as if he had cut himself off from all the violent feelings that drove him to kill his child. It was only when he spoke of his devoted mother that he came to life. She fell ill with tuberculosis when he was very young and was often away in hospital. He would walk long distances in order to see her. His mother died when he was eight years old and he was left in the care of his very violent father, who beat him up and terrified him. We were both able to recognize that he had seen his 'little waif of a daughter' very much as he had seen his pale sick mother in hospital and, though he wanted to keep her as an angel in his mind, he was also able to admit that he had felt abandoned by her and had missed her. He may well have felt guilt as well, as children of that age tend to do when they lose a parent. It seemed likely that the unconscious rage he felt about his mother was finally discharged on his daughter who, like his mother, appeared helpless and neglected, evoking in him his own desperate needs and his old pain. In this state, her father, Mr Brown, had not been able to find in himself the love his child needed from him. Instead, he had coped with his own pain by identifying with his father and his destructive rage, a rage which at least had the positive effect of giving him the power to inflict the pain he had once suffered so much.

It is very likely that when Mr Brown tortured his child to death, he did not 'see' her before him. What he saw and felt were his own feelings and memories being brought back to life, those unbearable moments of pain and fear which had been 'split off' in his mind, locked away from daily experience, just as they were during the interview. Splitting is a dissociative process which allows us to cut off from feelings of terror and helplessness. It is by not remembering feelings of terror or pain that both children and adults find the strength to survive loss, abuse or trauma. However, though the trauma may appear forgotten, the awful memories and sensations continue to operate out of consciousness, often bringing to their current relationships the hidden memories of their past. Both in children and adults, the re-enactment of past traumatic experiences is seen as a characteristic manifestation of psychological trauma, or post-traumatic stress disorder. It is also recognized as a major cause of violent behaviour (Zulueta, 1993).

Though my ideas about Mr Brown's motives for torturing his child might appear rather speculative, we do now have the evidence we need to begin to understand why the way parents relate to their children can predispose them to violent behaviour towards others.

We owe it to John Bowlby and his followers to have made us aware of the attachment behavioural system that we share with other primates (Bowlby, 1988). It is because of this behavioural system that the human infant selects a primary attachment figure (which need not be the mother) whose whereabouts require constant monitoring. The developing child remains in close proximity to this caregiver and, with time, secondary attachment figures develop an increasingly important role.

The attachment system is activated either by internal cues, such as illness, or external threats which drive the child to seek protection from his caregiver. If the latter is not available, the infant protests strongly before showing despair and, finally, becoming detached. At this point these infants will no longer respond to the return of their parental figures and might even appear to snub them. As we will see, this so-called 'avoidant' response is crucial to our understanding of destructive human behaviour.

The development of these attachment bonds is achieved by a complex process of physical and emotional attunement which, if disrupted in childhood through deprivation, loss or any other form of trauma, has long-term effects on the way we feel about ourselves, on our capacity to form relationships, and on how we perceive others. It is important to realize that the attachment behavioural system is continuously active. As development takes place, infants learn to be alert to the physical and emotional accessibility of their caregivers: some may be experienced as either rejecting or unpredictable, in which case different strategies for gaining or maintaining access will be developed. These different responses to the caregiver have become the focus of much research in the field of attachment behaviour.

Ainsworth and her colleagues were the first to show that the way one-year-old infants behaved when separated and then reunited with their caregivers was related to how sensitively the latter had responded to the infants' needs during infancy (Ainsworth et al., 1978). What they found, using the Strange Situation test, was that 63 per cent of these middle-class American children showed a secure attachment. They were able to form good relations, to tune into the needs of others, that is, to empathize.

On the other hand, 20 to 25 per cent of infants were found to be insecurely attached and showed an 'avoidant' response to their caregivers' return after a brief separation. In other words, they showed no distress when separated and ignored their parent on their return, though their rapid heartbeat belied their apparent indifference. These babies had been emotionally deprived or rejected, or both.

The remaining 12 per cent of infants tested were described as 'insecure–ambivalent': they were very distressed when their caregivers left and took a long time to be soothed when they returned. In subsequent studies, another group of infants were identified who displayed a strange 'disorganized' response to their returning parent, a mixture of 'avoidant' and 'anxious-ambivalent' behaviour. This particular form of attachment behaviour has been observed in abusive families and, more specifically, in infants' response to their parents' traumatized and often dissociated state of mind (Main and Hesse, 1990). What these infants seem to suffer from is a collapse of their attachment behavioural strategies. Current research appears to show a link between this attachment behaviour and actively violent behaviour in later life, either criminal or self-destructive.

However, our current interest lies in the study of 'avoidant' infants, whose potential for destructive behaviour is of particular interest to our understanding of how apparently normal individuals like those seen in Milgram's and Zimbardo's studies are capable of torturing and even killing in particular social conditions. The study of attachment relations in this group of people provides us with links between the infant's attachment behaviour and the formation of internal relationship models or 'templates' for future relationships. A study was done on 19 pairs of four-year-old children at play. In those pairs where either one or both partners were 'avoidant' children, there was victimization, both verbal and physical. The victimizer was always an 'avoidant' child while the victim could be either 'avoidant' or 'anxious–ambivalent'. This suggests that it is the relationship as a whole which becomes the template for the individual's future attachments. A rejected or abused child can behave as either a victim or a tormentor, depending on the circumstances. Another, extremely important point is that the secure children were never victimizers or victims (Troy and Sroufe, 1987).

What is becoming clearer is that patterns of attachment are self-perpetuating, which allows the individual to preserve a sense of continuity in terms of his or her self. For this to be maintained cognitive distortions need to take place so that individuals see the world and others very much as they need to see them. Thus, for the insecure person whose self-esteem is low, the other can often be experienced in terms of a dehumanized object that can be used to bolster up his fragile self. What this implies in terms of the attachment bond is that it can be perverted into one of control and manipulation of the 'other' such as to give the person concerned both excitement and power. Torture provides the torturer with just such a perverted form of intimate attachment.

As we have seen, the boundaries between the effects of psychological trauma and insecure attachment patterns are blurred. The rejection the avoidant child is exposed to elicits similar defensive patterns: the child learns to dissociate or 'cut off' in order to remain 'on the right side' of mother. The price he pays is that he cannot integrate his feelings of fear and rage, which can be triggered off by the unmet needs of another. For such individuals to be able to do unto others what was done to them is a way of being in control and getting satisfaction and even excitement. These adults who were once 'avoidant' infants differ, however, from active criminals in that what they have learnt from their parents' behaviour is to obey. The price to pay in order to maintain a relationship with a rejecting, fearful parent on whom the infant depends totally is to cut himself off from feelings of fear and rage and to obey, to do what pleases his parent. Such individuals will later make good soldiers who obey their commanders in order to please them but for whom the 'other' in this setting can be experienced only as the infant was made to feel when rejected or threatened by his parent: as a dehumanized being. Such an individual will therefore be capable of aggressive, cold-blooded attacks on a dehumanized 'other' in order to be in power, as his parent was once over him.

As O'Brien says in George Orwell's novel *Nineteen Eighty-Four*:

> '*The real power . . . is power . . . over men. How does one man assert his power over another, Winston?. . . By making him suffer. Obedience is not enough. Unless he is suffering, how can you be sure that he is obeying your will and not his own? Power is in inflicting pain and humiliation. Power is in tearing human minds to pieces and putting them together in new shapes of your own choosing.*'

(Orwell, 1949, p. 211)

Unfortunately, this terrible observation applies as much to insecure individuals in relation to those with whom they are involved as it applies to rulers bent on maximizing their power to bolster their personal insecurity or that of their government.

The psycho-social context of torture

Cultural traditions of violence exist the world over and have done so for thousands of years. While child abuse is now regarded as deviant in the West, it is still accepted and fostered in many non-Western countries. For instance, in a rural peasant society in India, ritual punishment by suspension is regarded as necessary to obtain submission, and in Taiwan severe beating is regarded as beneficial for obedience. There is hardly a non-Western society which does not administer some forms of physical abuse which are regarded as normal in the rearing of its children (Zulueta, 1993, pp. 213–14), and necessary if people are to become obedient and compliant. The few exceptions to this rule are restricted to hunter-gatherers living in small non-hierarchical groups in the rain forest.

In Western societies, child abuse is considered 'idiosyncratic' – that is, at odds with our cultural norms – though that does not by any means indicate that abuse does not take place (see below). Non-Western cultures often view parents in the West as unable to care for their children properly. They condemn the practice of isolating children at night, of allowing infants to cry without immediately responding to their needs as well as keeping them waiting for their food.

Though parenting behaviour has been studied worldwide, most of the detailed research on its effects has been conducted in Western countries. So what kind of upbringing do children in the West receive? We have seen from one study (Ainsworth *et al.*, 1978), that about a quarter of American children are likely to belong to the 'avoidant' group. This study has been replicated in other countries such as Sweden, Germany and the United Kingdom. This means that perhaps a quarter of our population have been subject to rearing practices which are detrimental to their capacity to 'tune into' others and to form satisfactory relationships. They are also aggressive toward others.

Such high numbers of 'avoidant' children in our society do suggest high levels of generally neglectful or rejecting parents. We now know that levels of child abuse are of the order of 6 per cent and rising. In what was West Germany, 1000 children died in 1988 as a result of being beaten up by their parents. In Britain, at least four children die every week as a result of abuse and neglect (Meadows, 1989), and one child in ten is sexually abused (Zulueta, 1993, p. 216).

However, the most interesting findings regarding Western forms of upbringing are reported by Gelles in the USA. Knowing that about 90 per cent of all parents use physical punishment on their children, he carried out a study of what violence did take place in American families. Violence was defined as 'an act carried out with the intention, or perceived intention, of physically injuring another person' (Gelles, 1978). Extrapolating the figures from his study, Gelles estimated that, of 46 million children between the ages of 3 and 17 years old living with both their parents in 1975, 46.4 per cent had been pushed, grabbed or shoved, 71 per cent had been slapped or spanked and about 7.7 per cent (about 3.5 million) had been kicked, beaten or punched by their parents. About

4.2 per cent (around 1.9 million) had been 'beaten up'. Lastly, Gelles found that about 2.8 per cent (around 1.2 million) of American children had had their parents use a gun or a knife on them.

With the exception of the last figures, these are patterns of regular violence in the American home. These are low estimates of what takes place since they are based on self-reports. Mothers are more likely to hit the child with something or to spank or slap the child. Boys were more likely to be the victims of violence. Gelles concludes that violence 'well beyond ordinary physical punishment' is a widespread phenomenon in child–parent relationships. In case we find his definition of violence over-inclusive, he points out that if one million children had knives or guns used on them at school, we would consider the problem very seriously, but because it happens at home there is far less awareness. What is so striking is that often these acts of violence were seen by the perpetrators as being carried out in the best interest of their victims. And yet, as we now believe, the consequences of such violence carried out by those held to be the child's loving caregivers are potentially a very serious cause of violent behaviour.

Straus points out how physical punishment in the USA (and in many other countries) is a universal phenomenon involving nearly all Americans as either perpetrators or recipients. He believes this is so because it is 'central to the primacy and continuity of the socialization process'. He believes that physical punishment legitimizes violence since it is a legally permissible physical attack on children (though presumably the use of knives or guns is not).

> Since physical punishment is used by authority figures who tend to be loved or respected and since it is almost always used for a morally correct end when other methods fail, physical punishment teaches that violence can and should be used under similar circumstances. The intriguing question is whether this legitimization of violence spills over from the parent–child relationship to other relationships in which one has to deal with persons who persist in some wrongdoing, such as a spouse or a friend.

(Straus, 1991, p. 134)

In his 'cultural spillover' theory, Straus attempts to show that such a causal connection exists. For example, the more physical punishment was authorized in schools, the higher the rate of assault by children in the same schools. The theory gained credence when associations were found between legitimate violence, violent attitudes and rape across the American states (Baron et al., 1988). It was found that in a western state of America whose citizens scored highly on three tests of violence (violence in the media, violence in state legislation and participation in violent pursuits such as hunting), women were eight times more likely to be raped than women in an eastern state whose inhabitants scored low. 'This suggests that legitimate violence tends to be diffused to relations between the sexes, resulting in an increased probability of women being raped' (Baron et al., 1988, pp. 100–1). The authors suggest that to reduce the incidence of rape, for instance, attention must be paid to socially approved violence and not just criminal violence. This is seen as an enormous task because economic and racial inequality, physical punishment, mass media violence, capital punishment and other forms of legitimate violence are woven into the fabric of American culture and increasingly into that of other Westernized cultures.

Links between cultures and their direct effect on the attachment bonds of children and parents have been clearly shown when studying infant attachment patterns across different cultures. In northern Germany, for example, a team of researchers found that one-half of the infants were classified as insecure–avoidant as opposed to a quarter in the USA (Grossman et al., 1985). The authors ascribed this difference to the fact that, in that part of Germany, people believed in 'keeping their distance' so that as soon as the infant became mobile, most mothers thought their children should be weaned from close body contact. The ideal for this part of the world was to produce an independent non-clinging infant who made few demands on the parents but who rather unquestioningly obeyed commands. This reminded the authors of similar attitudes described by Kurt Lewin about the time of the Second World War (Lewin, 1948, p. 27). The needs of the child were sacrificed to produce the ideal north German adult. As we now believe, the unconscious pain and anger associated with this upbringing makes the 'avoidant' infant a potentially more violent person than his more secure counterpart. Alice Miller, who has written widely on the causes and effects of child mistreatment (Miller, 1987), would probably have said that it is the 'avoidant' infant who could make the good Nazi, both obedient and yet yearning for revenge.

Unfortunately, such individuals are also likely to make good torturers.

As we have seen, cultural forms of upbringing provide a ready source of people whose childhood background makes them potentially good torturers under the appropriate conditions.

Torture as an institution

Torture is usually part of the state-controlled machinery to suppress dissent. To understand the torturer it is important to understand the character of the state whose agent he is. If we recall the Milgram and

Zimbardo experiments, the act of torture is carried out when it is made legitimate by someone in authority. This is why torture can be used so often as an integral part of a government's security strategy. It can begin in response to a threat by guerrillas, as in Guatemala, where it was used as a police method of interrogation. When the army entered the conflict it was used on a much greater scale, and by 1975 torture became routine treatment for any peaceful opponent of the government. The rationale behind this torture is to obtain information, to break down, to humiliate and to frighten those close to the victim and thereby to maintain control over the population.

If we assume that a large reservoir of potential torturers does exist in most countries in the world, it is interesting to see how General Massu and his like go about selecting the best individuals for the job. The trials of the accused torturers in Greece in the mid-1970s provide valuable information on this process (Amnesty International, 1977). Peasant or working-class conscript soldiers from known anti-communist families were selected for special training by the military police. Further screening was used in selecting the few who were to be trained as torturers. They were also offered special privileges as members of an 'elite corps'. They were initially unaware of the duties of the corps. Their early training consisted in beating and being beaten by fellow conscripts. They were then humiliated by being forced to eat the straps of their berets and made to kneel and swear allegiance in front of pictures of their commanding officers. They were also forced to pretend to make love to a woman in front of other soldiers. By this stage, these individuals may well have suffered some degree of psychological trauma which meant that, if given the possibility to do so, they could re-enact what had been done unto them on dehumanized others with no difficulty. The dehumanization of their future victims was achieved by indoctrinating them into believing that they had an elevated role, which was to protect the state against 'subversives'. The whole process of torture was redefined as an essential aspect of the 'war' against 'communists'.

This dehumanization of the enemy is essential for the institution of torture to be maintained, and is achieved by labelling the potential victims, in this case as enemies or communists. A torturer from Chile explained in 1984 how torture was carried out:

> 'The youngest were the regulars on the machine. They lasted longer. No remorse, no feelings. It was enough to tell them "that is your enemy; a communist" and for them it was just like a football match. They had to beat the other side.'

He went on to explain how the dehumanization of the victim was maintained:

> 'You don't look at their face even when you put the prods in the mouth; you keep their eyes covered. The secret is not to look in their eyes. The other secret is not to draw blood. You leave that for the sick bastards or the young brutes. You can watch the body arch and bounce under electricity, but never draw blood . . . '

(Graham-Yooll, 1984, p. 11)

The same man said that he had never tortured: 'Torture is inflicting pain for personal pleasure. I dealt punishment to my enemy under orders from my superior.'

As mentioned earlier, it is essential for torturers to know that, even if their acts are criminal, they are sanctioned by the state, which will take responsibility for what they do. We can remember how crucial it was both for Mr Prozi and Mr Batta to know that they had no responsibility for what happened to their victim. One could say they showed a propensity to act under orders. Despite his doubts, Mr Prozi obeyed to the end once he knew he did not have to be responsible for what happened to the learner. Having abrogated personal responsibility, he then behaved and spoke like a child to the experimenter, as if the latter was his superior, such as a parent or a teacher. Mr Batta had no qualms about what he did as long as he knew that in the eyes of the person in authority he was behaving like a 'good boy'. How do we explain adult men and women performing in this manner?

We have seen how children who are systematically rejected or threatened learn to cut themselves off from their feelings of fear and anger so as to remain close to their parent. These feelings, though no longer consciously felt, are still present and active. They were demonstrated in the four-year-old pairs of victimizers or victims of Troy and Sroufe's experiment (1987). In the Milgram and Zimbardo experiments we witnessed how, by giving people the legitimate power to abuse the 'other', some subjects may have unconsciously re-enacted an earlier abusive power relation – but this time in identification with the aggressor rather than the victim they once were.

One may then ask how the presence of an authority figure like the experimenter acts in some people as a 'switch' to bring about obedience and abuse of the 'other'. To judge from the studies examined so far it was the scientific status of the experimenter which made some of the subjects feel that what took place under his orders was legitimate. This legitimacy could be considered the equivalent of parental approval for the child: it would allow the insecure child finally to feel that he or she has the possibility of being approved, provided, of course, that the parent's wish is carried out or that the experimenter is obeyed. The more insecure the person is, the more desperate the need to obey authority and so become part of the group of those in power, of those who know how to remain in power by dehumanizing the 'other', by inflicting pain and even killing. This process was illustrated in the formation of torturers in Greece. In view of the extent to which corporal punishment is practised, it comes as no surprise to discover that people will tend to believe that 'power is might', and will provide a reservoir of potential torturers.

What we saw happening in the Milgram experiments was very much like what takes place in the torture chambers of the world. In a similar act of dissociation, the torturer can unconsciously exert his power over his victim. In this way he can belong to the group of those in authority and at the same time revenge himself for what was done to him in childhood and during his training, as we saw happening with the Greek torturers, who were abused and humiliated. In the torture cells, the legitimizing role of the experimenter is taken over by the doctor who attends to the victims of torture. His presence makes those who work with him feel that things are being done scientifically but what he illustrates is the most profound perversion of the doctor–patient relationship: his main role is to make sure that his patient is fit enough to endure further torture.

Many have noted that torturers are all men, but we now know from the Milgram and Zimbardo experiments that women too are capable of tormenting the other if they are given the opportunity. This was illustrated in the Nazi concentration camps. No one, whatever their sex or age, is invulnerable to the devastating effects of a damaged behaviour system.

While it is clear that not everybody could become a torturer, what we have learnt is that there are plenty of people in our societies whose past painful upbringing can provide those who seek power with the means to terrify and oppress through the use of torture. To change this would require a fundamental change in the way children are raised, a change which most of us would currently consider quite unrealistic despite the epidemic levels of social violence that now exist in the Americas and elsewhere.

Milgram's experiments do, however, provide us with what could be a more immediate way of possibly reducing the numbers of torturers. Having seen how crucial it is for those who carry out these terrible activities to feel that they are not responsible for what they are doing, it clearly is important that they should know that they will have to account one day for what they have done. If obedience to orders is no longer a valid justification for raping and electrocuting your fellow citizens, some may think twice before becoming torturers. This is why Amnesty International's campaign for the establishment of a permanent International Criminal Court, and for governments to support the Ad Hoc War Crimes Tribunals for Rwanda and former Yugoslavia, is so important.

The subject of torture and its implementation is one that horrifies us all and yet we all tend to turn a blind eye to the pain and violence inflicted upon those who depend upon us in every way, as shown by the figures for violent child death. It is children's fear and accompanying rage which provide the breeding ground for tomorrow's dictators and torturers. We are not, as some would have us believe, born to torture and destroy.

As Bowlby reminds us, 'Human beings are pre-programmed to develop in a socially co-operative way; whether they do or not turns to a high degree on how they are treated' (Bowlby, 1988, p. 9), and the kind of society they grow up in.

References

Ainsworth, M.D.S., Blehar, M.C., Waters, E. and Wall, S. (1978) *Patterns of Attachment: A Psychological Study of the Strange Situation*. Hillsdale, NJ: Lawrence Erlbaum.

Amnesty International (1977) *Torture in Greece: The First Torturers' Trial*. London: Amnesty International.

Baron, L., Straus, M.A. and Jaffee, D. (1988) 'Legitimate violence, violent attitudes and rape: a test of the cultural spillover theory'. In R.E. Prentky and V.I. Quinsey (eds), *Human Sexual Aggression: Current Perspectives*, pp. 79–110. New York: New York Academy of Science.

Bloomstein, R. (1990) *The Torturer* (television programme, Independent Television).

Bowlby, J. (1988) *A Secure Base: Clinical Applications of Attachment Theory*. London: Routledge.

Gelles, R.J. (1978) 'Violence against young children in the United States'. *American Journal of Orthopsychiatry* 48, 580–92.

Graham-Yooll, G. (1984) 'The mind of the torturer'. *Observer*, 15 January, p. 11.

Grossman, K., Grossman, K.E., Spangler, G., Suess, G. and Unzner, L. (1985) 'Maternal sensitivity and newborn's orientation responses as related to quality of attachment in northern Germany.' In I. Bretherton and E. Waters (eds), *Growing Points of Attachment Theory and Research*. Monographs of the Society for Research in Child Development vol. 50 (1–2, serial no. 209), pp. 233–56.

Lewin, K. (1948) *Resolving Social Conflicts*. New York: Harper. (First published in 1936.)

Main, M. and Hesse, E. (1990) 'Parents' unresolved traumatic experiences are related to infant disorganized attachment status: is frightened and/or frightening parental behavior the linking mechanism?' In M. Greenberg, D. Cicchetti, and E.M Cummings (eds), *Attachment in the Pre-school Years*, pp. 161–82. Chicago: University of Chicago Press.

Meadows, R. (1989) 'The ABC of child abuse: epidemiology'. *British Medical Journal* 298, 727.

Milgram, S. (1974) *Obedience to Authority: An Experimental View*. London: Harper & Row.

Miller, A. (1987) *The Drama of Being a Child*. London: Virago.

Orwell, G. (1949) *Nineteen Eighty-Four*. Harmondsworth: Penguin Books.

Sabini, J. and Silver, M. (1982) *Moralities of Everyday Life*. Oxford: Oxford University Press.

Straus, M.B. (1991) 'Discipline and deviance: physical punishment of children and violence and other crimes in adulthood'. *Social Problems* 38, 133–54.

Troy, M. and Sroufe, L.A. (1987) 'Victimization among pre-schoolers: role of attachment relation history'. *Journal of the American Academy of Child and Adolescent Psychiatry* 26, 166–72.

Zulueta, F. de (1993) *From Pain to Violence: The Traumatic Roots of Destructiveness*. London: Whurr.

CHAPTER 7

The Methods of Torture and Its Effects

Duncan Forrest

Introduction

The wish to hurt another human being and the devising of methods of doing so are as old as recorded history. If we think of torture as a system of deliberately harming others short of fatal injury, the available ways of doing so are almost limitless, though in practice usually limited by local custom and depending on the sophistication of the organization employing them and their perception of any risk of being found out.

Enumeration of methods of torture may be thought to run the risk of being used as a handbook for the unscrupulous or deranged. This cannot be denied, but would-be torturers would have no difficulty in finding techniques without referring to a book such as this. The true aim is to dispel the myth that torture is a thing of the past and to show readers that it is still employed in all its variety in many countries and there is still much evil against which to campaign.

The environment of torture

Arrest

In my work with torture survivors at the Medical Foundation for the Care of Victims of Torture in London, I have gleaned stories from a large number of patients and witnesses which give a clear picture of some common practices worldwide.

Arrests are often made in secret, the victim spirited away in the middle of the night or from a lonely place. The authorities are then able to deny that there has been an arrest and the victim 'disappears'. Or there may be a great show of force, with dozens of uniformed or plain-clothes armed policemen or soldiers surrounding the victim's house, either in the middle of the night or in broad daylight. In those circumstances, where there is no secrecy but rather a deliberate escalation of terror, the whole household may be beaten up with kicks, punches, blows from truncheons and rifle butts. The women of the household may be raped before the targeted ones are taken away, often injured as they are dragged along the ground and thrown into a jeep. They may be blindfolded and handcuffed or bound with ropes. During transport they may lie on the floor and be trodden on, beaten and kicked. On the other hand, many detainees have gone of their own free will to the police station to 'clear up a misunderstanding', only to find themselves in detention.

Village round-ups

In countries where a repressive government is faced with armed rebellion, whole areas are subjected to periodic displays of power. Typical of this manifestation of oppression is the Kurdish south-east of Turkey. Villagers are thought (not always correctly) to be assisting the rebel forces with food and sanctuary. The villagers have for generations been subjected to suppression of their culture, forbidden to speak Kurdish or indulge in their cultural practices. The schoolteachers are instructed to inform on pupils when they inadvertently reveal any Kurdish activities in their homes, or their parents' sympathetic attitudes to the rebels. At regular intervals of a month or so, police, gendarmes or soldiers may descend on and surround the village. The whole population is assembled in the village square and the men and boys stripped and insulted, beaten with truncheons, punched and kicked and subjected to *falaka* (beating the soles of the feet), after which the victims are made to carry a policeman or (even worse humiliation) their wife round on their backs over the rough ground. Some report that these humiliations in front of their families are worse than the physical pain. When the invaders leave, they usually take a few of the men deemed to be ringleaders with them for a few days' further beating in the police station.

Similar behaviour is seen in the Tamil north-east of Sri Lanka where previously the Indian Peace-Keeping Force and still the Sri Lankan army assume that all Tamil men and youths as young as 14 as well as some women are, if not active members, at least sympathizers with the Tamil Tigers. They raid the villages and take all the young males, after beating them up in view of the rest of the village, for interrogation that involves gross physical and psychological abuse. One Tamil youth told me:

> 'While they were questioning me and accusing me of being a Tiger, they hung me up and beat me. They cut my wrist with a bayonet saying, "Next time we catch you, this will show us that you are one of them." Then they threw me out.'

Many who are released in this way are promptly captured by the Tigers, who rightly or wrongly assume that they have given away secrets to the army. From then on their lives are forfeit, suspected as they are both by the Army and the Tigers. Others are killed in 'fake encounters'.

Conditions of detention

Whatever the conditions of detention, a most potent source of fear is the isolation of detention incommunicado, perhaps with blindfolding or hooding. In many countries the police stations and interrogation centres are in a condition of neglect and the cells are overcrowded and filthy. There are no toilet facilities except perhaps for a hole in the floor or a bucket in the corner. Ventilation may be almost entirely absent even in a tropical climate. There are often deliberate attempts to make life intolerable. The cell may be kept in total darkness or, alternatively, with a constant bright light. The floor may be flooded ankle-deep in water. The cries of others being tortured may ring through the building. Guards bang on the door frequently throughout the night to prevent sleep. In any case, the cell may be too small for sleep, a single cell 1 metre square or a crowded cell with detainees shoulder to shoulder with just enough room to take turns to squat down.

The interrogation/torture room

Interrogation and torture can take place anywhere: in the open air, a schoolroom or a hospital. When it is in a police station or security headquarters it may be arranged at one or other extreme. The room may be a neat and formal interrogation room with an officer sitting behind a desk and the detainee seated facing him, perhaps with a bright light shining in his eyes, or he may be blindfolded or hooded. But every time he fails to answer a question 'correctly', a pair of guards standing behind him slap, punch or hit him with a truncheon or whip, burn him with a cigarette or administer an electric shock.

At the other extreme is the room that is blatantly used for torture. On entering, the victim, even if blindfolded, is aware of the overpowering smell of death. The walls are smeared with blood and there are hooks on the walls and ceiling for suspension. Various items of equipment are displayed prominently round the room. In this environment, there may be no interrogation but just threats and abuse to accompany the main object, which is to destroy the individual's resistance.

One main factor, whatever the physical conditions, is the disorientating nature of the process brought about by the absence of any normal sensory reference points, the relentless questioning going on continuously for hours, the 'bad' alternating with the 'good' interrogator.

A popular way of potentiating the psychological effect of these surroundings is to keep the victim waiting in an adjoining room where he can hear the cries and screams of other victims. One Iranian man reported to me that every evening he was taken with five or six others to a waiting-room where they spent all night hearing screams while waiting for their turn to be expertly tortured. Twenty years later he is still unable to sit in a doctor's waiting-room for more than a few minutes before suffering a panic attack.

Prison

Most formal torture takes place in the few days after arrest, but many survivors report that conditions in the prison to which they are transferred are almost as bad, and random torture still takes place. Some special prisons for political prisoners are deliberately kept in conditions in which death is the expected outcome. Makala Prison in Kinshasa, Zaire, and the secret detention centre of Tazmamert (now closed) in Morocco have been well documented (Johannes Wier Foundation, 1993). A striking description of conditions in the latter centre was given by three brothers, Bayazid, Midhat and Ali Bourequat, who were held there from March 1981 until their release under an amnesty in December 1991:

> 'In Tazmamert we used to call out to the other prisoners from one cell to another. We shouted – when we could. When we got very weak, we'd call once every three days or once a week. We were isolated; we didn't see each other till the day of our release 10 years later. The cells were 3 m by 2 m. . . . The cells were made of cement – they'd left it like that; you could feel the bumps. There was a cement bed 2 metres square at the end of the cell. At the entrance was a hole for the toilet and 14 holes about 10 cm in diameter in the wall leading to the corridor. There was no light or water . . . nothing. . . . In building 2, 26 out of 33 men died.'

While many ex-detainees report that interrogation with beatings and torture ease off after transfer to prison, there is often random beating, possibly for the guards' gratification and exercise of power, or else systematic abuse ordered from above with the aim of humiliating and further destroying the individual's personality (Figure 7.1). Sexual abuse, both of males and females, is a prominent feature of this environment. Prison torture is often carried out in the night when the guards come on duty drunk.

Methods of torture

The basic tools of the torturer are his fists and boots. Nothing else is really needed to inflict suffering but most police or security forces carry

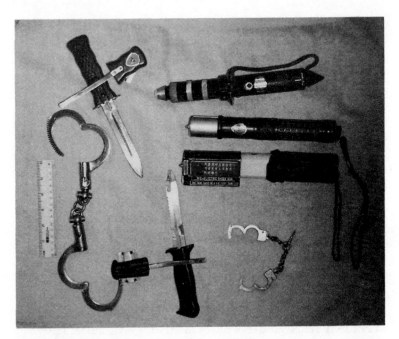

Figure 7.1. Knives, handcuffs, thumb cuffs and electroshock batons used by Chinese police and prison guards, smuggled out of Tibet by Palden Gyatso, a monk who spent 33 of his 62 years as a political prisoner.

equipment with more potential, such as truncheons, *lathis* (long, stout bamboo canes) or rifles, legal and legitimate if used in the way for which they were designed, but capable of inflicting serious blunt injury if used as offensive weapons. Canes are also used in South Africa, where the *sjambok*, a hard leather whip, was formerly the symbol of police violence. Simple beating, especially to the head, is the most frequently used form of ill-treatment (Goldfeld *et al.*, 1988). The Presidential Guard in Zaire wear a *cordelette*, a long, stout woven belt with heavy metal buckles. It was originally designed for use by commandos to scale walls, but it makes a particularly vicious whip. Some guards weave metal bosses or spikes into the length of the belt, so that it inflicts even more painful injuries. Other items that come easily to hand are knives, broken bottles, cigarettes and branches cut from thorn bushes or stinging plants.

In countries where the official position is that torture is forbidden, governments might condone techniques that border on torture (see Chapter 4). Simple measures can be very effective. In Northern Ireland in the 1970s, 'confessions' were obtained by deprivation of sleep, food and drink, enforced prolonged standing leaning against the wall, hooding, the use of continuous noise and other methods of 'depth interrogation' (Amnesty International, 1984; British Medical Association, 1992).

In Israel, 'moderate physical pressure', first legitimized by the Landau Report (1987), still invites interrogators to question and punish by isolation, deprivation of sleep, toilet facilities and food, hooding, violent shaking, prolonged confinement in tiny cells (the 'coffin', the 'refrigerator') or handcuffing to the wall in a position which makes it impossible either to stand up straight or sit or lie down (*shabah*). During the night of 21–2 April 1995 a Palestinian, 'Abd al-Samad Harizat, was arrested from his home by members of the Israeli Defence Force (IDF) on suspicion of membership of Hamas, the Islamic resistance movement. On 22 April he was taken to hospital in a coma. Three days later he was dead. The autopsy showed a brain haemorrhage, caused by being violently shaken while in detention. It is too soon to predict what the future holds in store in Israel.

Natural resources are often used. In Angola, prisoners have been staked out in the sun, made to look at the sun, smeared in honey to attract ants or locked in a tin shed or derelict car all day in the tropical sun. Pressure-hosing with cold water, deprivation of blankets or clothing in cold weather and placing between ice blocks are all punishments that have been reported from many different countries.

Often equipment is home-made. Whips are made of electric cable or rubber fan belts fastened onto a wooden handle. One man reported to me how he had been beaten with such a whip. At the beginning of the session he was shown one side of the flat handle on which was written 'Welcome'. After the whipping, he was shown the other side, which had written on it 'See you again soon'.

Sandbags or plastic tubes filled with sand or metal give a sickening blow but leave no mark.

Submersion under water or foul liquid to the point of drowning (*la bañera*, *submarino*) or covering the face with a plastic bag (dry *submarino*) are widely used.

Making the victim lie on the ground and then piling weights on the chest was used in England in the Middle Ages (see page 22). It is still in use today in the Middle East.

Other equipment is obtained from local sources. In India the *manja*, the common wooden bed frame, is used to tie down victims for beating. The *ghotna*, a stout wooden pole about 4 inches in diameter and 4 feet long, is used for grinding corn or spices. It comes in useful at the police station, where it is used in a number of ways to cause pain. It can be placed behind the knees and then the legs bent forcibly over it; it can be placed between the thighs and then the legs tied together; but its most common use is to roll it up and down the thighs while two or more policemen stand on it. The pain that this treatment causes is excruciating and it does irreparable damage to the muscles (Forrest, 1995). The same treatment is sometimes delivered with a square-section table leg or a metal cylinder. One survivor reported being rolled on by one of these with '75 kg' printed on it, presumably to amplify the psychological effect.

Another common method used in India and Pakistan is *cheera* (tearing), in which the victim's legs are spread apart until the muscles tear and great bruises form in the groin.

Beating is often concentrated on sensitive parts of the body such as the genitals. One of the oldest methods, traditional throughout the Middle East, even for punishment for children, is *falaka* (*falanga*, *bastinado*), where the soles of the feet are beaten with truncheons, sticks or whips, usually with the ankles held or tied up in the air. The intense pain, though starting in the feet, strikes right up to the head. Afterwards, the victim may be made to walk round on rough ground or to piggy-back the heaviest policeman or another. The huge swelling and bruising are often controlled by immersing the feet in salt water or forcing the victim's shoes on. Many other examples of beating are given in Chapter 5.

Electric shocks, which are usually concentrated on the genitals, nipples or lips (which are not only the most sensitive parts of the body but also the most private and personal ones), as well as the fingertips, toes or ear lobes, may be generated in the simplest way straight from a mains plug by touching the skin with bare wires or probes (*picana*), or from a 'black box' capable of delivering graduated shocks. The magnetos which are found in many police stations in Turkey are alleged to be manufactured in a state-run factory. Electric truncheons or cattle prods are used in many police stations and prisons.

Restraint can be achieved in many ingenious ways with nothing more than a length of rope. African 'five-point' tying immobilizes the victim, who is arched backwards, every movement tightening the ropes round the wrists, ankles and neck. Tying the thumbs together with one arm over the head and the other behind the back causes intolerable pain, aggravated with every breath.

Shackling with handcuffs, leg-irons or chains is common (Amnesty International, 1995a). They may be used to prevent escape or simply to add to the detainee's pain and humiliation. If left on too long or fastened too tightly, they can cause deep wounds or cut off the circulation and nerve supply to the extremities, leading to gangrene and ending in amputation.

In Denmark a detainee, Benjamin Christian Schou, suffered irreversible brain damage while being restrained in the 'leg-lock', in which

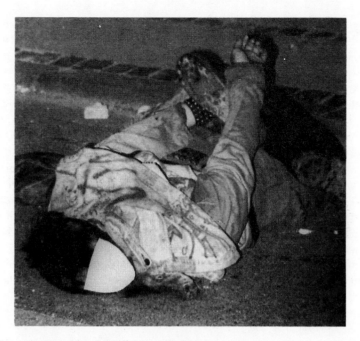

Figure 7.2. Denmark: a detainee immobilized in a leg-lock.

handcuffs are applied behind the back, then one foot wedged behind the other knee and the second foot hooked under the handcuff (Figure 7.2). This method can severely interfere with respiration if the victim is left lying face down, as well as putting pressure on the wrists for which the cuffs were not designed (Amnesty International, 1994). The practice was reportedly banned immediately after AI's report was published.

Suspension to assist beating is practised in many countries. It takes many forms, of varying sophistication. In some hot climates, the victim may be hung from a ceiling fan so that he slowly rotates as he is beaten. Where there is no regard for injury, ropes or wire may be used, causing deep scars, but in other countries, where the detainee must be taken to court, elaborate steps are taken to disguise the practice. In India, turban cloth or soft cotton cord is used, or ropes may be wrapped in soft cloth. The beating may be conducted over clothing to prevent the lacerations though not the pain. With these precautions, external evidence can be avoided.

Suspension by the wrists or ankles is bad enough, but the pain is much worse if the whole weight of the body is taken by limbs which are put into strained positions, such as spread-eagled or in 'Palestinian hanging', where suspension is by the wrists tied behind the back. There is intolerable strain on the shoulder joints, which may become dislocated, and the victim often faints after a few minutes. Interrogation rooms in countries such as Turkey and Iran have hooks or pulleys on the walls or ceiling ready to suspend detainees.

Common to many countries and with a corresponding number of nicknames such as '*la barra*' (the bar), '*el pollo*' (the chicken), '*pau de arara*' (the parrot's perch), is the device of tying the wrists together around the bent knees and then pushing a pole behind the knees. Suspended like this, apart from suffering extreme pain the victim may have the blood and nerve supply to the legs cut off and, of course, it leaves the victim vulnerable to beating all over the body and especially the soles of the feet.

The possibilities for ingenuity in planning physical abuse are unlimited and especially disturbing when modern technology is diverted from its legitimate original purpose to assist torture (see Chapter 9). The headquarters of the Dubai Special Branch commissioned (from a British firm) its 'prisoner disorientation equipment', nicknamed 'House of Fun', a high-tech room fitted with a generator for white noise and strobe lights such as might be seen in a disco, but turned up to a volume capable of reducing the victim to submission within half an hour (*Observer*, 13 January 1991).

Regarded by many as the worst torture, causing the victim the ultimate humiliation, indignity and lasting psychological damage, is rape and other forms of sexual assault. In many countries, women are routinely raped, often within sight or sound of their spouse or children. Men and women have truncheons, bottles or electric batons pushed into the anus, sometimes causing internal rupture. Men are forced to have sex with their wives or other prisoners, male or female. In many police stations and prisons, the guards regularly and casually rape male and female prisoners without restraint. In the former Yugoslavia, mass rape has been a deliberate policy. Though practised by all sides, it appears to have been most systematically used by Serbian soldiers and irregulars against Muslim women. The Special Rapporteur in the former Yugoslavia reported that 'rape was being used as an instrument of ethnic cleansing. . . . There are reliable reports of public rapes, for example, in front of a whole village, designed to terrorize the population and force ethnic groups to flee' (Amnesty International, 1995b, p. 134).

When we come to consider the possibilities for gross injury, there are no limits. Pliers are used to pull off finger- or toenails, dental drills are used to attack teeth, and acid or caustic substances are poured over the skin. Many corpses are discovered with evidence that before death they suffered horrendous mutilation such as having the ears, hands, genitals or tongue cut off or eyes gouged out.

Some torture survivors report that, after initial intense pain in the region struck, the whole body is engulfed in pain. Then a state of dazed numbness often ensues and this may continue for hours (though all sense of time is lost) or be followed by unconsciousness. There is, of course, great variation in individual pain thresholds.

Many report that they developed strategies to minimize the pain during torture sessions. Most of these are psychological: methods of directing the thoughts, for example, trying not to be dominated by the obvious power of the torturer, and developing contempt or pity for him. There are physical techniques too, such as overbreathing, which eventually leads to a trance-like state.

It is not possible to mention here every means of physical abuse. More are detailed in Chapter 5.

Psychological abuse is inherent in the concept of torture, and every torture session includes some degree of mental cruelty. In many cases it starts right from the moment of arrest, which is accompanied by threats and insults. In strongly God-fearing subjects, the most telling abuse is often religious. One deeply religious Sikh reported to me that the severe physical torture he endured was less distressing than having his five sacred objects removed, his hair and beard shaved, cigarette ash blown into his face and whisky poured down his throat. Sexual threats and insults may be directed at the female members of the family or impugn the manhood of a male detainee.

The circumstances of confinement have a great influence on the ability of the authorities to break down a prisoner's resistance. Detention incommunicado, especially with the victim uncertain of his whereabouts and blindfolded or hooded, and denied access to family or lawyers, claims that nobody knows his whereabouts, and the conviction that there is no hope of escape or rescue all produce maximum fear and uncertainty and make it absolutely clear that the captors have complete control over life or death.

One of the most terrifying psychological weapons is the mock execution. It gives enormous scope for sadistic ingenuity and has been practised in many forms throughout history. One of the most elaborate recorded hoaxes was that perpetrated on the Russian author Fyodor Mikhailovich Dostoyevsky in 1849. The novelist and 20 associates were paraded in a public square with great ceremony. A general, who was a notorious stutterer, laboriously read out the death sentences. As the firing squad took aim, an aide galloped up with a sealed envelope containing the Tsar's commutation which the general read out, once more with agonizing slowness. The whole charade had been planned in detail and set up by Tsar Nicholas I (Hingley, 1978). Similarly elaborate hoaxes are still acted out for the same purpose of humiliating and breaking the spirit.

Often, the subject of the deception hears the sound of shots and takes some time to realize that he is still alive. It is quite possible to destroy a captive purely by this and other psychological means.

Tsar Nicholas I features again in the first recorded case of a political dissident being incarcerated in a psychiatric institution. In 1836 the philosopher Pyotr Chaadayev was declared by the Tsar to be suffering from 'derangement and insanity' after he had published a letter critical of the Tsar (Bloch and Reddaway, 1977).

It is well known that more recently in the USSR prior to 1991, dissidents were frequently committed to psychiatric institutions, particularly Moscow's Serbski Institute, using the reasoning that anyone who doubted the policies of the state must be insane. They were diagnosed as suffering from 'sluggish schizophrenia', by definition an incurable condition but without any psychotic symptoms, and recognized by Soviet psychiatrists but no others. They were inappropriately treated with huge doses of mind-altering drugs which caused frightening and often painful effects (Reich, 1985). Now that the USSR has disintegrated, systematic use of the practice seems to have ceased in Russia and other Eastern European countries, but former detainees do not appear to have been rehabilitated or granted any compensation. There have been recent reports from Cuba that political dissidents are still being held in psychiatric institutes, where the appalling conditions are possibly used for punishment. Recently, a small number of cases of the political use of psychiatry have surfaced in China, where forcible confinement has been used to silence vocal critics (Amnesty International, 1995c).

Of course, it is not only individuals that the regime may be seeking to destroy. Whole communities are psychologically terrorized by death threats, 'disappearances', death squads and other displays of naked power.

Effects of torture

Physical effects

The physical results of torture are too numerous to document in full, but the immediate after-effects have been graphically described by many ex-detainees, who tell of being thrown back into their cell unconscious at the end of a session only to be woken by having a bucket of cold water thrown over them. Many describe how they are covered in bruises, bleeding, with broken teeth and perhaps broken bones, unable to stand, and relying on fellow-prisoners to tend their wounds. In the insanitary atmosphere of a prison cell, perhaps ankle-deep in water and sewage, wounds fester and fail to heal.

Heavy blows to the head may result in coma, blindness or deafness.

Abdominal blows may rupture liver, kidney or spleen, with potentially fatal effect unless the victim is operated upon urgently.

There is seldom any help to be expected from the prison guards, except in some cases where the victim seems to be in danger of dying and is taken to the prison hospital or perhaps a nearby civil hospital. There he may be held under armed guard, chained to the bed while wounds are stitched, limbs plastered and perhaps internal injuries repaired by open operation. Doctors and nurses are powerless to treat their patient satisfactorily and usually he is returned to prison long before he is ready for discharge.

Unfortunately, most of the immediate physical appearances of torture are not very specific and, if the police are accused of brutality, they will cynically try to explain the injuries away by alleging that the detainee injured himself deliberately, or accidentally by falling down the stairs while trying to escape.

When a detainee escapes or is released, his condition may be seen and described by relatives or other witnesses. Often he is unable to walk and is taken home by car or carried by relatives, to remain in bed for weeks or months. He may have lost a great deal of weight, have digestive trouble owing to the poor or contaminated prison food, or respiratory diseases such as tuberculosis, which tend to run riot in the appalling conditions of many detention centres.

A local doctor or traditional healer may be called in, but often ex-detainees are afraid of drawing attention to their condition and have to rely on family or friends to give what help they can. More than one Indian refugee has reported to me that he was turned away from a civil hospital because he was a 'police case'.

Physical signs usually fade quickly with rest. After a couple of weeks the worst of the swelling and bruising will have disappeared and the aches and pains will have diminished.

The *late* after-effects, which are usually all that are seen in refugees, may be gross or very slight. Beating, if it has broken the skin, may leave characteristic scars across the back or over bony points, but often nothing more remains than could be accounted for by normal accidental injury (see Chapter 11).

A very high percentage of torture survivors complain of neck stiffness, backache, pain in the limbs and difficulty with walking, often for years after their last detention. Though there is a tendency to slow improvement, severe disability often remains, limiting the capacity to do anything more than light work. Survivors usually attribute these pains to beating and confinement in cramped, damp, unsanitary conditions. Probably all these have a potent effect, but it is difficult to be sure of the precise causes in individual cases. It is very likely that convulsive movements in trying to escape the lashes also result in muscular strains. More specific damage is caused by more severe tortures such as 'Palestinian hanging', which almost always leaves the victim with pain and limitation of movement due to permanent damage to the shoulder girdle.

Falaka also causes very characteristic late symptoms due to damage to the foot by the direct blows of sticks to the soles of the feet and also the resulting gross swelling of the soft tissues of the soles and heels. For years afterwards, the victim may be unable to walk more than a few hundred metres or climb stairs without stabbing or burning pain in the feet. After an active day, pain increases in bed at night, spreading up from the soles to the calves and thighs.

Direct violence, restraint or suspension can cause nerve damage in limbs, resulting in numbness and paralysis which can be either temporary or permanent.

Blows to the side of the head, either random or calculated (*teléfono*), can rupture ear-drums and cause deafness. Head blows can also cause blindness due to a detached retina or ruptured optic nerve. Concussion, especially if repeated, can lead to chronic epilepsy, loss of short-term memory, confusion or dementia.

Violent beating with or without crushing injury, such as is inflicted by the *ghotna*, can release such quantities of muscle breakdown products into the bloodstream as to cause the victim to suffer kidney failure, fatal unless promptly treated by dialysis (Malik, 1993).

Repeated ducking under water, which is often grossly contaminated (*submarino*) can lead to permanent lung damage.

Many torture survivors complain long afterwards of indigestion which may go on to actual peptic ulceration. They usually ascribe this to poor prison food and drink, and these undoubtedly have an effect, but the main cause is probably stress, which is a potent cause of peptic ulcer.

Many other pains experienced after torture have a similarly strong psychosomatic origin. Headaches, neck- and backache are very common, often attributed to blows round the head but also probably aggravated by stress, muscular tension and sleeplessness.

Torture survivors from Africa and South-East Asia tend to 'somatize' their symptoms; that is, they attribute their pains to some persisting injury inside the body. If only it could be removed, the pain would disappear. They often ask for shrapnel fragments or bullets, apparently harmless, to be removed, or scars, which must be reminders of the past, to be tidied up by plastic surgery.

Psychological effects

Many pains can rightly be described as psychosomatic, and there are also truly psychological symptoms which are often similar to those associated with post-traumatic stress disorder, as listed in the American Psychiatric Association's *Diagnostic and Statistical Manual of Mental Disorders* (DSM-IV, 1994). Of course, not all causes of stress are similar. Torture is not a one-off accidental event like an air crash, but has similarities to child or wife abuse in that its origin was repetitive and above all, intentional.

When looking at the late psychological effects of torture in refugees from all around the world, one should recognize that to the effects of torture have been added the stressful effects of exile and separation and the anxieties of living as a member of a minority, usually an impoverished one. Another caveat in applying a psychological diagnosis is that concepts embodied in the DSM-IV are couched in Western European terms and may not be appropriate for use when dealing with refugees from the Third World (Bracken *et al.*, 1995).

Nearly all torture survivors show some psychological symptoms, though these may not last, and it is perhaps unwise to attempt to link the symptoms together as a 'torture syndrome' (Turner and Gorst-Unsworth, 1990). What they suffer is not a disease but 'a normal reaction to an abnormal experience'. The degree of apparent damage varies enormously, and is not always related to the severity of the torture. Some highly committed political activists who have been detained many times develop some immunity to torture-related stress and regard torture as a price they have to pay for their convictions (Başoğlu and Paker, 1995). Some individuals seem to be completely destroyed and may never again be normally functioning social beings, while others eventually appear to cope with the consequences and have little evidence of permanent damage. There are even some whose experiences have a beneficial effect. Bracken reports the case of a man he was asked to see:

> *A 40 year old Ugandan man who had been a prominent politician in the past was arrested and brought to an army compound. He was held for seven days. During this time he was beaten and humiliated while being interrogated. After his release he was referred by a friend who assumed that he would be in need of some form of psychiatric help. When interviewed, however, he denied any great distress. He told us that he was a Christian but that prior to his imprisonment his faith had not meant a great deal to him. While he was in detention he felt a strong identification with the figure of Jesus Christ who had also suffered torture and humiliation. He found that his own suffering and his identification with Christ brought him closer to his religion and since his ordeal the quality of his spiritual life was*

intensified. He indicated that because of this the overall effect of his experience had been positive for him.

(Bracken et al., 1995)

The saying 'tortured once, tortured for life' does not therefore seem always to be applicable. Of course, since the symptoms may be hidden, it is necessary that they be recognized – which is not always easy, since the victim tends not to want to talk about his experiences, and his behaviour may be misunderstood. The effects can surface many years later, as graphically shown in survivors of the Holocaust or Japanese prison camps fifty years ago, many of whom, having apparently managed reasonably well during an active career, have suffered psychological breakdown after retirement.

There are assumptions about the nature of the destructive process that severe torture involves. Torture demolishes or dismantles, deliberately, the systems of integration, cohesion, control and defence against dissolution, both physical and mental, that people ordinarily maintain, mostly without thinking about it, to keep themselves together as independent beings.

Once dismantled, these systems may reconstitute themselves, overall or in certain respects, depending on how extreme was the original damage and the degree of stress to which the individual was subsequently exposed. Physical healing may be sufficient to allow a body to function reasonably well so long as not too much is asked of it. But tiredness or other physiological changes may alter the limits, and the same may be said of mental integration, once regained.

It is wrong to see these two spheres as distinct. They are closely linked, and physical performance is always fundamentally determined by mental state. The forced demolition of mental integration, of the whole personality, either completely or in part, introduces an essentially new element to an individual's experience and knowledge of himself. Such an experience is invariably associated with extreme anxiety, where the sense is of utter helplessness, of the disappearance of all those means of adaptation by which one ordinarily maintains one's integrity and defends oneself from danger.

Those who have been severely tortured have learnt that such disintegration remains a constant possibility given the necessary circumstances. They become watchful and apprehensive, fearful of any circumstances that remind them of those surrounding their torture: small rooms, locked doors, threatening behaviour, even officials asking questions. They fear any change which reduces their control of the world and of others' actions.

Particularly, they fear night-time and sleeping because that is the time when those integrative controls – conscious awareness and control of thoughts – which ordinarily hold them together are voluntarily dismantled. People who have been tortured fear the night and sleeping because then their memories of persecution return and become unmanageable, because they have lost both their conscious control of them and the reassurance they often find in the presence of others. With their conscious sense of time in abeyance they are back in their terrifying past time and helplessness. Many survivors develop elaborate stratagems to try to avoid or control these possibilities. They resist sleep, take sedatives or drink, listen to the radio, read. In sleep a person becomes individual and alone, and the circumstances of torture are also solitary: one is alone with one's tormentors and one's pain, even though others may be near and being tortured as well.

Another effect of torture is that it constitutes a forced and destructive intrusion on a person's privacy. A life which generally represented the results of affectionate care, a generous granting of individual independence, now contains baleful elements which dispute that affection, replace it with hatred, and assert an alternative possession.

Communications and their control are central to all aspects of the matter. From the beginning, an individual's inner life is linked to the world of others by messages passed in both directions using means appropriate to all the senses. Free-living people are mostly able to control their passage, their exchange. Tortures, of whatever form, are communications, and are intended to leave their meanings within the victims in the permanent damage both to their bodies and to their minds.

People who have been tortured develop a relationship with their experiences. They live them, reproduce them in their relationships with others, in whole or in part, remain preoccupied with them consciously and unconsciously, and re-enact them every night as the time to sleep approaches, and in their nightmares.

Torture survivors often show anxiety, poor concentration, intrusive thoughts and poor memory during the day and sleeplessness and nightmares at night. Many also suffer panic attacks with sweating, palpitations and overbreathing, flashbacks of the events, aggression, inability to mix socially, depression and suicidal thoughts or actual suicide attempts. At first they are unable to talk of their experiences and many have not even told their spouse or family any details, especially if there has been sexual abuse. Many victims have been insistently told by their torturers during episodes of physical or electrical assaults on the genitals that they will in future be impotent or sterile. Naturally, this has a profound and lasting effect on sexual relations, even though there may be no detectable physical damage.

Many survivors show paradoxical feelings of guilt. This may be because they imagine that they have betrayed their companions or let down their organization, but it seems often to be a feeling that has been deliberately inculcated by the torturers, who have formed a bond with their victims.

While many of these symptoms may be identical to those seen after different types of trauma, certain features may indicate that torture is the cause, for instance, of panic attacks triggered by the sight of police or the sound of screams, or nightmares featuring precise episodes from the victim's torture history.

Though the effects of torture which we see in torture survivors are extremely distressing, it has to be remembered that we do not see the worst cases, those whose release was in death. Their suffering can only be imagined.

The lasting psychological effects on the families of torture victims, and on the community from which they have been torn, are also important. They are most extreme where there has been a 'disappearance'. The relatives remain in a sort of limbo as long as the victim's fate remains uncertain and the authorities continue to deny responsibility. For years afterwards the relatives, unable to mourn properly, continue to feel the possibility of the return of their loved one and continue to entertain recurrent images of meeting him on the street or of seeing him walk through the door. Until they obtain positive proof of death or survival they will continue in a state of 'frozen mourning' (Amnesty International, 1995b; Summerfield, 1995; see also Chapter 10).

In summary, it is important to emphasize the extreme diversity of the picture of torture, in its methods and effects. There is great variation around the world, in the political climate and the legal constraints (if any) put upon its practice, the methods used and its effects on the people it involves directly or indirectly.

References

American Psychiatric Association (1994) *Diagnostic and Statistical Manual of Mental Disorders*, 4th edition (DSM-IV). Washington, DC: American Psychiatric Association.

Amnesty International (1984) *Torture in the Eighties*, pp. 13–17. London: Amnesty International.

Amnesty International (1994) 'Physical restraint: Denmark'. AI Index: EUR 18/05/94.

Amnesty International (1995a) 'Cruel, inhuman and degrading punishment: the use of fetters in Pakistan'. AI Index: ASA 33/20/95.

Amnesty International (1995b) *Human Rights Are Women's Rights*. London: Amnesty International.

Amnesty International (1995c) 'Psychiatry: a human rights perspective'. AI Index: ACT 75/03/95.

Başoğlu, M. and Paker, M. (1995) 'Severity of trauma as predictor of long-term psychological status in survivors of torture'. *Journal of Anxiety Disorders* 9, 339–50.

Bloch, S. and Reddaway, P. (1977) *Russia's Political Hospitals: The Abuse of Psychiatry in the Soviet Union.* London: Gollancz.

Bracken, P.J., Giller, J.E. and Summerfield, D. (1995) 'Psychological responses to war and atrocity: the limitations of current concepts'. *Social Science Medicine* 40, 1073–82.

British Medical Association (1992) *Medicine Betrayed*, p. 40. London: Zed Books.

Forrest, D. (1995) 'Patterns of abuse in Sikh asylum seekers'. *Lancet* 345, 225–6.

Goldfeld, A.E., Mollica, R.F., Pesavento, B.H. and Faraone, S.V. (1988) 'The physical and psychological sequelae of torture'. *Journal of the American Medical Association* 259, 2725–9.

Hingley, R. (1978) *Dostoyevsky: His Life and Works.* Quoted in Kelly, L. (1981) *St*

Petersburg: A Travellers' Companion, pp. 161–3. London: Constable.

Johannes Wier Foundation (1993) *Tazmamert: fort militaire secret du Maroc.* Amersfoort, Netherlands: Johannes Wier Foundation for Health and Human Rights.

Landau Commission (1987) *Report of the Commission of Enquiry into the Methods of Investigation of the General Security Services Regarding Hostile Terrorist Activity.* Jerusalem, Israel.

Malik, G.H. (1993) 'Acute renal failure following physical torture'. *Nephron* 63, 434–7.

Reich, W. (1985) 'The world of Soviet psychiatry'. In E. Stover and E.O. Nightingale (eds), *The Breaking of Bodies and Minds*, pp. 206–22. New York: Norton.

Summerfield, D. (1995) 'Raising the dead: war, reparation, and the politics of memory'. *British Medical Journal* 311, 495–7.

Turner, S. and Gorst-Unsworth, C. (1990) 'Psychological sequelae of torture: a descriptive model'. *British Journal of Psychiatry* 157, 475–80.

CHAPTER 8

The Agencies Involved

Mike Jempson

Introduction

Systematic torture seems so far removed from acceptable social behaviour that there is a real danger of seeing it merely as an aberration conducted by sick individuals in secretive surroundings. However, torture is more often the consequence of a mind-set among those with power that their ends justify any means of ensuring the compliance of those whom they seek to control. Among their subordinates this translates into a licence to ill-treat supposed or actual 'opponents'.

The most likely villains

Under a military regime the torturers are most likely to be drawn from the ranks of the armed services or, more specifically, from élite security units charged with eradicating opposition. The security services are equally likely to supply the torturers under a civilian government, but other law enforcement officers, including the police and prison staff, will also be involved.

Torture is frequently associated with over-reliance upon confession evidence in court. There are some countries, such as Mexico, where a confession is necessary for conviction. When an uncorroborated confession is enough to convict, when the police are under pressure to produce results, and when detainees may be held incommunicado for long periods, the risk of torture in police custody increases greatly. Under such circumstances formal or informal systems of immunity from prosecution may be enjoyed by police or security forces. Where torture has occurred, similar patterns of denial can be expected, with the accused exonerated after internal investigation, often by their own colleagues, and swift rejection of requests for independent inquiries (Figure 8.1).

Alongside those directly responsible for torture are others who must be considered equally culpable: senior law enforcement officers and members of the judiciary, and doctors and medical staff who fail to intervene when

Figure 8.1. Colombia: the soldiers who killed 11 members of the Burgos family (shown here) in 1990 were acquitted despite being ordered to stand trial by a supreme military tribunal.

they become aware that human rights and internationally recognized standards of behaviour are being breached by the authorities. Between them they provide silent endorsement and so contribute to the blanket of immunity necessary for the torturer to have confidence in his task.

But behind or, more properly, above them all there is a hierarchy of responsibility: the direct superiors who issue orders or allow their subordinates a 'free hand'; those further up in public service who devise strategies of control and supervise training; and members of the government, who determine policy, set goals and devise legislation. The chain of command between the torture chamber and the government may not be direct, but the licence to torture is evident from the administrative systems that operate.

When a government declares a 'state of emergency' – itself seen as an admission that 'normal rules' no longer apply – because civil and political unrest, armed rebellion or other forms of paramilitary activity threaten its authority, torture inevitably joins the armoury of those charged with restoring 'law and order'. The security services are granted wide-ranging powers of arrest and detention covering often the flimsiest suspicion of dissent and sympathy for, if not actual involvement in, subversive activity.

In India the police have been accused of the systematic use of torture in dealing with both criminal and counter-insurgency investigations.

Official denials have provided a first layer of impunity, reducing the likelihood of thorough investigation of torture allegations, let alone prosecution.

The police are also able to rely upon section 23 of the 1861 Police Act, which survived India's independence from colonial rule, to justify any action they take in response to political pressure to obtain results at local, regional or national level. It requires every police officer 'promptly to obey and execute all orders and warrants lawfully issued to him by any competent authority'. In territories where the government faces violent political opposition, such as Punjab, Jammu and Kashmir, Assam and other northern states, the Armed Forces (Special Powers) Act has been invoked, granting the security forces draconian powers and immunity from prosecution. Section 4 provides that:

> Any commissioned officer, non-commissioned officer or any other person of equivalent rank in the armed forces may . . . fire upon or otherwise use force, even to the causing of death, against any person who is acting in contravention of any law or order for the time being in force in the disturbed area prohibiting the assembly of five or more persons or the carrying of weapons or of things capable of being used as weapons . . .

Section 6 states:

> No prosecution, suit or other legal proceeding shall be instituted, except with the previous sanction of the central government, against any person in respect of anything done or purported to have been done in the exercise of the powers conferred under this Act.

As Amnesty International has so often pointed out, a 'state of emergency' should be an extension of the rule of law, not an abrogation of it.

When political activists are targeted for surveillance or apprehension because they are asserting 'rights', especially territorial rights which are regarded as invalid or potentially divisive by the government, there is a danger that all their rights will be overridden by the security services. In Israel, for example, the Occupied Territories are subject to Military Orders, which were amended on 20 July 1994 to reduce the maximum period of detention without judicial review from 18 to 11 days but which continue to deny detainees their right to be heard promptly by a judicial or other authority. Detainees may be denied access to a lawyer for the first 30 days, renewable for two further periods of 30 days. The Israeli authorities have agreed that visits by the International Committee of the Red Cross (ICRC) may be allowed after 14 days, but there are obvious dangers of ill-treatment under these regulations (see also Chapter 11).

Even where special laws granting the security services extra powers are not in force, there may be tacit acceptance that questionable methods may be necessary to enforce 'law and order'. Many of the real culprits never set foot in a torture chamber and have the resources to exonerate themselves in a court of law, if indeed they were ever to be apprehended. When notorious regimes are brought down, the guilty men at the top are the first to take flight, choosing exile in countries from which extradition is least likely; others swiftly obtain a licence to remain at liberty, using the remnants of their power to negotiate amnesties. Some of those most directly involved – security service personnel, police officers, gaolers and informers – may receive rough retributive justice at the hands of the communities they have terrorized, or themselves become victims of torture as the cycle of terror turns full circle.

The longer the delay in bringing those involved in torture to justice, the more complicated the issues of identification and 'degrees of responsibility' become, reducing the likelihood of successful prosecution, as the continuing controversy over the pursuit and arraignment of alleged war criminals from Rwanda, Bosnia-Herzegovina or even Nazi Germany has shown. Too often it seems as if the impunity which allowed torturers to conduct their vicious assaults is extended long beyond the 'extenuating' circumstances which supposedly 'justified' their behaviour in the first place. Protected by their colleagues and vulnerable only to the often uncorroborated evidence of the victims who survive, those who torture live in a cocoon of denial that must eventually destroy their own self-respect. Those who brutalize others are themselves brutalized.

Without the guarantee of immunity from prosecution, or even identification, recruiting people to conduct torture would be all the more difficult. But first there needs to be a pool of potential recruits. In December 1986 a former member of the national police in El Salvador explained how he had been recruited into an undercover 'death squad':

> 'I was assigned to the job of arresting people wanted by the government for subversive activity. . . . I was given photographs and descriptions of people wanted by my government, and their addresses as well, but I was not furnished with the names of these people. . . . I told my superiors that I simply couldn't do this kind of work because it was against my conscience and my moral beliefs. . . . I had learnt that many times when people were taken in this manner and delivered to the police, the arrested people disappeared, and frequently their dead bodies turned up later. . . . [I was] dismissed from the police service . . .

> 'Someone from the Salvadorean army visited my home. He compelled me to accompany him . . . [a] major told me that he needed my service and that he was going to change my name. . . . I felt I was not being asked to

volunteer for something; my services were being recruited under duress. . . . I did not express opposition, because I felt instinctively that my life was on the line. . . . He introduced me to two undercover, or plain-clothes, officers. . . . He said, "They are your father, mother, child, they are your everything." Then he said, "No questions." I was told I was now a member of a government death squad . . . there was no turning back. From that moment my life changed completely. I could not see my wife and children any more except for five minutes in the middle of the night or during the early morning. [They] were placed under surveillance. When . . . [after a detainee had been killed] I told my superior . . . that it was not my job to murder people, or to participate in a murder . . . [he] and three other men grabbed me and hit me in the face with a pistol. . . . I said . . . "I don't want to work with you any more." He said. . . ". . . do you love your wife and kids? If you love them you will work with us, or we will kill your wife and kids." I fled the country. . . . '

Authorizing torture

When the use of torture is condoned by a regime it is rarely expressly permitted. Rather there is a blurring of the distinctions between the executive, the legislature, the judiciary, the military and those responsible for civilian law enforcement.

There are many ways in which a leadership may let it be known that their officials may 'do what is necessary' to achieve specified goals. Promoting the use of brutal interrogation techniques through training programmes is perhaps the most obvious, but insistence upon total obedience and the imposition of tough sanctions upon those who disobey is signal enough.

Indoctrination and propaganda that demonizes those who are to be regarded as the 'enemy' and encourages the view that those who do not share the dominant culture or who oppose the political ideology of the regime are in some sense subhuman further helps to relieve the natural anxiety that most people feel about hurting others. Security service personnel and law enforcement officers may themselves be gradually exposed to more and more extremes of violence as a means of desensitizing them to the sufferings of others.

Having 'approved' the use of excessive force, or turned a blind eye to it, the authorities complete the process by offering rewards for results in the form of personal recognition including bonuses and special status. Agents of the state themselves know that they will be judged by results, and that any special laws that empower them also protect them. But they are also aware that their immunity is likely to last only as long as the current regime remains in power. By identifying their personal and family interests with those of the state they become the perfect cipher: dependent, obedient and ruthless. Torture and terror can quickly become their method of demonstrating unquestioning loyalty.

This remains true even when the efficacy of torture has been exposed as a sham. Detainees are most often subjected to torture on the ostensible grounds that they are withholding information that is vital to the security of the state. Often it would appear that the torturers know this is not true. Victims may be required to recant their political or religious views, or to confirm information already known to their tormentors by informing on their colleagues. They continue to be beaten and injured as a matter of political expediency. It demonstrates to doubters that a regime has the means and the will to crush opposition and provides the servants of the regime with an opportunity to confirm their loyalty.

The classic conditions under which torture might be expected to flourish – a definable enemy, a real threat to the lives of the civilian population, and an urgent need to elicit information about the enemy's capabilities, tactics and intentions – occur when a country is at war. Normal social and legal arrangements take second place to the military and political objectives of the protagonists. The justification for the suspension of peacetime laws and conventions is the saving of civilian lives. The interrogation of suspected agents of an external enemy becomes a military and a political priority. Even so, more than 150 states have ratified the Geneva Conventions (1864, 1868, 1906, 1929, 1949) that govern the treatment of non-combatants, the sick and wounded, and prisoners of war during military campaigns. They reject torture as a legitimate means of obtaining information from detainees. All the more alarming therefore that 'national security' is so frequently cited in defence of legislative measures that provide cover for torturers, or as an explanation for human rights abuses by state officials during peacetime or in the midst of civil war. It is one of those catch-all terms used by an élite to justify almost any type of behaviour or clandestine activity carried out by agents of the state. Once the term is invoked, no further explanation is considered necessary. As with 'the fight against terrorism', such terms imply a morally neutral space in which all manner of normally unacceptable behaviour may be conducted, free from rebuke or judicial remedy.

Of course, the problem is that the people who determine what may or may not be regarded as 'subversive' are those most at risk if their 'opponents' gain credibility or overturn their power base. Sheltering beneath the all-enveloping cloak of such expressions, the élite are able to dismiss critics as ill-informed or even a threat to the stability of society. When those in power fob off their challengers by claiming 'We know something you don't', what remains unspoken is more sinister: 'That is what makes us powerful.' More often than not, over-reliance upon secrecy implies lack of confidence, the fatal weakness of every bully.

Many 'freedom fighters' and 'terrorists' are as guilty of human rights abuses as the governments they oppose. None the less, an established government has a special responsibility for those who share its territory but not its point of view. If opposition is not tolerated, and violent dissent is not dealt with under due process of law, then a state of *de facto* civil war exists. And political opponents having been categorized as 'the enemy within' to justify any suspension of civil liberties, a self-fulfilling prophecy unfolds. However bestial the behaviour of a militant minority, retaliating in an equally objectionable manner challenges the values represented by the rule of law, legitimizing criticism of the regime. Once the security forces are given *carte blanche* to seek out and destroy dissidents, the citizenry are given a licence to become informers and *agents provocateurs*. If dissidents are stigmatized as less deserving of respect before the law, it is not hard to persuade the majority that they deserve all manner of unjust and inhuman treatment. The enemy having been 'dehumanized', normal rules of behaviour no longer apply: old scores can be settled with impunity, breeding further distrust and division and justifying more stringent security measures.

The enemy may not have political motives. Drug trafficking is big business, and police know that they are up against powerful adversaries in their war against the drug barons. Public opprobrium has helped to justify excesses by those engaged in the fight against the illegal trade in drugs. The narcotics divisions of police forces in Greece and Mexico are among many who have tortured suspects to gather information about supply and distribution networks.

Total control

Torture is not a remote phenomenon. It lurks beneath the surface wherever power is exercised without transparency and accountability. One individual acting in the belief that he has authority to inflict pain upon another is a manifestation of power at its crudest, when those who control a society feel they have the right to insist that all opposition should be silenced.

The torturer demonstrates his total control by denying his victim's humanity; and torture is most likely to occur in a society where the government attempts to assert total control over the citizenry. Each is the corollary of the other.

Simply establishing a panoply of measures to underpin the authority of government – including special laws and intelligence and security services at all levels of society and throughout a country – might be considered sufficient to cow a population. But to be really effective the system must display evidence of its ruthlessness.

Under President Suharto of Indonesia a comprehensive security structure enforces compliance with the state ideology, *Pancasila*, the 1945 Constitution and key 'national goals' of stability, security and order. Deviation by individuals or organizations from the five principles of *Pancasila* – belief in God, humanitarianism, national unity, democracy and social justice – is punishable by law. Interpretation of what constitutes compliance or deviation rests with the state and its institutions. Small wonder that the Chief of the State Intelligence Co-ordinating Agency could announce in February 1994, with apparently unintentional irony: 'Local human rights groups are all right so long as they do not deviate from the official policy line.' Troops are deployed throughout the country, supplemented by élite combat teams and paramilitary groups primarily concerned with counter-insurgency. Organizations like the Kopassus (Special Forces Command), Brimob (Police Mobile Brigade), the Army Strategic Reserve Command (KOS-TRAD) and the police riot squad have been responsible for many human rights violations, including torture and extrajudicial executions. They are serviced by an intelligence-gathering network operating within the formal military command structure and a range of semi-autonomous bodies such as the Co-ordinating Agency for the Maintenance of National Stability (Bakorstansus).

When the military seized control of Myanmar (Burma) in September 1988 under the guise of the State Law and Order Restoration Council (SLORC), its very name was an indication that it would brook no opposition. Days later over a thousand unarmed demonstrators were shot dead by the security forces. Hundreds of thousands of people have been killed, tortured or forcibly conscripted since SLORC refused to hand over power to the National League for Democracy (NLD) which won the general election of 1990. NLD General Secretary Aung San Suu Kyi was held under house arrest until the summer of 1995. This highly centralized structure allows tight control from the top, while distancing the leadership from human rights abuses that take place in local detention and interrogation centres run by a plethora of internal security services.

A variation of the total control mechanism operates in Cuba, where the Communist regime encourages every citizen to see himself or herself as a defender of the Revolution, and claims that over half the population are trained to defend the country in the event of external attack. Many civilians are armed and encouraged to take a proactive role in confronting 'any sign of counter-revolution or crime'.

China, the most populous country on earth, also has a highly centralized and ideologically driven administration. Over the years it has experimented with a variety of techniques to suppress dissent and assert the authority of the ruling Communist Party over all aspects of everyone's life. The judicial system itself exemplifies the extent to which terror has become institutionalized. Few cases are brought to court without confession evidence, and many convictions are obtained solely on the basis of uncorroborated confessions extracted from detainees after they have been charged. But torture is not just the prerogative of the police. In a society where 'reform through labour' and 're-education through labour' are the *raison d'être* of many penal institutions it is not surprising that allegations and evidence of ill-treatment persist. Many of those detained have not had the benefit of a trial. Those who express a negative attitude towards their sentence, their incarceration, prison staff or the regime can expect further punishment from their gaolers. Prison officers become judges as well as gaolers, with powers to mete out whatever 'instructive' ill-treatment they think appropriate. Although the police and prison warders are not completely immune from prosecution (407 cases of 'extorting confessions by torture' were dealt with in 1991 alone, and 24 prison wardens and guards were sentenced to imprisonment for administering 'corporal punishment' in 1990 and 1991), the system is wide open to abuse, especially since weapons of torture, including a variety of painful shackles and electric batons, are standard issue.

Policing change

Having ousted the corrupt and discredited regime of President Marcos, first at the ballot box and then through a popular, non-violent uprising, the government of President Corazon Aquino in the Philippines sought to quell opposition using methods similar to those of her predecessor (Figure 8.2). The Citizen Armed Force Geographical Unit (CAFGU) was established in 1987, but many of its members had served in the Civilian Home Defense Force (CHDF), disbanded by presidential decree in the same year after winning notoriety for its vicious assaults on civilians under President Marcos. At neighbourhood level civilian self-defence organizations (CVOs) were set up, ostensibly to defend local communities. Working alongside CAFGU and smaller politically motivated vigilante groups such as Alsa Masa (Masses Arise), these poorly trained and often undisciplined groups have operated reigns of terror with impunity as part of the 'total approach' to counter-insurgency initiated by the Aquino government. In effect they function as an unofficial extension of the military, although their supposed autonomy allows the administration to deny complicity when their excesses are exposed.

Figure 8.2. Philippines: Renato Tabasa Zabate of the United Farmers' Organization was abducted by armed men in September 1991. Schoolchildren found his body five days later, gagged and bound and with 31 wounds.

After the violent removal of a government, subjugation of dissent becomes a military and political priority. Terror becomes the most effective weapon of ordinary soldiers and their immediate superiors. When Lieutenant-General Omar Hassan Ahmad al-Bashir mounted his coup against the elected government of Sudan on 30 June 1989 he announced the formation of the National Salvation Revolution Command Council (NSRCC), declared a state of emergency, suspended the Constitution, dissolved trade unions and political parties, closed down the independent press and suspended all secular associations. The NSRCC then embarked upon an ambitious programme to reshape a pluralist society according to a political agenda derived from its interpretation of Islam. It has resorted to repression to maintain control. Hundreds of prisoners of conscience from all walks of life have been arrested; torture in secret detention centres is widespread; and political opponents have lost jobs, homes and prospects and sometimes their lives after unfair summary military tribunals. Thousands of people have 'disappeared' during a war with southern-based rebels, a civil war

131

prosecuted with ruthlessness on both sides. The military and security forces have been purged and parallel military and security forces ideologically aligned to the NRSCC have been set up: the paramilitary Popular Defence Force, and Security of the Revolution, staffed by members of the National Islamic Front.

In 1991 a similar initial display of force and a rapid deterioration in respect for human rights followed the overthrow of the elected government of President Jean-Paul Aristide in Haiti.

An unpopular government, even when elected democratically, may also resort to inhuman and degrading treatment in an effort to retain control during a period of sudden change. When the newly elected President Carlos Andrés Pérez introduced austerity measures in Venezuela during 1989 there was widespread unrest, and responsibility for law and order was passed to the military. Within three years there were two attempted military coups, and in May 1993 the President was suspended on charges of corruption and an interim president, Ramón José Velásquez, was elected.

Throughout this period of uncertainty reports of human rights violations increased dramatically. Civilian law enforcement agencies, special sections of the armed services – the Directorates of Military Intelligence (Dirección de Inteligencia Militar, DIM) and Army Intelligence (Dirección de Inteligencia del Ejército, DIE) – and the National Guard (Guarda Nacional) have all been accused of torturing detainees. The National Guard investigates drug offences, handles external security in prisons, and provides support for the police during civil disturbances.

The rule of the mob

A regime that embarks on the subjugation of its population may wish to distance itself from terror tactics by laying blame for torture, mutilation and extrajudicial killings at the door of vigilantes and death squads. It is a phenomenon found throughout the world. Using colourful names designed to strike fear into the community (White Hand, Secret Anti-Communist Army, Black Cats) they function efficiently and are rarely brought to trial. These *ad hoc* terror groups 'do unofficially what cannot be done officially', relying upon the authorities for instructions and protection. Evidence from former death squad members has revealed that these shadowy organizations are a sinister extension of the political role of the security services. Many are serving soldiers or police officers authorized to abduct, interrogate under torture, execute and dispose of the bodies of their victims, sometimes working in conjunction with armed civilians. Their existence provides the authorities with an excuse to increase surveillance and security and to blame casualties on vendettas between rival terror groups.

Once the use of death squads has become embedded in the operational techniques of the security forces, it is difficult to eradicate. After a lull in death squad activity in El Salvador following the election of the civilian President Duarte in 1984, there was a resurgence in the late 1980s as senior members of the military made use of the technique to undermine the authority of a government whose policies they opposed.

Not all governments find it necessary or appropriate to hide behind shadowy paramilitary groups when torture is considered an effective means of asserting their authority. Most governments would prefer not to risk international opprobrium by formally sanctioning torture, but find it convenient to acknowledge the 'will of the people' when charged with human rights abuses.

One consequence of the Gulf War was the rough justice handed out to individuals suspected of collaborating with the Iraqi forces during the invasion of Kuwait. In the months after the Iraqi withdrawal, armed Kuwaiti civilians, often with the knowledge of government officials, conducted a brutal campaign of reprisals against those thought to have collaborated with the Iraqis during the occupation. Arbitrary arrest, torture and extrajudicial execution were particularly common during the initial period of martial law that followed Kuwait's liberation. Despite the Kuwaiti authorities' statement that nationality played no part in the arrests, according to reports received by AI most of the victims were Iraqis, Jordanians, Sudanese, Yemenis, Somalis and stateless Palestinians and *Bidun* (Bedouin), many of whom had worked in Kuwait for generations (Figure 8.3).

The rise in nationalism in Europe, especially since the collapse of Russian communism, has also given rise to resentment and racist violence towards minorities. Social and political pressures related to immigration may induce law enforcement officers to exceed their power, safe in the knowledge that a large body of opinion within the country endorses or tacitly accepts their behaviour. Western European countries that are seen as a safe point of entry for political and economic refugees escaping oppression and poverty at home have also been the focus of complaints about ill-treatment and racist abuse by police officers, immigration officials and prison staff.

Racist violence and anti-foreigner sentiment have scarred the Federal Republic of Germany since unification. The attitudes of individual police officers towards foreigners, reflecting those of a society undergoing dramatic change, have given rise to complaints about harsh treatment meted out to foreigners suspected of even minor infringements of the

Figure 8.3. Kuwait: Fatima Ramez Tafia, a young Lebanese woman initially sentenced to death by the martial law court, now serving 10 years despite recommendations by three review counsellors that her sentence be suspended for lack of substantial evidence.

law. Information obtained by AI points to a pattern of police ill-treatment throughout Germany. Victims have included people of Algerian, Iranian, Kurdish, Moroccan, Romani, Senegalese, Sri Lankan, Turkish and Vietnamese origin. In many cases the officers concerned have gone unpunished. Failure to acknowledge the extent of such ill-treatment, to bring to justice those responsible and compensate the victims, and to put in place appropriate mechanisms to safeguard against ill-treatment make it more, not less, likely that such abuses will continue.

AI has documented similar instances of police ill-treatment of foreigners in France and Italy, where many people from North Africa and the Middle East have sought asylum or a new life. Racist attacks by civilians offer perhaps the most striking evidence that such violence is not solely the prerogative of agents of the state. When police officers, government officials or the military conduct torture openly or fail to intervene when civilians 'take the law into their own hands', mob rule has its way. Systematic attacks by villagers on their Roma neighbours in Romania are evidence enough of that. And in the chaos of the disintegration of former Yugoslavia cruelty and ill-treatment was not confined to those wearing uniforms.

When the state embarks upon political programmes focused around ethnic status, pogroms are almost inevitable. The target community is utterly vulnerable to any indignity or injury that the agents of the state and their supporters within the majority population choose to visit upon them. As part of their 'total conflict' policy in south-eastern Turkey, the authorities have 'enlisted' the assistance of village civil defence corps in their campaign against the armed insurgents of the Kurdish Workers' Party (PKK). Local people risk ill-treatment from both sides. The ineptly named anti-terror branches of the police lead the way in promoting torture as a means of asserting the authority of the state. Control of the media and harassment of journalists, human rights activists and other external observers are among the techniques used by the government to keep a lid on domestic and international criticism of its policies. Yet the government admits that the security forces have difficulty in distinguishing between insurgents and non-combatants, and because civilians are paid to fight against the PKK they and their families frequently suffer reprisals. On all sides degrading treatment and torture have become the language of loyalty to the cause. It is one of the consequences of passing responsibility for security directly to the civilian population.

Similar techniques are employed by the government of Indonesia in its suppression of dissent. In Indonesia's occupation of East Timor, the security services have employed a tactic known as the 'fence of legs' during which villagers are forced to 'sweep' an area ahead of troops, to flush out rebels and inhibit them from returning fire. The Regional Commander of Aceh in northern Sumatra declared in November 1990:

> 'I have told the community, if you find a terrorist, kill him. There is no need to investigate him. Don't let people be the victims. If they don't do as you order them, shoot them on the spot, or butcher them. I tell members of the community to carry sharp weapons, a machete or whatever. If you meet a terrorist, kill him.'

Under such conditions it is easy for people to convince themselves that they can be safe only if they take no part in politics or if they collaborate with the agents of the state. When the identity of 'the enemy within' is nebulous and defined largely by attitudes of mind, it is not difficult to generate mass anxiety and even hysteria.

A society can quickly become paranoid, uncertain about who can be trusted, and whose interpretation of events has the most validity. Fear and uncertainty offer immense scope for abuses of human rights. Those who sympathize with or act in defence of the victims of a repressive regime are immediately suspect, and liable to similar ill-treatment. When basic human rights go out of the window, those who campaign for them become enemies of the state who must be silenced.

Conclusion

One of AI's concerns is that the spread of torture is facilitated by the sharing of security and interrogation techniques through intergovernmental and inter-agency transfers and training programmes involving personnel from foreign military, security and police services. Both the United Nations Convention against Torture of 1984 (Chapter 1) and AI's 12-point Program for the Prevention of Torture (see page 198), adopted in 1984, stress the importance of monitoring domestic interrogation methods and prison conditions, and insist that the training of public officials should make clear that any form of cruel or degrading treatment constitutes unacceptable behaviour.

The revulsion that most political leaders publicly express about torture should mean that it is possible for those involved in torture, whether directly or by association, to be apprehended and tried wherever they take refuge and regardless of where their offences were committed, as AI advocates. Although that would seem to require an almost unprecedented degree of international co-operation, the UN Convention already provides the basis for common judicial instruments to make torture a heinous offence regardless of frontiers or domestic politics, and ensure that there is no 'safe haven' for torturers. Only the unswerving implementation of sanctions against those who order and those who conduct torture is likely to begin the process of eradicating it from the arsenal of political weaponry.

CHAPTER 9

The New Trade in Technologies of Restraint and Electroshock

Steve Wright

Introduction

Instruments of repression and torture have been associated with the apparatus of power as long as human history has been recorded. Centuries of research and development have been expended in devising ever more cruel and inhumane means of extracting obedience and information from reluctant victims, or achieving excruciatingly painful and long-drawn-out deaths for those who would question or challenge the prevalent status quo.

The early history of torture is covered in Chapter 2. The present chapter examines some of the reasons for the advent of new technologies and their role and function in maintaining illegitimate regimes. It describes recent findings on the research, development, procurement and proliferation of modern technologies. Many of them are designed primarily for containment and riot control, but they readily lend themselves to cruel, inhuman or degrading treatment if not outright torture in the hands of the torturing states. Also identified in this chapter are some of the companies involved in the manufacture and supply of these instruments. The chapter concludes with a look at some of the new technologies of political control which lie on the horizon and describes what Amnesty International (AI) is currently doing to prevent such technologies, training and techniques being used in the gross violation of human rights.

Repression technologies: role and function

What has changed over the centuries is the increasing requirement for speed in breaking down prisoners' resistance and the adoption of sophisticated methods based on a scientific approach. The advent of modern torture technique can be traced back to the Russian NKVD, which used sensory deprivation and multiple levels of brutality to induce

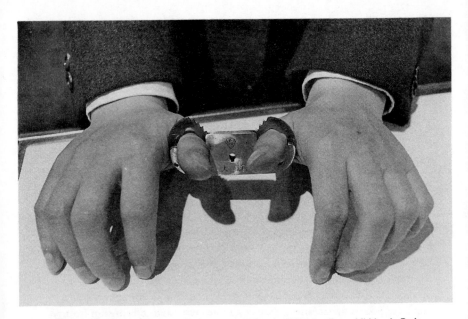

Figure 9.1. Chinese thumb cuffs demonstrated at the Milipol police exhibition in Paris. Photo, David Hoffman

stress before 'conveyor'-style questioning by relays of interrogators for days on end, thereby industrializing state terror. These approaches had the dual requirement of extracting information and breaking down personality in order to elicit public confessions as the era of the 'show trial' opened up. Such torture techniques can themselves be regarded as part of an evolving technology which can be further researched and developed before being transferred elsewhere. Modern torture technology can be conceptualized as having three components, namely hardware, software and liveware (the human elements), which are all woven together to form manipulative programmes of socio-political control.

The hardware can include both modern and medieval prisoner restraining, disabling and repressive technologies, for example leg shackles, thumb cuffs (Figure 9.1), suspension equipment, blunt trauma-inducing drugs (e.g. Aminazin, apomorphine, curare, suxamethonium, haloperidol, insulin, sulfazin, triftazin, tizertsin, sanapax, etaperazin, phrenolong, trisedil, mazjeptil, seduksin and motiden-depo (Plate and Darvi, 1981)), electroshock weapons, electrically heated hot tables, whips, iron-chain-filled rubber hoses, cat-o'-nine-tails, clubs, canes, specially designed torture devices and interrogation rooms using white noise (Sweeny, 1991a, 1991b), and stroboscopic or UV light (*New Scientist*, 1973).

Much of this equipment is home-made, but some of the newer technologies are purpose-built and may be used by successive law enforcement agencies after one torturing regime is replaced by another. For example, the 'Apollo machine' which was devised by SAVAK, the Shah's secret police in Iran (it delivered an electric shock to sensitive parts of the body, while a steel helmet covered prisoners' heads to amplify their screams), was also used by the succeeding regime's religious police (Mather, 1982).

Helen Bamber, Director of the British Medical Foundation for the Treatment of the Victims of Torture, has described electroshock batons as the 'most universal modern tool of the torturers' (Gregory, 1995). Recent surveys of torture victims have confirmed that after systematic beating, electroshock torture is one of the most common factors (London, 1993; Rasmussen, 1990). If one looks at the country reports of AI, electroshock torture is the Esperanto of the most repressive states, and current examples of its use have been found from Greece (Council of Europe, 1994), to China (Amnesty International, 1992b; Ballantyne, 1992, 1995) and Saudi Arabia (Amnesty International, 1994). According to the manufacturers, the new pulsed variants of electroshock weapons were developed in the 1980s on the basis of biomedical research. An independent survey by the UK Forensic Science Service (FSS), commissioned by the Home Office, examined the possible hazardous effects of a range of different electroshock devices on the human body (Robinson et al., 1990). The FSS study reported that receiving a typical discharge from an electroshock prod for up to half a second startles and repels the victim; one to two seconds and the victim loses the ability to stand up; three to five seconds and loss of skeletal muscle control is total and immobilization occurs. The effect can last for between five and fifteen minutes. The FSS study also reported that modern pulsed electroshock weapons are more powerful than the old-fashioned cattle prods by nearly two orders of magnitude.

Portable electrified shields have been manufactured since the mid-1980s for prisoner capture and control. They comprise a transparent polycarbonate plate through which metal strips are interlaced. A button-activated induction coil in the handle sends 40,000 to 100,000 volts arcing across the metal strips, accompanied by intermittent indigo flashing sparks and an intimidating crackle as the air between the electrodes is ionized. They work by charging up and then instantaneously discharging a capacitor, to produce a chain of high-impulse shocks. A sales video shows how the victim can be instantaneously thrown to the ground on impact, completely incapacitated.

Apart from such hardware, there are also numerous standard operating procedures which form the 'software' component of the trade in repression technology. Examples of training supplied to authoritarian regimes include the low-intensity conflict training used to capture, stress and 'soften up' dissidents (Watson, 1980), advisory support, and technical assistance, including teaching of scientific methods of 'deep' interrogation procedures, torture and the more brutal forms of human destruction.

Research and development in modern torture techniques and technologies has focused upon methods which cause suffering and intimidation without leaving much in the way of embarrassing long-term visible evidence of brutality. However, researchers in torture rehabilitation centres are gradually evolving more sophisticated methods for detecting and verifying the use of torture (Karlsmark *et al.*, 1988; Rasmussen and Skylv, 1993). A vast range of torture techniques have been recorded, many of which are discussed further in Chapters 5 and 7. The names of these techniques signify how systematized this behaviour has become. Some torturing states evolve their own lexicon of systematized abuse. For example, in China there are *dian ji* (electrical assault), *gui bian* (down on knees whipping), *jieju* (chains and fetters), *shouzhikao* (finger cuffs), *zhiliaio* (rod fetters), *menbanliao* (shackleboard), and so on (Human Rights Watch, 1992; Amnesty International, 1992b).

The flow of modern repressive 'technique' includes expertise in courses on low-intensity conflict management which cover operations deemed to be 'counter-terror'. Some of these approaches are formally coded. Excellent discussions of the codification of counter-terror procedures and their proliferation in practice are provided by Chomsky and Herman (1979) and McClintock (1985a, 1985b, 1992).

Intense interrogation methodologies border on torture, particularly when they incorporate scientific approaches based on psychopharmacology or sensory deprivation (McGuffin, 1974; Shallice, 1973, 1974), or involve levels of physical terror and softening-up processes of intimidation which sap the will of the prisoner to resist. For an account of the techniques of sensory deprivation deployed by the British Army in Northern Ireland and AI's formal response, see British Medical Association (1986). What has evolved from this quest for ever more powerful techniques to break the human spirit is a classical form of operant conditioning designed to teach the target psyche debilitation, dependence and dread (Biderman and Zimmer, 1965). Occasionally, hard evidence of such research comes to light (Anon, 1993). (See also Chapters 4 and 6.)

Such approaches are designed to intimidate the wider population rather than just to extract specific information from any one individual; they are heuristic and can be taught to others (McHardy, 1976; *The Times*, 1980).

In any bureaucracy of repression, there are personnel schooled in the ideological attitudes necessary to keep such systems in operation. In some cases this schooling takes place literally, for example at the infamous School of Americas based at Fort Benning in Georgia, otherwise known as the 'school for dictators' or '*La escuela del golpe*' (the coup school). It has been accused of training death squads in Guatemala and in Honduras, for example Battalion 3-16 (Walker, 1994). The *Baltimore Sun* recently obtained Freedom of Information Act documents on Battalion 3-16 in Honduras (which used electroshock and rubber suffocation devices on prisoners) confirming that the unit had been trained in interrogation techniques by the CIA (*Baltimore Sun*, 11 June 1995). They include the various foreign technical advisers, counter-insurgency and low-intensity conflict strategists, paramilitary, intelligence and internal security police training officers, and the merchants who actually supply the equipment, as well as the 'white-collar mercenaries' who act as key technical operators in the bureaucracy of any repressive system that uses systematic torture as an instrumental tool of the administration. This 'liveware' category includes all the people who are conditioned by fear or training actually to put into practice the software and hardware components of a particular policy of repression (see Chapter 6).

The export of some of this 'security' training has now become a commercial proposition (Gordon, 1987), and it is a characteristic of the trade in torture technology and expertise that it has become intensely privatized (Klare and Arnson, 1981).

The United States connection: transhipment and the bypass of controls

Sadly, it no longer comes as a surprise to imagine that Western liberal democracies might be colluding with the torture trade. Yet during the 1980s some clues were afforded by reports that US companies such as Technipol were freely advertising thumb cuffs, leg-irons and shackles. The Danish Medical Group of AI found that electronic prods manufactured by the US Shok-Baton Company had been used in the violation of human rights (Amnesty International Danish Medical Group, 1987), and a repentant Uruguayan torturer confessed that he had used US-made electroshock batons (Cooper, 1984).

In fact, scores of US companies either manufacture or supply electroshock devices or thumb cuffs and leg-irons, for example AB Electronics (electronic restraint devices), AFY Distributors (electroshock batons), Amazing Concepts (Intimidator electric shock weapons), Armas No Mortales (electroshock weapons), B. West Imports (paralyser Stun Batons), Custom Armoring Corp. (Nova Electronic riot equipment), Federal Laboratories Division (electronic batons), Hiatt Thompson (restraint devices), Nova Technologies (electronic restraint and stun devices), Paralyzer Protection (electric shock stunguns and batons), Ranger Joe's (stun guns), Reliapon Police products (Nova Electronic restraints and shields), S & J Products (electronic restraint devices), SAS R&D Services (electronic batons), Sherwood Communications Associates Ltd (Equaliser and Lightning stun guns), Stun Tech., Inc. (electronic immobilization weapons), Taser Industries (electronic dart shock weapons), The Edge Company (Thunderbolt stun gun), American Handcuff Co. (leg-irons), C & S Security (gang transport chains), Defense Technology (leg-irons), Gulf State Distributors (leg-irons), Peerless Handcuffs (leg-irons and transportation chains), Smith & Wesson (belly chains and other restraining equipment), Technipol International (leg-irons and thumb cuffs), Tobin Tool and Die (shackles), W.S. Darley (leg-irons and belly chains) – to name but a few firms who have advertised their wares. This information has been collected from company brochures, *Police and Security News* (various volumes) and *Thomas' Register* (1992).

Back in 1984 it emerged that US export regulations even had special customs codes for such items as 'specially designed instruments of torture' (US Department of Commerce, 1984). There was even some suggestion (in 376.14) that the government could distance itself from human rights violations through 'judicious use of export controls' (US Department of Commerce, 1983).

Alarmed by the possible scale of the trade in such technologies, in 1993 the Omega Foundation, a UK human rights organization based in Manchester and dealing with military, security and police concerns, sought comprehensive US export trade statistics from the US government, via a Freedom of Information Act request, which was put down on Omega's behalf by the Federation of American Scientists (FAS). The new category codes in the export administration regulations have been, if anything, extended, to include, *inter alia*:

- 'saps, thumbcuffs, thumbscrews, leg irons, shackles and handcuffs, specially designed implements of torture, straight jackets etc (OA82C)' and

- 'stun guns, shock batons, electric cattle prods and other immobilization guns (OA84C)' (United States Department of Commerce 1994).

The statistics of the export licences of such repressive equipment show that from September 1991 to December 1993 the US Commerce Department approved over 350 export licences under commodity category A82C. The further category OA84C aggregates together data on electric shock batons with shotguns and shells. Over 2000 licences were granted from September 1991 to December 1993. While the licences represent a snapshot of permissions for the sale to go forward, they do not indicate actual delivery, nor are they comprehensive, since countries in NATO, such as Turkey, do not require a licence (Arms Sales Monitor, 1995). FAS points out that aggregating data in this way, by lumping non-controversial data such as those on helmets with controversial data on equipment often used for torture such as shock batons, effectively frustrates public oversight.

Given the nature of some of the recipients – Saudi Arabia for example, where AI has already recorded instances of Iraqis being tortured with electric shock batons (Amnesty International, 1994) – many people will suspect the worst.

The United Kingdom 'torture trail'

Britain's involvement in the supply of prison, restraining and execution equipment was first brought into sharp focus in 1983, when a memo on sensitive services was leaked from the Crown Agents (Eburne, 1983). It was more concerned with avoiding government embarrassment than promoting human rights where trade concerning execution ropes, leg-irons and other restraining equipment was concerned. Two journalists from the *Daily Mirror* newspaper were offered a quantity of leg-irons and gang chains by Hiatt & Co. Birmingham (Merritt and Lisners, 1983). The then Minister of Trade's response created a furore when he said, 'If this country did not export them someone else would' (*Hansard*, 1983). Since that time AI has campaigned for a complete ban on the sale or transfer of equipment which is used for torture, the death penalty or other grave human rights violations. The UK government was pressured by public opinion to ban the export of leg-irons, shackles, belly chains and gang chains in 1984.

Yet more than a decade later, in January 1995, it was possible for UK Channel Four Television to show a special edition of the *Dispatches* programme which revealed a startling willingness on the part of British companies to supply banned electroshock weapons (Gregory, 1995). While several European companies are already known to have been involved in either the manufacture or the supply of electroshock devices – including Browning (Belgium); Equipol, France-Selection, Nerai & Cie SARL (France); Bonowi, ERO, Micro and Security Electronic, NOWAR, PK Electronic, Romer, Sicherheitstechnik Schmid, Solid Company (Germany); Alpha Safety (Luxembourg); Auto Alloys, Ensign Ordnance, Miracles of Science, and Tactical Arms International (UK)

(Ballantyne, 1995) – it was not widely realized that such an extensive manufacturing and supply base existed. The information was openly available from company advertising brochures and the *International Defence Directory* (1993, p. 1004; 1995, p. 956).

After they were used in a spate of muggings, electronic stun weapons were banned in the UK in 1988. They were deemed to be a prohibited weapon under the terms of section 5 of the Firearms Acts 1968–1992: 'A person commits an offence if, without the authority of the Defence Council, he has in his possession or purchases or acquires or manufactures or sells or transfers prohibited weapons.' Moreover, Trade Minister Richard Needham advised in October 1993 that the export of such electroshock equipment is controlled by the Export of Goods (Control Order) 1992 and export without a licence is prohibited. He also said that import of such weapons is restricted to those persons legally authorized to hold them in the UK. Section S1.41 of the Criminal Justice Act 1988 provides for criminal sanctions against anyone 'who manufactures, sells or hires or offers for sale or hire, or exposes or has in his possession for the purpose of sale or hire . . . a weapon to which this section applies . . .'. Anyone advertising weapons for sale in the UK, even if the sale is to take place elsewhere, is potentially caught by the 'expose for sale' provisions, which have been very widely interpreted by the courts. In 1994 the UK Trade Minister unequivocally agreed that 'any export of equipment that can be used for torture is quite unacceptable'. He said, 'We must ensure that such trade is stopped, and whenever it comes to our notice, we insist it is stopped. . . . we will take whatever action is necessary to ensure that the export of anything that could be used for torture ceases' (*Hansard*, 12 January 1994, col. 165).

Set against this legal background, the ease with which *Dispatches'* undercover TV actors managed not only enter the heart of the British defence industry, but also to be given privileged access to a secret network of electroshock weapons manufacturers and suppliers and to come away with over £4 million of orders is extraordinary indeed. The orders reported in the programme (10,000 electroshock shields and 5000 shock batons from British Aerospace (BAe) and 15,000 electroshock units from ICL Technical Plastics) are prodigious quantities to let go – particularly to Lebanon – without some very searching questions. But perhaps the insight this programme gave into the procurement and proliferation of electro-control technology is even more astonishing. Philip Morris, the Sales Manager for Royal Ordnance, agreed to use the Royal Ordnance's worldwide procurement network to bring the electroshock deal together, irrespective of the equipment's country of origin or its eventual destination; Ordnance would organize the whole package. British Aerospace, Royal Ordnance's parent company, invited their clients to meet up at the secretive Covert Operation and Procurement Exhibition (COPEX), held at Sandown Park racecourse in November 1994. A wide range of internal security equipment was on display. Foreign invitees included delegations from China, Algeria, Bosnia-Herzegovina, Colombia, Iran, Saudi Arabia, Sri Lanka and Turkey.

The *Dispatches* TV team followed through that rendezvous with a meeting at Royal Ordnance's own offices in Chorley, Lancashire, where they were shown a 40,000-volt shock baton made in Ireland together with an electronic riot shield made in Tennessee, USA, by Nova Technologies which could immobilize 120 people without a battery charge. During the discussions while the £3.62m electroshock package deal was being struck, Philip Morris made an astonishing confession in front of his boss, Martin Trengrove, the Royal Ordnance's General Sales Manager. He revealed that Royal Ordnance had sold 8000 German electroshock batons as part of the Al Yamamah deal negotiated with Saudi Arabia at a cost of £20 billion, the biggest UK arms deal in history and paid for in oil. The *Dispatches* programme team concluded that given that the £500,000 cost of the electroshock deal was paid for in oil, and because BAe would have had to invoice the MoD for payment and the UK government would have had to issue an export licence, they must have known what was going on (Lashmar, 1995).

A further insight into the complicity of British companies in this trail was afforded by the programme's interview with the boss of ICL Technical Plastics in Glasgow, Frank Stott. This company is usually associated with the manufacture of riot shields and rubber batons (including sjamboks). Stott sits on the board and is a founding member of the Association of Police and Public Security Suppliers. The undercover *Dispatches* team managed to visit the factory in Glasgow which produced electroshock weapons, for which Stott said the firm had been granted permission by the Scottish Office. He said the Glasgow police were aware of his activities but had asked him to keep very quiet about his involvement in the electroshock equipment trade. On the programme, he claimed that he used to sell shock batons to the apartheid regime in South Africa and to Abu Dhabi for the Gulf States; and a year after the Tiananmen Square massacre, he sold electric-shock weapons to the Chinese authorities via Hong Kong, with the UK government's blessing, and said that the trip was supported by the Department of Trade and Industry. This was despite the government's ban on all arms sales to China. Mr Stott claimed that the Chinese had an ulterior motive for buying his electroshock weapons: they wanted them to copy. It is

Figure 9.2. A Taiwanese extensible electroshock baton.
© Omega

instructive to note that one of the Taiwanese products shown on the *Dispatches* programme, an extending electroshock probe (Figure 9.2), has been awarded a British patent (no. GB214906A).

Such 'vertical proliferation' is a fearful consequence of the UK government's inadequate control of export and transfer of security equipment. The *Guardian* newspaper has reported (Ballantyne, 1992), that Chinese workshops such as the Safety Electronic Equipment Branch of the Tianjin Bohai Radio Works are producing 80,000 shock weapons a year to enable the Chinese authorities to continue violating human rights. According to Pierre Sané, the Secretary General of AI, the use of shock weapons in China today 'has become so endemic that it is almost impossible to document and follow the cases of the number of victims'. Electroshock weapons are carried by all prison camp guards in China. Pierre Sané has called for governments to investigate and to put in place new mechanisms, such as public disclosure in advance, to halt the trade in electroshock equipment to states which use it to torture. On 19 January 1995, the European Parliament made the following resolution (Doc EN\RE\264264474):

– *aware of the European Parliament's concerns regarding the export of repressive technologies to regimes that violate human rights,*

– **disturbed at** *recent revelations that such technologies are being produced in at least three European Union (EU) countries, namely Germany, Ireland and the United Kingdom, companies such as Equipol, France Sélection Neral et Cie SARL (France), Tactical Arms International UK and British Aerospace are all known to have supplied electroshock units,*

– **horrified at** *the information that these technologies have been exported amongst others to Saudi Arabia, China, the Gulf States and South Africa under the apartheid regime,*

– **aware that** *these technologies have been used in gross violation of human rights,*

– **aware of** *government complicity in these transactions that have been formally banned by the governments concerned, for example ICL Technical Plastics in Glasgow, which produces electroshock weapons with permission from the Scottish Office, according to Frank Stott, the Head of ICL,*

1. **Requests** *a statement from the governments concerned regarding the allegations;*

2. **Urges** *support for Amnesty International's call for a full investigation into the extent of the trade in the EU;*

3. **Calls on** *the Commission to bring forward proposals to incorporate those technologies within the scope of arms export controls and ensure greater transparency in the export of all military security and police technologies to prevent the hypocrisy of governments who themselves breach their own export bans;*

4. **Instructs** *the President to forward this resolution to the Council, the Commission and the EU Member State Governments.*

Eight months after the *Dispatches* television programme was shown, UK government ministers admitted that an electroshock baton export licence had in fact been issued for transhipping some devices via the UK, but refused to name the supplier or recipient countries (Pallister, 1995).

New technologies of political control on the horizon

AI is increasingly aware that a new generation of military, security and police (MSP) technologies is emerging, which speed up the process of bringing new victims to the torture chamber if such equipment falls into the wrong hands. Examples are sophisticated surveillance and human tracking technology and databases, discreet order vehicles for rounding up dissidents, and a new array of specialized capture, containment and public order equipment (Ackroyd *et al.*, 1980; Amnesty International, 1992a; Wright, 1987,1991). Some of the technologies mentioned in this chapter, particularly the electroshock equipment and the interrogation chambers (Sweeney, 1991a, 1991b), are variants of so-called non-lethal weapons. A new generation of such capture, paralysing and incapacitating devices is already being evolved (Kiernan, 1993; Wright, 1994). These developments could lead to a sinister new generation of very questionable technologies used for restraint and containment: for example, the irritant-laced fence-making equipment that was made available during the US troop evacuation from Somalia (*Washington Post*, 24 February 1995, p. A8).

A belt capable of delivering a powerful electric shock by remote control has been developed in the USA. The training material for the Remote Electronically Activated Custody Technology Belt (REACT) published by Stuntech Inc. of Cleveland, Ohio, describes the actual restraint process and then states:

> 'the additional factor of a psychological deterrent is discussed and further explored. After all, if you were wearing a contraption around your waist, that by the mere push of a button in someone else's hand, could make you defecate or urinate yourself, what would that do to you from the psychological standpoint?'

The potential of this device for deliberate torture is obvious.

Such technologies are now being transferred between countries in a way that was not possible in the days of the old power blocs. For example, International Commercial Services advertised electroshock batons in the COPEX 92 catalogue after establishing offices in Budapest, Washington and Moscow.

AI now needs to keep a close monitoring brief on the sale and transfer of these weapons as they emerge on the stands of MSP exhibitions around the world.

Amnesty International's call for tighter legislation on military, security and police exports

On the basis that prevention is better than cure, over recent years AI has attempted to persuade countries which supply MSP equipment and training not to do so where it can reasonably be demonstrated that this will contribute to grave human rights violations. In Britain this has led to some successes. For example, the worldwide publicity generated by AI about the use of UK leg-irons in Malawi's jails helped to secure the release of political prisoners there in 1992–3 (Norton-Taylor, 1992). AI's campaigns have promoted better conduct and preventive measures for the control of MSP transfers; for example, the UK government tightened the export ban on all types of leg cuffs and oversized cuffs in 1991 when AI publicity showed that 'enlarged' cuffs could be used as leg cuffs.

AI's policy is

> to oppose by all appropriate means any transfer of MSP equipment, personnel, training or technology, including financial or logistical support for such transfers, to governments and political non-governmental entities that can reasonably be assumed to contribute to grave human rights violations.

AI calls publicly for a cessation of any such MSP transfer when any one of the following conditions can be verified:

- *the sole practical use for the MSP transfer is to commit grave human rights violations (e.g. a torture chamber or thumbscrew);*

- *the transfer of the type/class of equipment has been shown in the past to contribute to such grave violations in the receiving country (e.g. electroshock batons to China);*

- *the transfers support those specific military, paramilitary or security units which are significantly responsible for such grave violations (such as death squads).*

AI also asks searching questions about supplier governments and companies in relation to the use to which intended MSP transfers will be put by the receiving country in order to draw attention to the danger of an MSP transfer being used for the grave violation of human rights.

In 1994 AI's EU Association vigorously lobbied member states of the European Union to implement human rights criteria to prevent any MSP transfers to other countries being used to commit human rights violations. All AI national sections are being asked (Amnesty International, 1995) to call for legislation which should:

- **require** *the human rights situation in receiving countries to be taken into consideration prior to decisions being made about MSP transfers;*

- **prohibit** *MSP transfers from taking place unless it can be reasonably demonstrated that such transfers will not contribute to human rights violations with Amnesty International's mandate;*

- **ensure** *that the sender should take responsibility for the use of MSP transfers in practice;*

- **include** *provisions which are precise in their terms and concrete in their procedures, avoiding ambiguities and minimizing the scope for interpretation which could contradict the purpose of the law;*

- **enables** *the legislature to be notified of all information necessary to enable it to exercise proper control over the implementation of the law;*

- **publicly** *disclose in advance all MSP transfers;*

- **require** *reports to be issued on the human rights situation in all potential receiving countries;*

- **establish** *effective channels for receiving information from non-governmental organizations.*

It seems likely that this area of AI's work will grow in the future since it is one issue where strong critical action in the supplier nations can have a powerful impact on reducing the flow of repressive technologies to states which systematically practise torture.

References and Further Reading

Ackroyd, C., Margolis, K., Rosenhead, T. and Shallice, T. (1980) *The Technology of Political Control.* London: Pluto Press.

Amnesty International (1992a) *Repression Trade (UK) Limited: How the UK Makes Torture and Death Its Business.* London: Amnesty International UK Section.

Amnesty International (1992b) 'Torture in China'. AI Index: ASA 17/55/92.

Amnesty International (1994) 'Saudi Arabia – unwelcome "guests": the plight of Iraqi refugees'. AI Index: MDE 23/01/94.

Amnesty International (1995) *Trade Unionists and Military, Security and Police Transfers*, pp. 13–14. London: Amnesty International.

Amnesty International Danish Section Medical Group (1977) *Evidence of Torture.* London: Amnesty International.

Amnesty International EU Association (1994) *European Union: Human Rights and Military, Security and Police Transfers – When Will Established Criteria Be Implemented?* EU Ass/02/94, Amnesty International EU Association, 9 rue Berckmans, 1060 Brussels, July.

Anon. (1993) 'Compensating victims of brainwashing experiments'. *Torture* 3 (2), 63.

Arms Sales Monitor (1995) 'Commerce Dept. licenses export of torture devices'. no. 30, 20 July, pp. 1–3.

Ballantyne, R. (1992) 'At China's torture fair'. *Guardian*, 14 August.

Ballantyne, R. (1995) 'Shock tactics'. *Guardian*, 12 January.

Biderman, A.D. and Zimmer, H. (eds) (1965) *The Manipulation of Human Behavior.* New York: John Wiley & Sons.

British Medical Association (1986) *The Torture Report: Report of a Working Party of the British Medical Association Investigating the Involvement of Doctors in Torture.* London: BMA.

Chomsky, N. and Herman, E. (1979) *The Washington Connection and Third World Fascism: The Political Economy of Human Rights*, vol.1. Nottingham: Spokesman Books, for Bertrand Russell Peace Foundation.

Cooper, J.C. (1984) 'A torturer's testimony'. *Medicine and Human Rights*, no. 8, February–April, p. 6. (Published in London by the British Medical Group of Amnesty International.)

Council of Europe (1994) *Report to the Government of Greece on the Visit to Greece Carried out by the European Committee for the Prevention of Torture and Inhuman or Degrading Treatment or Punishment*, CPT/Inf (94) 20, Strasbourg/Athens, 29 November.

Eburne, S. (1983) 'Sensitive services: matters being monitored by Monitoring of Sensitive Services Committee', circular letter to all Crown Agents staff, 11 March.

Franks, S. and Gabor, I. (1984) 'UK's torture trade has quietly resumed'. *New Statesman*, 21 September.

Gibson, J.T. (1991) 'Training people to inflict pain: state terror and social learning'. *Journal of Humanistic Psychology* 31 (2), 72–87.

Gordon, P. (1987) 'The killing machine: Britain and the international repression trade'. *Race and Class* 29 (2), 52.

Gregory, M. (1995) 'The UK torture trail', *Dispatches television programme*, Channel Four (UK), 11 January.

Haritos-Fatouros, M. (1988) 'The official torturer: a learning model for obedience to the authority of violence'. *Journal of Applied Social Psychology* 18 (13), 1107–20.

Human Rights Watch (1992) *Anthems of Defeat: Crackdown in Hunan Province 1989–92*. Asia Watch Report. Washington, DC: Human Rights Watch.

Hunter, J. (1987) *Israel Foreign Policy, South Africa and Central America*. Boston: South End Press.

International Defence Directory (1993; 1995). Coulsdon, Surrey: Jane's Information Group.

Karlsmark, T. *et al.* (1988) 'Electrically induced collagen calcification in pig skin: a histological and histochemical study'. *Forensic Science International* 39, 163–74.

Kiernan, V. (1993) 'Weird weapons: conquering without killing'. *New Scientist*, 11 December, pp.14–16.

Klare, M.T. and Arnson, C. (1981) *Supplying Repression: U.S. Support for*

Authoritarian Regimes Abroad. Washington, DC: Institute for Policy Studies.

Lashmar, P. (1995) 'No pain, no gain'. *New Statesman and Society*, 20 January, pp. 22–3.

London, L. (1993) 'Evidence of torture: political repression and human rights abuses in South Africa'. *Torture* 3, 39–40.

McClintock, M. (1985a) *The American Connection*, vol. 1: *State Terror and Popular Resistance in El Salvador*. London: Zed Books.

McClintock, M. (1985b) *The American Connection*, vol. 2: *State Terror and Popular Resistance in Guatemala*. London: Zed Books.

McClintock, M. (1992) *Instruments of Statecraft: US Guerilla Warfare, Counter-insurgency, Counter-terrorism, 1940–1990*. New York: Pantheon Books.

McGuffin, J. (1974) *The Guineapigs*. Harmondsworth: Penguin Books.

McHardy, A. (1976) 'War game training for civil servants'. *Guardian*, 28 October.

Mather, I. (1982) 'Religious torturers use Shah's police techniques'. *Observer*, 14 November.

Merritt, J. and Lisners, J. (1983) 'Fury over slave trade leg irons'. *Daily Mirror*, 25 November.

New Scientist, London (1973) 'Building a better thumbscrew', 19 July, pp. 139–41.

Norton-Taylor, R. (1992) 'British chains used in torture'. *Guardian*, 15 January.

Pallister, D. (1995) 'Minister admits torture baton export licence'. *Guardian*, 12 August.

Plate, T. and Darvi, A. (1981) *Secret Police: The Inside Story of an International Network*. London: Hale.

Rasmussen, O.V. (1990) *Medical Aspects of Torture*. Copenhagen: Laegeforeningens Forlag.

Rasmussen, O.V. and Skylv, G. (1993) 'Signs of *falanga* torture'. *Torture* 3 (1), 16–17.

Robinson, M. N., Brooks, C.G. and Renshaw, G.D. (1990) 'Electric shock devices and their effects on the human body'. *Medicine, Science and the Law* 30 (4), 285–300.

Shallice, T. (1973) 'The Ulster depth interrogation techniques and their relation to sensory deprivation research'. *Cognition* 1 (4), 385–405.

Shallice, T. (1974) 'Solitary confinement: a torture revived?' *New Scientist*, 28 November, pp. 666–7.

Sweeny, J. (1991a) 'UK firm equips torturers'. *Observer*, 13 January.

Sweeny, J. (1991b) 'Tortured logic'. *GQ Magazine*, June, pp. 90–1.

Times, London (1980) 'Training to resist questioning justified', 16 January.

Thomas' Register (1992) New York: Thomas.

United States Department of Commerce (1983) Crime Control and Detection Commodities – Export License Requirements, Section 376.14, *Export Administration Regulations – Special Commodity Policy and Provisions*, 1 October.

United States Department of Commerce (1984) Commodity Control List 5999B, *Export Administration Regulations*, Supplement no. 1 to 399.1-CCL-103, 15 June.

United States Department of Commerce (1994) Commerce Control List OA80D–OA86F, *Export Administration Regulations*, Supplement no. 1 to 799.1-CCL-236, June.

Walker, M. (1994) 'US Army's "coup school" faces calls for closure'. *Guardian*, 8 April, p. 12.

Watson, P. (1980) *War on the Mind: The Military Uses and Abuses of Psychology*. Harmondsworth: Penguin Books.

Wright, J. (1994) 'Shoot not to kill'. *Guardian*, 19 May.

Wright, S. (1984) 'The hard sell'. *Guardian*, 21 June.

Wright, S. (1987) 'Public order technology: less-lethal weapons'. In B. Rolston and M. Tomlinson (eds), *Civil Rights, Public Opinion and the State*, pp. 70–96. Working Papers in European Criminology no. 8. Belfast: European Group for the Study of Deviance and Social Control.

Wright, S. (1991) 'The new technologies of repression: a new case for arms control?'. *Philosophy and Social Action* 17, January–June, 1–20.

CHAPTER 10

The Treatment of Survivors of Torture

John Denford

Introduction

There are many motives for torture, many different methods and many degrees of severity. The effects of the traumatic experiences on survivors take many forms: physical, psychological, social or cultural. They may be short-lived or of long duration, obvious or insidious. One of the ways that torture can be dealt with, apart from by campaigning for its abolition, is to provide treatment facilities for the victims.

It follows that, for a service for torture survivors to be truly comprehensive and efficient, it must be wide-ranging and flexible, and its organization coherent and well controlled. Rehabilitative work with survivors requires an understanding by all concerned that such work is part of a broader human rights commitment addressing these issues.

The Medical Foundation for the Care of Victims of Torture

There are several different ways in which a service for torture survivors may be developed and function. This chapter outlines one way, suitable for a Western country of refuge, but not necessarily so for other, non-Western countries. The underlying principles must be the same, though. The Medical Foundation for the Care of Victims of Torture, based in London, was founded in December 1985 to continue work first carried out by volunteer practitioners who were members of the Medical Group of the British Section of Amnesty International. It has grown rapidly from an organization that was largely voluntary to one which, although still having a large proportion of volunteer health professionals, employs more than 40 paid staff, part-time and full-time, headed by Helen Bamber. It is funded entirely by voluntary donations, and by grants from the London Borough Grants Committee, the European Union and the United Nations Voluntary Fund for Victims of Torture, and a number of sympathetic trusts and institutions. It sees its independence from national government funding as an important advantage for its clients.

Clients include people from some 65 different countries whose experience of violence may be as recent as yesterday or as remote as the Second World War. Refugees and asylum seekers are seen for brief or extended help. There are currently 8000 clients on the records, of whom about 1000, including new referrals, are seen each year.

Commitment to rehabilitation

Since our inception, we have worked to establish a model of care and treatment which seems appropriate to the special needs of each client. Through a combination of medicine, casework and a range of psychological, social and physical therapies, the aim is to encompass the needs of the whole person. By integrating self-help principles with the specialist services of a multi-professional team, we have found that almost all clients can be helped in some way to overcome problems that are frequently severe and sometimes apparently intractable (Turner, 1989; Bamber, 1995).

Referral

People come to the Medical Foundation for help and advice with their special needs. They may be referred by their general practitioner, a human rights or refugee organization, any other health or social worker, another Medical Foundation client or a friend, or they may refer themselves. Many clients are living in the limbo of temporary admission to the UK. If they require a medical or psychological report to support their asylum application, it must be requested by their solicitor.

Assessment

The caseworker who sees a new client on first arriving at the Medical Foundation must assess the needs as comprehensively as possible, often at more than one meeting. The needs which are most urgent are identified. A plan of action is made, and the case is taken to one of the general clinical teams for discussion and clarification of aims, and appropriate allocation for further work. Throughout the time of their involvement with the Medical Foundation, clients retain their connection with one caseworker, usually the one who made the original assessment, who takes overall responsibility for them, acts as a guide, an organizer of the assistance and therapeutic work, and provides a continuing relationship through which the work is mediated and further assessment can be made if necessary.

General service

Many clients have suffered extensive physical trauma. In these and other cases of torture, there may be massive psychic trauma which, if unattended, will almost certainly be compounded rather than alleviated by time. The principle of work is positive intervention through medical attention and through sustained and structured emotional support in all those cases where people express a need that allows engagement in constructive terms.

In all cases where physical trauma is implicated, positive intervention begins with a medical consultation. The physician conducts a sensitive medical examination in which the principal therapeutic factor is one of engagement rather than imposition. We find that this plays a part in legitimizing help-seeking behaviour across a wide range of cultures. Furthermore, as a specialist in physical disorder, the physician has a direct and practical role to play as well as an indirect symbolic one, in helping to restore to individuals the privacy and integrity of their own bodily processes. The separation of body from mind is nowhere less appropriate than in the treatment of torture, where the body has been abused to gain access to the mind. An integrated physical and psychosocial approach is developed from this basic principle of positive intervention involving the combined endeavours of a multi-professional team.

The concept of cure is in many cases inappropriate. Such post-traumatic sequelae are not the conditions of illness so much as a form of bondage through which the torturer ensures that his interventions will last over time. The rehabilitative aim is centred on the purpose of freeing the victims rather than curing them. Damage is in many cases profound and extensive, but in almost all that come to our attention there is something constructive to be done (Bamber, 1995).

Because many clients are insecure in their physical, mental or social state, we have found it valuable to provide a 'drop-in' service for crisis management. They may receive immediate medical treatment, referral to a psychiatrist, brief psychological interventions such as bereavement counselling, advice on legal or welfare rights, or practical assistance on housing, finance or clothing and basic living needs.

In most, if not all, of our treatments there is an ultimate reliance on the holding and potentially reparative powers of human relationships. The damage was done in destructive relationships; healing, other than of specifically physical hurt (and even that to a considerable degree), will occur through the influence of generally benign, though honest, integrative and rational, human links.

The body and the mind

Most torture is directed at people's bodies, at least in the first place, but all torture is associated with extreme mental pain or disturbance. Some torture is directed primarily at victims' minds, as in mock executions or being forced to witness violence to friends or relatives. For all victims, though, the distinction is probably academic if the assault is sustained. It is the *person* who is tortured. But it is also true that persons differ in their experience of their bodies. Some individuals live a much more physical existence than others, and some cultures focus far more on physical existence than on mental life. Urban, more sophisticated populations tend more to live in their heads than do rural or peasant ones. Again, some ways of life involve harsher physical experiences than others, and someone who has been used to hard physical labour, where actual physical hurt is frequent, can be expected to react differently, though not necessarily more successfully, to physical torture than someone who has had a sedentary or professional job.

Clients of the Medical Foundation come from many different countries with many different languages and cultures, and need skilled interpreters for our workers to communicate effectively with them. Similarly, they require an equivalent flexibility of therapeutic response from us. In particular, difficulty is often experienced by client and therapist in finding the same meaning for words used to describe suffering. It has increasingly appeared to us that our Western European assumptions may be inappropriate for many of our clients. Those who come from cultures where damage is thought of primarily in physical terms communicate generally in practical and physical language.

For many people, expectations are first for physical and practical help. They wish to be reassured that all physical ills are being dealt with. It is important, therefore, for appropriate examination, laboratory tests and X-rays to be arranged and treatment commenced for overt physical disorders. If, however, after thorough investigation, no clear 'medical' diagnosis can be made, the client is left in an unbearable limbo, unable to accept that the pains are 'not real'. For many of these clients, whose only recent physical contact has been hostile, painful and abusive, treatment by various forms of physiotherapy, exercise, massage, breathing techniques, postural and dietary advice, or complementary therapies such as osteo-pathy, homeopathy, aromatherapy and the Alexander technique, can be, once trust has been established, extremely rewarding, provided of course that they are administered by a gentle, understanding and knowledgeable therapist (Hough, 1992).

In many cultures, any suggestion of psychological disturbance is associated with the notion of madness and is the subject of serious prejudice. Consequently, people from such backgrounds are very upset by such suggestions, and avoid offers of help which appear to them to imply that meaning. Such people also tend to conceive of their troubles in physical terms and present them as such. These factors require us to accept the physical channel of communication as a starting point in many cases, and only slowly, as a secure connection with the therapist is built up through physical treatment, approach psychological disturbance. It seems likely that in many of our clients, an appropriate language for mental suffering, and concepts to match it, have to be developed between a client and therapist as necessary preliminary work.

For these reasons many of our more prolonged efforts at rehabilitation combine physical and practical means with psychological and social, sometimes loosely, sometimes very closely, particularly in those which attempt to integrate physical contacts with discussions of body experience and pain, and eventual work that is effectively psychotherapeutic. Using the link between body and mind, some of the therapists at the Medical Foundation have developed original methods of somato-psychotherapy and movement psychotherapy, combining processes such as the Alexander technique, Dalcroze Eurythmics, Master's Psycho-physical method or Gindler work with psychotherapeutic methods (Blackwell, 1989; Melzak, 1992, 1993, 1994; Callaghan, 1993). Clearly, such treatment requires a therapist with sound training in physiological as well as psychological theory and practice (M. Korzinski, personal communication, 1995).

Many torture victims have developed defence mechanisms to protect themselves during torture sessions. These may be physical, as in over-breathing, which can lead to a trance-like state. Others use psychological methods to take the mind off the pain, sometimes very successfully. These defences can continue to be used in exile, sometimes usefully but often aggravating the physical or mental symptoms. The therapist must learn to recognize these strategies and put them to positive use.

Groups
Many of our remedial efforts are suited to group settings. The financial advantages are obvious, and there are important therapeutic and social gains in such methods. There are difficulties in using groups which base their structure and working on conventional group psychotherapeutic models. Language difficulties limit their use, and distrust of any group discussion, particularly with others from the same country, is frequent; anything but an individual connection with a professional worker is unknown in many traditional cultures, and the idea that significant help may come through association with other sufferers also tends to be rejected. The difficulties with group treatments are minimized if it is

possible to use therapists who are from the same culture and language as the clients. However, group methods can be devised that do not rely on language.

Our experience has been that developing groups of clients and getting the eventual advantages they can give has much more often been successful when the initial (and continuing) primary focus of the group's attention has been a practical task, with meanings which clients value because they are associated with the lives from which they have been exiled, activities which tend to objectify the difficulties they have (so that they can be worked on out there, in the task), and that yield significant gains of self-respect. Tasks around which we have built successful groups have included allotment gardening, preparing meals and story-telling, craft work and football. Shackman and Tribe (1989) have shown the benefits that grow from women's discussion groups.

Participants inevitably establish links with each other, and the group life that develops allows opportunity for interventions on many levels and in relation not just to the present time but to past experience as well.

Psychotherapy

We assume that there is a psychotherapeutic (or psycho-integrative) element in all our contacts with clients, due to the integrative effect of the relationships offered. A very large proportion of our clients want immediate help with practical and physical problems which are the result of both their original ill-treatment and their subsequent exile. A much smaller proportion want immediate but limited help with the psychological results of their torture, and an even smaller group appear to need much longer-sustained psychotherapy in order to adapt successfully to life as they now find it.

In most cases a finite course of treatment is offered, but the client can always come back later if necessary. Long-term individual help is provided only when it is specifically asked for, or when disturbances are of such a nature and degree that this appears the only response offering hope of containing disturbance or reducing it. However, it is only through such detailed and sustained treatments that the realities of the destructive experiences our clients have suffered and the widespread and fundamental damage that can follow, both in themselves and in all their associates, family and friends, can be fully appreciated. It is also only through such treatments that the slow and complicated processes through which relief and rehabilitation and the return of effective living capacity become clear and can be achieved.

I am indebted to Schlapobersky and Bamber (1988) for the case history which follows:

A young man had been held in prison for more than three years, and tortured. Before his detention when aged about 20 years, he had been physically strong – a sportsman – and reasonably happy. Now he was anorexic, far below his optimal weight, had a poorly healed fracture of one wrist, and damaged, painful soles of both feet. He had recurrent headaches, disordered sleep and morbid ruminations. Any discussion of his ill-treatment produced dramatic convulsions for which no organic cause had been found.

He told of having been blindfolded and thrown into a cell with a former friend whose toes had been severed. Later he was taken to a small room. The walls were bloodstained and the floor strewn with broken glass. Three men stripped him naked, bound his hands and feet and hung him upside down from a bar on the ceiling. He was beaten with wire cables and his feet were cut. They burnt him with lighted cigarettes between his fingers and on the backs of his hands. A bloodstained blanket was stuffed in his mouth to muffle his cries. Urine was passed into his mouth. They punched him there, broke six teeth and pulled out the stumps with pliers. A day later he was tied to a pole along with five other prisoners. When the shots rang out, he alone was left alive. Then he was locked in the back of a van with the corpses.

Our work began with a detailed examination and history by a doctor and caseworker. Much time was spent establishing familiarity and trust before neurological tests were done (in the presence of the caseworker). A physiotherapist and osteopath treated his feet and wrist and he had breathing and relaxation exercises. He was given a special pair of soft shoes and a bicycle. His consequent increased mobility was a major factor in his rehabilitation.

Individual psychotherapy was begun, using a family friend as interpreter. This translator shared the treatment, potentiating its effects and continuing its processes away from the formal sessions, but always under the supervision of the psychotherapist and caseworker.

First, everything was done to establish secure therapeutic relationships. His early history was examined. Only after six months were the details of his torture explored. This provoked convulsions. A routine was established with the interpreter: our client was firmly held and massaged where muscles had gone into spasm. Meanwhile the subjects which had provoked the seizure were kept under discussion. The assistance of friends and family was enlisted to sustain this effort. He and his therapist turned increasingly to examination of the symbolic contents of his vivid and tormented dreams.

Much later, when he had learnt enough English to dispense with the interpreter, he would pass a large dictionary back and forth between himself and the therapist. It seemed to symbolize the link between himself and the therapist, as well as a bridge between his past and present lives. He began to be able to grieve for people he had loved who had been tortured and executed.

He was 'stuck' with images of their grotesque deaths, unable to remember beyond those images to reach the whole people they had once been, as though he was still in bondage to the torturers who had caused such revolting distortions of living beings whom he knew. It was necessary to reconstruct their earlier intact images; by discussion to re-create them in detail in his imagination, and to incorporate them anew, before he could begin to mourn their loss and bury them as dead. His slow but consistent progress was evidenced by a gradual return to normal of his moods and of his sleeping and eating patterns. His weight increased and he no longer had seizures when talking about his imprisonment. He joined a long-term therapy group, became interested in women again and began to plan a programme of study. He was treated intensively for a year and less so for a second year. After a gap of a few months he returned with a recurrence of nightmares. After a course of grieving counselling he was able to lead a full and useful life.

This account illustrates the main features of such treatments:

- *The need to establish trust and a good working alliance.*

- *The good sense of sharing work between different professionals with different skills and enlisting the assistance of interpreters, family and friends.*

- *The need for patience and sensitivity in approaching extremely painful matters.*

- *The importance of practical and physical help in allowing a therapeutic process to begin.*

- *The need for flexibility in the therapeutic approach: medical, social, behavioural and psychodynamic means were all used.*

- *The central importance of grieving as a process through which a person can come to terms with his or her losses and find the courage and hope to take up life again with some conviction. It could be reasoned that all therapeutic efforts bear on that as a final common path through which the energy of all the others is directed; that when the person begins to be able to take that task on himself actively, he has rediscovered his own potentially creative emotional sources and their power, on which his eventual recovery will depend.*

- *The need, in many cases, for a quite protracted therapeutic availability, which may include allowing some more economical, lower-key or even relatively infrequent access to a worker. This may be provided by a therapeutic group, or an activity group, or by reviews of progress at quite long intervals. Such availability indicates the continuation of the relationship, with individuals or the institution, which is an important source of continuing stability and reinforcement of the original therapeutic work.*

Asylum

Applications for medico-legal reports are assessed by an asylum team, working closely with a legal adviser. Those who seem, on paper, to have a case which could be assisted by a report are allocated to an examining doctor and usually wait a short time for an appointment. More urgent cases, such as those threatened with deportation, may demand immediate action. Medical examinations are carried out by a group of experienced doctors of appropriate expertise, including the necessary clinical knowledge of torture and the relevant cultural background. Sometimes it is necessary to go into prisons and detention centres where asylum seekers are held. The problems and skills of reporting on asylum cases are further dealt with in Chapter 11.

An additional service of the Medical Foundation (also dealt with in Chapter 11) is collection of the evidence which accumulates concerning particular countries where persecutions continue despite official denials by the home government (and sometimes by the UK government). Material on Zaire (based on the cases of 92 clients) has recently been published (Miller *et al.*, 1995), and other countries will be covered in future. Such activity is part of our aim to increase the awareness of governments and the public of the incidence of torture and to work for its prevention.

Training

The Medical Foundation devotes much energy to training a variety of professionals, but does not use a specific training model, creating workshops and training sessions according to the stated needs of those who request help. We have a holistic model of practice which forms the backbone of our training, taking into account exile as well as torture, and the social and political contexts of clients' experience and lives.

A fundamental principle behind our training is to develop and build on the skills and expertise that participants already have, to use participatory methods of training which draw on participants' own case material and enable them to practise and develop different ways of working. Effective training brings about changes in skills, knowledge and attitude. It may also lead to workers lobbying for changes in service delivery within their own organizations.

Training is provided in many aspects of care for torture survivors, to many different groups of workers. One simple fact is that the numbers needing help are very large, so that their needs are far beyond the capacity of one small clinic to provide. All agencies within the community, health, social and educational services, in particular, need to acquire the necessary skills since they are all likely to come in contact with refugees who have been tortured. Organized courses range from half-day or one-day workshops for different health workers, intercultural associations and councils, to eight-day training courses, for example for workers with refugees from the former Yugoslavia.

Overseas

Similar principles have been applied in the development of certain overseas projects, notably in Uganda. This experience has shown that in countries with a record of torture, the needs of torture survivors who remain in their own country differ in a number of important ways from the requirements of those who have sought refuge in alien lands, and there are many differences in setting up a centre in a Third World country as compared to a developed country. Bracken *et al.* (1992) have described their experience in Uganda, and the following extracts are quoted *in extenso* from their paper, since they illustrate problems which might arise in other Third World countries.

> In 1987 the London-based Medical Foundation for the Care of Victims of Torture, under the auspices of the Uganda Ministry of Health, began a small project in Uganda to provide care specially for victims of war-trauma and torture. The original aim of the project was to set up a centre in the capital, Kampala, where referred clients could be assessed and treated. There are a growing number of treatment centres for victims of torture around the world, many of which emphasise the specialist nature of the treatment provided (Somnier and Genefke, 1986). There have been calls for such centres to be opened in Africa (International Commission of Health Professionals, 1988). Experience in London and elsewhere has pointed to the particular severity and chronicity of the psychological problems after torture, and thus it was decided that there should be an emphasis on the psychological aspects of rehabilitation in the proposed project.
>
> The original team consisted of two expatriate doctors (a gynaecologist and a psychiatrist) and a Ugandan social worker. An office was opened in Kampala and meetings were held with many different groups and

individuals in order to discuss the problems faced by war victims and the ways in which they might be helped. Many such victims were sent from various sources, such as hospitals, church groups and other aid organisations. Visits were made to those areas of the country worst affected by war and violence. Much time was spent in a part of the Luwero Triangle, an area to the north-west of Kampala which became notorious in the 1980s as Uganda's 'killing fields'. Here up to half a million civilians were unaccounted for following counter-insurgency measures by Obote's forces.

It became apparent after some time that there were certain difficulties in establishing a specialist centre for torture victims in a country such as Uganda. The first concerned the very scale of the problem. Many areas within the country had been affected by war over a period of 20 years. Hundreds of thousands of people were killed and many more were left bereaved or suffered the effects of torture or other traumas. Few people escaped at least some degree of personal suffering. Many of the people who suffered so severely were from rural areas far from Kampala; even for those within travelling distance (such as the Luwero Triangle area), a Kampala-based centre would be largely inaccessible due to poverty, poor roads and lack of transport. Of those villagers who did manage to find their way to the Kampala office, many were disappointed by the inability to offer much in the way of financial assistance.

It also proved very difficult to make decisions as to who constituted a 'client' and who did not. To reserve the service for those who had suffered systematic torture during periods of detention would be to ignore the suffering of thousands of Ugandans. On the other hand, to offer a free medical service with a very wide brief would have resulted in more clients than could reasonably be catered for.

Possibly the most serious problem was the danger of undermining local individual and community responses to the results of trauma by the very act of establishing a 'specialist' centre. War and violence are not new phenomena in Africa and communities have been coping in one way or another with their effects for centuries. Emphasis is placed on the maintenance of very strong family bonds in most African societies and many of the effects of violence are dealt with within the family group.

Most African societies also have an extensive network of traditional healers. As many forms of distress are perceived as having a supernatural dimension which cannot be adequately dealt with by western medicine, resort is very frequently made to such healers. The distress associated with trauma is often not conceptualised as a medical problem, and local family networks and traditional healers are felt to be the appropriate agents to deal

163

with it. The establishment of a specialist centre to deal with victims of violence runs the risk of undermining these systems by suggesting that there is an established western expertise in this area, and that traditional concepts and practices have little value. Such a centre would also be contrary to the aims of a primary health care approach which attempts to enable local communities and health workers to define and to deal with their own health needs.

It was clear, therefore, that the establishment of a specialist centre along the lines of those operating in Europe and North America was not the most appropriate response, and an approach which would strengthen and support local efforts and avoid undermining this confidence of local health workers was needed.

Accordingly, a trial was set up in the previously prosperous Luwero Triangle.

Many of the survivors had been witness to horrific massacres, often involving members of their own families. Many of them had been tortured or spent time in prison or internment camps where conditions were generally appalling. Many women had been raped. People had spent long periods hiding in the bush, without shelter and with very little food. There were stories of survival by eating grass or chewing old animal skins. Many died of starvation and disease as a result. Over 60 per cent of the people had lost at least one first degree relative, while virtually everyone had had their homes destroyed and property looted. It was obvious that memories were still vivid and over 75 per cent reported sleep difficulties associated with memories of the war.

However, there was no great increase in psychiatric breakdown and overall there was less psychological disturbance than had been originally anticipated. In Uganda, as in other societies in times of war, an increase in social cohesion appeared to have operated as a protective factor. . . .

The significance of post-traumatic symptoms depends to a large extent on social and cultural factors. Nightmares are almost universally reported after the experience of traumatic events. In western societies they are usually understood to be the result of some internal psychological disturbance. As such they are seen to be amenable to treatment with psychotherapy or chemotherapy by both the patient and his or her physician. In Uganda nightmares are generally conceptualised as the direct effect of some supernatural involvement, coming from the spirits of the dead. Treatment needs to be responsive to this concept.

Many clients presented with somatic complaints . . . which were the actual way in which the people experienced and described their distress. Therapy needs to take this into account.

While most people were able to deal with the effects of violence within the context of family and local community, some appeared to be more at risk of developing long-term problems following their various traumas. These included refugees who were separated from their own homes and whose communities had therefore been disrupted, children who had been exposed to violence either to themselves or to members of their families, soldiers who had been repeatedly exposed to combat, people who had suffered severe forms of systematic torture, and, lastly, women who had been the victims of sexual violence. For various reasons, many people in these groups had not had the benefit of the protective effects of social cohesion and solidarity. Over 50 per cent of the women who had been raped had never spoken about their experience, facing their trauma alone because of the community's inability to allow discussion of rape and because of the political position of women whereby their particular suffering was not given recognition.

Many were suffering gynaecological and psychological symptoms and 26 per cent were HIV-positive (Giller *et al.*, 1991, pp. 156–60).

Two initiatives were developed: first, to develop a teaching programme to enable local medical assistants and nurses to deal more effectively with some of the consequences of violence, and second, the setting up of a service for victims of rape, providing a medical and counselling clinic which moves from village to village. Confidentiality and trust are obviously crucial, and therefore this work is carried out only by women. In 1990 the organization of these projects was taken over by a small Ugandan team of social and health workers.

The lesson of the Uganda enterprise seems to be that, when setting up new units, especially in Third World countries, or places where the customs and conditions are remote from the parent organization, great flexibility must be exercised. Also, it is relevant that the Uganda enterprise was set up in conjunction with the government, which by that time was keen to assist rehabilitation of its traumatized population. There are many countries where repression is still active or at least smouldering, and any overt attempt to help victims could draw unwanted attention to the local workers, perhaps hazarding their safety. Great sensitivity must be exercised in these conditions.

Countries where civil war or an oppressive regime have devastated the population leave thousands of survivors requiring rehabilitation. Buwalda (1994) has described the situation in the Philippines, and Shackman and Reynolds (1994) draw on that experience to give practical advice for training indigenous workers struggling with the problems in countries such as Croatia or Bosnia-Herzegovina.

Conclusion

A system of care for torture survivors must be carefully geared to the needs of each individual and take a holistic approach to the client's needs. Different environments, whether in the country of origin or that of refuge, must influence the type of organization established, sensitive to the client's cultural and emotional differences and the country's system of government and range of facilities. An important aspect of care is the facilitation of the client's introduction to the health and social services available and, if necessary, aid in the asylum process. An important by-product is the publication of research into individual and national data on the incidence and methods of torture in various countries.

References

Bamber, H. (1995) in *Torture: Human Rights, Medical Ethics and the Case of Israel*, pp. 117–29. London: Zed Books.

Blackwell, R.D. (1989) 'The disruption and reconstitution of family, network and community systems following torture, organised violence and exile'. Paper presented at the 2nd International Conference of Individuals, Centres and Institutions Concerned with the Care of Victims of Organised Violence, Costa Rica.

Bracken, P.J., Giller, J.E. and Kabaganda, S. (1992) 'Helping victims of violence in Uganda'. *Medicine and War* 8, 155–63.

Buwalda, H. (1994) 'Children of war in the Philippines'. *Development in Practice* 4, 3–12.

Callaghan, K. (1993) 'Movement psychotherapy with adult survivors of political torture and organised violence'. *The Arts in Psychotherapy* 20, 411–21.

Giller, J.E., Bracken, P.J. and Kabaganda, S. (1991) 'Uganda: war, women and rape'. *Lancet* 337, 604.

Hough, A. (1992) 'Physiotherapy for survivors of torture'. *Physiotherapy* 78, 323–8.

International Commission of Health Professionals (1988) *Healing in Africa*. Geneva: ICHP, pp. 155–63.

Melzak, S. (1992) 'Secrecy, privacy, repressive regimes, and growing up'.

Bulletin of the Anna Freud Centre 15, 205–24.

Melzak, S. (1993) 'Thinking about the internal and external experience of refugee children in Europe, conflict and treatment'. *Proceedings of Conference on Children, War and Persecution*, Hamburg, October.

Melzak, S. (1994) 'You can't see your reflection when the water is full of soap suds'. Medical Foundation for the Care of Victims of Torture, Ref: 052/SM.

Miller, C. *et al.* (1995) *Zairian Asylum Seekers in the UK: Their Experiences in Two Countries*. London: Medical Foundation for the Care of Victims of Torture.

Schlapobersky, J. and Bamber, H. (1988) 'Torture as the perversion of a healing relationship: rehabilitation and therapy with the victims of torture and organized violence'. Paper presented to the American Association for the Advancement of Science.

Shackman, J. and Reynolds, J. (1994) 'Training indigenous workers in mental-health care'. *Development in Practice* 4, 112–22.

Shackman, J. and Tribe, R. (1989) 'A way forward: a group for refugee women'. *Group Work* 2, 159–66.

Somnier, F.E. and Genefke, I.K. (1986) 'Psychotherapy for victims of torture'. *British Journal of Psychiatry* 149, 323–9.

Turner, S. (1989) 'Working with survivors'. *Psychiatric Bulletin* 13, 173–6.

CHAPTER 11

The Documentation of Torture

Duncan Forrest, Bernard Knight and Morris Tidball-Binz

Introduction

The first thing a government or agency accused of inflicting torture on an individual or groups does, typically, is to deny it. If evidence is produced, it may be dismissed as concocted, malicious or misinformed. If an alleged torturer is brought to court – itself a rare event – he will have no difficulty in finding witnesses to attest to his innocence. It is therefore vital, if any accusation of torture is to be sustained, for the evidence to be supported by impartial, incorruptible and credible sources. If Amnesty International (AI) or any other human rights organization is to have any credibility, it must make no claim that has not been objectively corroborated by some independent individual or organization. Of course, torture cannot usually be proved 'beyond reasonable doubt', the level of proof needed to convict, and most AI documents and campaigns are at the level of 'credible evidence of torture'. Even with that lower level of proof, only a minority of abuses can ever be accepted for campaigning actions, let alone be fit for presentation in court. In spite of this, AI has no difficulty in finding large numbers of cases which stand up strongly, and the limit is AI's capacity to respond to the mass of instances of torture revealed.

In-country evidence

Obviously, it is best for evidence to be collected on the spot and immediately after an incident, when the circumstances and events are clear in everyone's mind and the physical signs are fresh. Unfortunately, in these circumstances, it is usually only the bystanders and relatives who are in a position to confirm the victim's story, and their word may not carry much weight with officials. It is therefore vital for the stories of bystanders and relatives to be collected and collated by some trustworthy body, able to overcome the natural fears and mistrust of the witnesses and with sufficient knowledge to be able to identify and record the facts.

Even in so-called free societies there are powerful pressures acting against anybody 'rocking the boat'. Fear of antagonizing colleagues or employers, or even of social discrimination, often prevents the reporting of human rights abuses. How much more difficult is it for persons living in an oppressive society, where their lives may be at risk if they make any accusation of torture or other abuse. Consequently, it is often only possible to obtain, and make public, information away from the country of origin (see below).

The local witness

One of the most important functions of torture inflicted for political, religious or ethnic reasons is the subjugation not only of those directly involved, but of the whole population of an area, and when this has been successfully achieved local people who oppose the regime may be dead, in hiding, in prison or simply terrorized. In spite of this, it is a remarkable tribute to the human spirit that citizens of oppressive societies are prepared to come forward with accusations against the police or army. Alternatively, it may be that others have been so overwhelmed by the mutilation and murder of their loved ones that they no longer care for their own life or safety. Unfortunately, alone, they will have little chance of influencing the authorities. They require an advocate to speak for them. Often the headman or elder of the village has the task of going to the police or prison to plead for a detainee or torture victim, perhaps with the result of obtaining release or at least better treatment, usually after payment of a bribe. Often such a person is the source of information being collected by an activist on behalf of a human rights organization.

Travellers and diplomats who have an intimate knowledge of the country can often give information on individual cases or widespread trends.

The human rights monitor

One of the most difficult tasks of this group must be to remain unemotional and impartial in the presentation of evidence, which is absolutely necessary if it is not to be dismissed out of hand. Much importance lies in local knowledge of local habits of the security forces and in deciding what conclusions can be drawn from the evidence. The story in different cases in a given district tends to be more or less the same. This is often interpreted by doubters as indicating that the alleged victims have colluded and concocted similar stories. It is more likely, though, that the similarities are due to the limited repertoire of techniques used by the security forces in that area.

Many human rights activists are community workers, teachers, journalists, students or lawyers, and these groups are most frequently targeted by the authorities, to be either discredited or eliminated by arrest, 'disappearance' or extrajudicial execution.

The local health worker

After release from torture, a victim is likely to seek assistance from a doctor, nurse or other health worker, or the security forces may take a prisoner to hospital for treatment if he has been beaten too vigorously, in order to make the detainee presentable for public appearance or even to prevent death or disablement. Health workers are thus the people in the best position to find and record evidence of torture.

The specialist

Doctors are often in an invidious ethical position, being employed by police or prison authorities, who naturally expect the doctor to present evidence that supports their policy. The doctor may be requested to write a certificate or autopsy report stating that the subject has no wounds or that the wounds have been caused accidentally or on a date prior to the detention. Refusal may lead to disciplinary action, loss of promotion, dismissal, threats or even imprisonment or death. Certificates which originate from such sources are therefore often inaccurate or meaningless.

In some countries, there are active groups of human rights lawyers who may collect information, though their reputation is often deliberately besmirched by the authorities in their own country.

The human rights organization

AI and similar human rights organizations have, over a period of years, built up a database for each country on patterns of abuse used by security, police and military forces, gleaned from individuals, religious and aid groups, the media, and inter- and non-governmental sources, which they can use systematically to measure and assess individual claims of abuse.

Fact-finding missions by organizations such as AI, Physicians for Human Rights, Human Rights Watch or the Johannes Wier Foundation seek interviews with relevant authorities such as Ministers of Justice and military and police authorities as well as individuals in the population. Not all organizations have the same methods or aims, however. For instance, the International Committee of the Red Cross (ICRC) has access to vulnerable individuals through prison visits, and it promises strict confidentiality of interviews. Its findings and concerns are reported to the government of the country, but the ICRC makes no public comment on its findings, which remain confidential between the ICRC and the government in order to maximize the chances of being able to continue visiting and protecting prisoners. AI does not systematically visit prisons and it does not say specifically whom it will see (other than government members it would like to interview). AI does not have the capacity to demand and carry out repeat visits on a regular basis and therefore must try, by maintaining a high degree of confidentiality, to avoid doing anything which could lead to an individual informant being identified and persecuted after the AI team has departed. AI gathers information on the understanding that it will usually publish data drawn from its mission findings and governments know that AI gives maximum exposure to its findings. The most valuable evidence is likely to be gathered during unaccompanied visits to villages, hospitals or clinics. It is usually easy for the authorities to prevent the team from seeing the real situation by making sensitive areas or organizations out of bounds. Nevertheless, these visits may gain useful information, often by implication from what is forbidden.

Evidence in countries of refuge

Valuable information can be obtained from refugees in countries which take them in. There are many organizations that assist refugees from one country or region, such as the Tibet Support Group UK and Sikh, Tamil or Kurdish groups, which build up a body of information about individual and country-wide abuses. The main drawback which must be recognized with such groups is that many of them have a political bias and so may be tempted to distort their information to serve their own political ends. Their reports also tend to be written in rather emotional prose which can detract from their credibility.

A valuable source of data is the voluntary organizations which have been set up in many countries of refuge to treat torture victims. Their aim is to mitigate the after-effects of torture, and one of these is the doubt and mistrust often shown by the host nation, something which makes the acceptance and assimilation of the victim more difficult and prolonged. There could be nothing so distressing for a survivor of torture who has, often with the greatest difficulty and danger, finally arrived at what should be a safe haven, only to find his story doubted and his appeal for political asylum refused. Consequently, organizations such as the Medical Foundation for the Care of Victims of Torture in London (see Chapter 10) find a considerable proportion of their energy devoted to documenting histories of torture and using the information gained for two purposes; first, to help individuals by providing medical reports which present the physical and psychological evidence of torture; and second, by collecting a large number of case histories from one country, to compile evidence of the current practice of human rights violations in that country. This can then be used to present evidence to the authorities in the host country that it is not safe to repatriate asylum seekers (Miller *et al.*, 1995).

Recording the evidence: recent torture *(Bernard Knight)*

The examination of *recent* injuries is more straightforward than that of old, fading and healing injuries, but the documentation needs to be no less accurate. The record of such an examination may be the only document available for the future and may not be supplemented by photographs. It therefore must convey with clarity the exact nature of the injuries described. Unfortunately, some doctors, including experienced clinicians, seem to be confused about the nomenclature of injuries with the result that their record of an otherwise excellent examination becomes of reduced value owing to ambiguity of terminology. Therefore, the well-recognized system of classification of recent injuries should be adhered to strictly. They are divided into the following categories:

Abrasions

Abrasions are the most superficial on the body surface and strictly speaking the term should be reserved for injuries that involve only the outer layer of the skin (epidermis), therefore giving rise to no bleeding. However, because of the corrugations of the dermis, many abrasions slightly penetrate the dermis and give rise to bleeding.

Abrasions are also called 'scratches', 'grazes' or even 'gravel rash'. The names illustrate the difference in their shape, as a linear abrasion or scratch is very narrow, while other abrasions may be of any size or shape. If they consist of numerous parallel linear abrasions, then these are 'brush abrasions', typical of friction against a rough surface.

As with all injuries, the documentation of abrasions should be exact, for both clinical and legal reasons. The length of a linear abrasion should be measured and the length and breadth of wider abrasions recorded. As well as the area, the position of the injury in relation to obvious anatomical points must be indicated. It is of little use recording that 'There was a large abrasion on the front of the chest', which conveys little to a reader six or 12 months later. A proper description would be: 'On the left side of the chest there was a large abrasion 14x7 cm in size with its long axis obliquely situated, passing from upper medial to lower lateral. Within this area were a number of parallel scratches about 1 mm apart, in the long axis of the injury. The centre of the abrasion was situated 19 cm below the left clavicle and 12 cm from the midline, just below a line joining the nipples.' Even without photographs, this conveys a good impression of what the injury looked like at the time of the examination.

Contusions

Contusions, better known as 'bruises', are caused by leakage of blood out of the blood vessels into the tissues below the skin surface. They may occur in any tissue, including organs. Usually they are placed under the skin and may be immediately under the epidermis, when they are called 'intradermal'; or they may be deeper in the connective tissue or fat, or even deeper.

As with abrasions, the documentation of bruises must include an assessment of their size and anatomical position and also the density of the bruise, whether it be faint or dense.

An important feature of bruises is their colour change with time, which may be important in determining the dating of the injury and whether or not different injuries are contemporaneous.

Older textbooks are too dogmatic and optimistic about accurate dating. There is personal variation in colour changes in bruises, which is also related to the amount of blood and the situation of the bruise. A fresh bruise is red, blue or purple. The colour depends on the amount of blood in the injury and the depth under the skin at which it is situated.

Recent research has shown that a yellow colour does not appear in less than 18 hours after infliction and may take much longer. It is therefore impossible to date a bruise by the appearance of a yellow or greenish colour until at least 18 hours. Also, a large bruise will have a variety of colours present at any one time, even if it is considerably older than 18 hours. Some bruises will not change colour for several days and may persist for a very variable period. Small bruises may vanish in a few days while large bruises may persist for many weeks, especially in old persons. However, if bruises of approximately the same size are of markedly different colours, then the examiner can confidently state that they were inflicted at different times.

Of course, where skin pigmentation is deep, the examination of bruises is rendered extremely difficult.

A particular type of bruise is the 'tramline' bruise consisting of two parallel lines separated by a pale area. This is characteristic of the impact of a tubular or square-section implement and is very commonly seen in abuse.

Lacerations

A blunt tearing of the tissues is a laceration, often confused with an incised wound (described below). A laceration is due to mechanical traction on the skin and subcutaneous tissues which exceeds the tensile strength so that the tissues part company. The edges are ragged and the margins often bruised or abraded.

It is difficult to cause lacerations on soft, mobile parts of the body such as buttocks or abdomen, and they are much more common where there is underlying bone, such as the scalp or face.

Where the scalp is hit with a blunt instrument, the 'anvil effect' of sandwiching the tissue against underlying bone may cause a very sharp-edged laceration, which can be mistaken for an incised wound. However, close inspection of the wound edge will reveal inversion, crushing, abrasion and bruising, albeit very narrow. A lens may assist in differentiation. In addition, the wound will exhibit tissue bridges crossing the gap, such as blood vessels, nerves and collagen; in an incised wound, these would have been cut through.

Lacerations due to punches and kicks also commonly occur in the face, especially in the tissue below the eye, where downward traction may cause tearing.

Incised wounds

Where an injury is caused by a sharp cutting edge, such as a knife, bayonet, razor, broken glass, etc., the resulting lesion is termed an 'incised' wound to differentiate it from blunt laceration. Incised wounds are further subdivided into 'slashes' and 'stab wounds'. In a slash, the length of the wound is greater than the depth, a stab wound being the reverse.

Slashes tend to be less dangerous to life than stabs because of the obvious shallower penetration, though they are potentially lethal if they transect large blood vessels or become infected. The edges of an incised wound are sharply cut and may be 'shelved', indicating an angled approach to the skin surface. The documentation of slashes is straightforward.

Stab wounds are more difficult, as the size of the stab wound on the surface is not necessarily that of the inflicted knife. Most knives are tapered, so the wound size will depend on the depth of penetration. In addition, the elasticity of the skin tends to pull the extremities together when the knife is removed, when some gaping occurs. The extent of this will depend upon whether or not the wound was in the line of, or at right angles to, the tissue, and on muscle tension.

All this should be carefully recorded, together with all dimensions and anatomical positions. Where surgical exploration or an autopsy has been carried out, then the depth of the wound may be explored. It is worth noting that the depth of the stab wound may be greater than the length of the blade, owing to indentation of the skin surface if the knife is forced in up to the hilt.

Gunshot wounds

Gunshot wounds are almost a separate study in themselves and cannot be dealt with here in any detail. The essentials are, first, to recognize them; they have often been mistaken for stab or blunt injuries. Once a lesion has been identified as a firearm injury, a distinction between a rifled weapon, such as a pistol, rifle or self-loading weapon, as opposed to a smooth-bore shotgun, should be made. It is also useful to try to determine the range and, where an exit and entry wound are present, to differentiate one from the other. The subject is too large for detailed discussion here. For more information one of the many standard texts can offer detailed advice (see, for example, Knight, 1991).

Burns

Dry burns can be due to all types of agent, from cigarettes to hot metal, from blowlamps to burning kerosene rags.

When burns are seen in the acute stage, there is usually little difficulty in determining the nature of these injuries, which may show erythema, blistering, skin desquamation and even charring. The later effects of scarring are dealt with below.

A recent cigarette burn is usually circular, though it may be elliptical if the cigarette is held obliquely. It is a red, angry lesion, sometimes consisting only of a slight swelling and erythema, but occasionally with small central blisters. Once again, documentation requires measurement, a detailed visual description and anatomical location.

Electrical injuries

Electrical injuries can again, in the acute stage, come in various shapes and sizes depending upon the nature of the conductor that was applied to the skin and the voltage of the supply. When a large conductor is pressed over a considerable area of skin, there may be no lesion whatsoever because of the lack of any heating effect from the diffuse entry of current. Where a firm contact is over a small area, a square centimetre or less, there is often a blister due to gas formation from boiling tissue fluid. Characteristically, the electrical lesion in the acute stages is often surrounded by a pale ring of constricted blood vessels, outside which may be a further reddened zone. This may surround the base of the blister.

Where a high voltage is applied without firm contact, a spark burn may occur. Here the electricity jumps an air gap and tends to cause a little papilla of fused keratin on the skin, again often surrounded by a pale ring and maybe a peripheral zone of reddening.

Where electricity is applied to a moist area such as the interior of the mouth, lips, penis, vulva, vagina or anus, the dampness of the contact may reduce surface resistance so that the heating effect is less or even absent, and therefore the characteristic injuries seen on dry skin may be replaced by only erythema or even no lesion at all. Much depends on the voltage and length of contact time.

Recording the evidence: long-term effects of torture *(Duncan Forrest)*
After the immediate effects of torture have faded it becomes much more difficult to assemble a convincing picture. Sometimes investigators on missions to oppressive countries are confronted with people who allege a long history of torture and present horrific scars and deformities, but whose stories are flawed by a fiercely partisan bias. It then becomes essential to weigh up the evidence from individuals with the overall picture from a number of sources.

Most individuals who have reached a country of refuge and allege torture are not examined in detail until long after the events, when the evidence of torture has long since faded. Those who escape their own country are a tiny minority of torture victims. The worst cases will have died under torture or never have emerged from prison.

In weighing up what evidence an individual presents, three elements have to be considered: the history; the physical evidence; and the psychological demeanour.

The history
This is the most crucial factor but is not always easy to elicit. A Turkish Kurd told me:

> 'I was detained many times between 1987 and 1993. I can't remember how often or all of the dates. Sometimes I was held for only a few hours but usually for three or four days. . . . Of course I was always beaten with truncheons and rifle butts and given falaka but I wasn't always tortured. . . . Sometimes I was given electric shocks. I was always blindfolded and could not see what was going on but could hear the noise of a magneto being cranked. . . . When I was given Palestinian hanging I often passed out so I don't know how long I hung there or everything they did to me.'

The history may be pieced together from a number of sources: statements to solicitors and immigration officials, or, from the country of origin, affidavits, newspaper reports or doctors' certificates (the value of which varies enormously). However, the most valuable evidence comes from an expert interviewer ready to devote several hours to an interview. In this way it is possible for detailed questions to be asked in order to obtain the maximum of relevant information as well as to assess credibility.

Most subjects have never before been questioned about their experiences in a sympathetic fashion and the questioner must take time to establish confidence and provide reassurance that the testimony will not be used against them or their family. Some are so psychologically damaged as to be almost mute so that the story has to be painfully pieced together, or else so hyperactive that the story comes tumbling out in a torrent, jumbled up with much irrelevant material. Often there are paradoxical guilt feelings or shame, so that some aspects are too painful to reveal, particularly of sexual abuse. Many victims of rape have never even told their spouse what happened.

The most important function of the history is to establish the credibility and honesty of the subject. The more horrific the story, the more likely it is to be dismissed as exaggerated, invented or the result of collusion with known torture victims. When the allegations seem similar to previous accounts from the same country or region, such doubts are reasonable but should not be accepted or dismissed without closer questioning. The more detail that is elicited, the more difficult it is for any deception to be kept up. Similarly, a story sometimes seems so incredible as to beggar belief. A Turkish Kurd told me (DF) how he had been put in a sack with wild cats and the sack then beaten to make the cats bite and scratch. This seemed so unlikely that it would have been dismissed out of hand had not a previous resident in the area provided strong evidence that it was a common torture in that particular police station at about the time of the subject's detention.

Though leading questions must be avoided, the questioner can enquire about details of detention, such as the size and shape of the cell and interrogation room, the personnel involved, details of restraint such as handcuffs, blindfolds or hoods, posture while being beaten, the implements used, and many other points. Very important is the victim's description of his state of health at the end of an interrogation session, including the presence of bruises, bleeding wounds or swollen or dislocated joints, as well as the state on release from detention, and the present state, perhaps several years later. By the time all this information has been gleaned, the questioner should have a fairly good idea how much credence can be given to the story, as well as the subject's psychological state. Multiplied many times with stories from individuals from the same area, a clear picture emerges of the state of affairs in a country which would be difficult for the authorities to refute, and it becomes clear that the similarity of stories by different individuals does not arise from collusion but from a rather limited stock of methods used in an area or region.

The world is made up not only of honest, straightforward people, but also liars, exaggerators, fantasists, the inhibited and those who, for a host of different reasons, may want to distort the truth, but that does not mean that they have not been tortured. For useful documentation, it is necessary for the investigator to unravel the stories in order to arrive at something approaching the truth.

Physical examination

After a lapse of time, examination can rarely *prove* that torture has taken place, and certainly torture can never be dated precisely to a particular episode of detention. Bruises fade after a few weeks and usually leave no trace. Cuts and abrasions leave a permanent scar only if they have penetrated the skin deeply. So *absence of scars does not negate a history of torture*. Even if there are scars, they are not usually specific for torture and could have been caused in some innocent way, by accident or infection. For instance, scars on the shins are no different whether they have been caused by army boots or football boots.

In some countries, tribal rituals or traditional medicine produce scars which can be confused with evidence of torture, so a knowledge of local customs is essential if the examiner is to avoid being deceived. Self-inflicted wounds are a potential source of error, but they usually follow fairly straightforward patterns. All that can be said in most cases is that the physical evidence is compatible with the history of torture, and does not in any way contradict the allegations.

There are, however, a few signs which can be said to be diagnostic of torture. Cigarette burns may be scattered at random and could be confused with old infections such as boils or acne, but, by some sinister psychological quirk, torturers often make cigarette burns in regular patterns – on the knuckles, in a row up the thigh or forearm or in a pattern on the shoulder. Their site often coincides with what would be expected from the victim's description of his or her posture when burnt (sitting facing the interrogator, lying on the ground, suspended, etc.). It can then be concluded that they could not have been caused accidentally and, if they can be distinguished from tribal markings and self-inflicted injury can be ruled out, it is possible to state that there is no other feasible explanation other than torture.

Musculo-skeletal abnormalities can sometimes also provide almost certain evidence of torture. Especially when the subject is a young man with no history of previous illness or injury, the pain and stiffness left by *falaka* (beating the soles of the feet) or suspension such as Palestinian hanging (see page 111) may be so characteristic as to rule out their having been caused by the normal wear and tear of manual labour or by any known rheumatic or neurological disease.

Psychological evidence

Psychological evidence can be elicited by ordinary questioning or by a formal, semi-structured protocol, based on the American Psychiatric Association's *Diagnostic and Statistical Manual of Mental Disorders* (DSM-IV), which is used in any situation of stress and consequent post-traumatic stress disorder. The results of stress are well-recognized, and can be tabulated. The problem is that the symptoms may be much the same whatever the initiating trauma. There are differences, of course. A single incident such as a plane crash will not cause the same late effects as an ongoing situation like warfare or repetitive torture. One important feature of torture is that *the victim knows that the injuries were deliberate*. In this, torture is similar to rape, wife abuse or child battering. In spite of differing influences, it may be impossible when documenting torture to disentangle the effects due to torture from those arising from other factors, such as civil war and displacement, or exile with its loss of family, dislocation into an alien culture with an unknown language and strange customs, lack of money, poor housing, perhaps hostility from the host population, and, most potently, uncertainty of the outcome of the asylum application.

One almost universal after-effect of torture that can prove more specific is the nightmare. Often nightmares are vivid and frightening and reproduce events in the victim's past, such as chases by police or beatings. If they can be described in detail, they can powerfully suggest that they reflect the underlying cause of the psychological disturbance.

With these exceptions, efforts to quantify the psychological after-effects of large groups of torture victims have not been very successful, though there have been several attempts (Turner and Gorst-Unsworth, 1990; Paker, Paker and Yüksel, 1992).

Recording the evidence – documenting gross human rights violations by examination of skeletal remains *(Morris Tidball-Binz)*

A body of experience in investigating gross human rights violations to seek truth, accountability and compensation has accumulated over the past 20 years as a result of the work of a number of human rights non-governmental organizations (NGOs) and some intergovernmental bodies, such as the United Nations. Such investigations have benefited from the increasing use of forensic sciences, including forensic archaeology and anthropology, for the recovery, identification and determination of cause and manner of death of fatal victims of gross human rights violations, which include torture, extrajudicial executions and 'disappearances'.

The systematic use of forensic archaeological and anthropological methods and techniques to investigate human rights violations was first applied in Argentina. The model has been successfully used thereafter in many other countries over the past few years. A summarized description of the development of forensic archaeology and anthropology as applied to human rights investigations in Argentina may therefore serve to illustrate the potential of this kind of research in the field of human rights investigations.

Under the military government which ruled Argentina between 1976 and 1983 the abduction and torture, frequently followed by murder, of political opponents became a systematic practice of the regime. Many of those abducted by the security forces were never seen again. They became known as *desaparecidos*, 'disappeared', a euphemism used by the ruling government, which repeatedly denied responsibility for the thousands who vanished under its rule.

The human rights crisis which affected Argentina during its military rule was by no means a unique phenomenon. Nowadays, the peoples in scores of countries suffer similar or even worse patterns of violations. While such actions are condemned by the international community, governments responsible – such as that which ruled Argentina between the late 1970s and early 1980s – operate with impunity, believing that such officially sponsored crimes will not be investigated and punished.

The Argentine Comisión Nacional sobre la Desaparición de Personas (CONADEP, the National Commission on the Disappeared), established in 1984 under the elected civilian government which followed the military regime, estimated that at least 9000 people had 'disappeared' in Argentina during the previous government's period in office. It found that most had been killed, in many cases after suffering long periods of torture in secret detention centres. The bodies of many had been dumped in rivers and the sea or cremated, but hundreds had been buried in unmarked single or mass graves in the paupers' sectors of county cemeteries. Human rights organizations such as Madres de Plaza de Mayo (Mothers of the Plaza de Mayo) estimated that the 'disappeared' numbered up to 30,000, and claimed that they could not be considered dead until their fate had been clarified and those responsible brought to justice. Most NGOs in Argentina now believe that all, except most of the children abducted by the military, were killed. The whereabouts of thousands remains unknown.

Since 1984 the Equipo Argentino de Antropología Forense (EAAF, the Argentine Team of Forensic Anthropology), an NGO formed by a small group of professionals and university students, has extended its efforts to recover, identify and determine the cause and manner of death of the 'disappeared' and other victims of past human rights violations, in Argentina and other countries. Many of its members received specialized training from other concerned forensic scientists, including anthropologists, some of whom visited Argentina in 1984, following an invitation by CONADEP and local human rights organizations interested in new methods to document human rights violations.

The search for the 'disappeared' posed a complex problem for Argentina's official forensic system, which had been unable and, many claim, unwilling to provide expertise to document human rights abuses effectively. For example, scores of skeletal remains reportedly belonging to the 'disappeared' were hastily unearthed with bulldozers during the initial months of the civilian elected government, under the supervision of coroners. With such procedures, valuable evidence, such as bullets, was lost, and the identification of the victims was mostly rendered impossible. The NGOs claimed that this was a result not merely of lack of technical skills, but of purposeful action by some authorities to destroy evidence, and called for an immediate end to such procedures. The hasty excavations, which received wide publicity, had a most negative impact on thousands of bewildered relatives of the 'disappeared', as a result of which some later rejected forensic investigations into the fate of their loved ones.

In an effort to overcome the problems inherent to the search for the 'disappeared', the EAAF developed a multidisciplinary approach involving archaeologists, anthropologists, medical doctors, computer experts and lawyers. Consequently, the scope of its forensic research became broader than that normally defined for the forensic anthropologist, namely, the application of the anthropologist's knowledge of human biological variation to problems of medical jurisprudence.

The usual research methodology used by the EAAF involves, first, a case evaluation based on preliminary research. This enables the team (which usually does not undertake any case without consent from the relatives of the victim or victims) to decide on the feasibility of the investigation. For example, it takes into account the applicability of international human rights standards to the case, such as the UN Principles on the Effective Prevention and Investigation of Extra-legal, Arbitrary and Summary Executions, to ensure, among other things, full access to all information necessary for the enquiry. The preliminary research includes, whenever possible, a detailed legal and historical analysis of every case based on information provided by the relatives, the courts, witnesses, historical records, etc., and the recollection of pre-mortem physical data of the victim(s), such as sex, stature, age at the time of death, dental records, etc. In some cases close relatives provide adequate samples for DNA testing, to compare with DNA extracted from recovered bones. All the above information is used for setting up an *ad hoc* data-bank, for future identifications of the remains under investigation.

Second, bearing in mind the frequent time limitations imposed during these excavations, methods and techniques adapted from field archaeology are used for the crime-scene investigation, including locating the site(s) of burial, as well as for recovering the remains of the victim(s), and all other significant evidence, in a timely manner.

Finally, laboratory research normally involves the standard morphological analysis of the recovered skeletal remains, including the techniques of radiology, physical anthropology, forensic pathology and odontology, aiming at establishing the identity and the possible cause and manner of death of the individual(s) (Figure 11.1).

Skeletal trauma, such as fractures or gunshot wounds, suffered by the individual immediately prior to or leading to his or her death may be readily identified during the examination of the bones, providing clues about the cause and manner of death.

Signs of torture which might be identified in the skeletal remains include: patterned rib fractures; amputations and/or fractures of fingers; fractures of limbs; and trauma to the teeth, such as enamel or tooth fractures. The degree of healing of these lesions may help reveal the time before death torture occurred.

Many victims of extrajudicial executions, including 'disappeared' people, are exposed to lengthy imprisonment in extremely harsh conditions before their murder. The prolonged deprivation of medical and dental care in individuals who had previously enjoyed adequate access to health care services may be apparent in skeletal remains showing evidence of recent and untreated septic bone erosions, and serious dental decay and periodontal disease.

Patterns of such types of skeletal trauma and pathology may be apparent in several related individuals recovered from mass graves or multiple burials, thus suggesting a practice, or even a methodology, of imprisonment, torture and execution by the perpetrators.

Unlike most normal criminal investigations in standard situations, the general methodology described above often requires substantial modifications according to the time and place of application. While legal, political and logistical factors may impose important limitations, the basic approach and technical requirements for carrying out these investigations are easily feasible in most situations, and of relatively low cost, and therefore applicable even in remote and under-resourced areas.

As a matter of principle, every possible effort is made by the investigative team to develop a close relationship, within professional boundaries, with the relatives of the victim(s) whose case is under investigation.

(a)

(b)

Figure 11.1. Proper excavation techniques (a) and detailed laboratory analysis of the remains (b) may help reveal the identity and the cause of death of the victim as well as to expose evidence of torture.

A constant flow of information and feedback from the researchers is proven to empower the relatives, who have usually been denied any information from the authorities about their loved ones, in accepting the final truth emerging from the forensic investigations, be it a confirmation or not of their expectations. Also, the process of accepting the truth appears to be less traumatic when the relatives are given an active role in the investigation.

This approach towards the relatives of victims of gross human rights violations has been successfully applied by the EAAF in different cultural and social contexts (and even with families who had previously rejected official investigations into the fate of their loved ones). Coupled with the team's independence, this clearly differentiates the group from most official forensic offices in countries where these had frequently been accused of curtailing the investigations into human rights violations.

To summarize, forensic archaeology and anthropology have proved increasingly useful for the scientific documentation of gross human rights violations. They help provide relevant and sometimes essential evidence to the courts, on the basis of which some of those responsible have been sentenced for such crimes in countries including Argentina, Bolivia and the Philippines. Such evidence is also of paramount importance for the relatives of victims, who may thus finally know the fate of their loved ones (Figure 11.2).

Juan Gelman, a distinguished Argentinian writer, has said:

> 'During all these years I knew he could not be alive, but one can never completely give up the dream that he might come home one day. I don't know if there is any worse torture than that. Burying my son, with his name on a gravestone above his tomb, has curiously, paradoxically, rescued him for us. He came out of the fog of the persons unknown.'

His son, Marcelo Gelman, a journalist, had 'disappeared' in 1976 after being abducted by the military in Buenos Aires. His skeletal remains, bearing the signs of torture and extrajudicial execution with close-range shots, were recovered, examined and identified by the EAAF in 1989.

Medico-legal reports for asylum seekers *(Duncan Forrest)*

With increasing numbers of refugees throughout the world, most countries, including all those of the European Union (EU), have erected barriers to immigration. These pay lip-service to humanitarian principles, but in many cases run directly counter to the Universal Declaration of Human Rights, which grants the right to seek asylum from persecution (Article 14), and the United Nations Convention on Refugees of 1951, which decrees that parties to the Convention (which includes the UK

Figure 11.2. A Kurdish woman mourns the remains of her brother killed by Iraqi soldiers. Exhumed from a secret burial site in 1992.

and other EU members) are legally obliged to offer protection to any asylum seeker who can demonstrate a 'well-founded fear of being persecuted for reasons of race, religion, nationality, membership of a particular social group, or political opinion' (Article 1). With the dissolving of frontiers between the states of the EU, it has become necessary to formulate harmonized rules, because refugees coming into the EU will be able to move freely within it. Accordingly, since the mid-1980s, secret meetings of EU members have laid down restrictive policies with the clear intention of greatly limiting the numbers being accepted. These include levying fines on carriers who land refugees with incomplete or false documentation, or sending the applicant back to the last 'safe third country' which he or she stopped at on the way. The trend was further potentiated by the passage of the UK's Asylum and Immigration Appeals Act 1993, which provides for a 'fast-track' processing of applicants whose application is 'manifestly unfounded'. Needless to say, none of these restrictions forms part of the international declarations. Even with these restrictions, many refugees would qualify for asylum, but their 'well-founded fear' is often denied by asylum officials (Amnesty International UK Section, 1995a). As this book went to press, the UK Parliament was considering new draft legislation, the

Asylum and Immigration Bill, providing for a substantial extension of the scope of the 'fast-track' mechanism established in July 1993 for applications deemed to be 'manifestly unfounded'. In particular, the Bill provides that this truncated and accelerated mechanism will cover applicants from a 'white list' of supposedly 'safe' countries which are deemed not to produce genuine refugees – including Ethiopia, India, Kenya and Pakistan. It also provides for the abolition of the existing right to appeal prior to expulsion in those cases where the applicant arrived not directly from the country of persecution, but via one or more transit or 'third' countries.

Obviously, the increased pressure on asylum seekers to prove their right to remain has grave psychological ill-effects, and this is most marked if the applicant has been imprisoned and tortured in his or her own country. Even more psychologically disturbing is the situation if the applicant is held in detention in the country of refuge. The Home Office of the UK has resorted to this expedient with increasing frequency, ostensibly only as a last resort if the applicant is deemed likely to abscond, but in reality as a very powerful deterrent to any refugees thinking of coming to the UK (Amnesty International UK Section, 1995b).

Because of this added pressure, it has become increasingly common for asylum seekers' solicitors to request a medical report to assist the case. Three essential facts need to be remembered: first, as stated before, it is virtually never possible to *prove* by medical examination that torture has taken place; second, the absence of scars does not negate a claim of torture; and third, even if a history of torture is admitted, this does not give an automatic right for asylum. Nevertheless, a medical report which adds to the credibility of the applicant's story, especially if there is external evidence which is compatible with the history, may help the case. Usually, of course, the report is requested months or years after the last episode of torture and so the evidence has faded. Sometimes, therefore, there are no external signs remaining. This does not rule out any value in a report, for the history may make it seem likely that there would be no scars – for instance, if the victim reports that, in spite of severe bruising, he suffered no deep wounds. Often there are few physical signs but severe and obvious psychological disturbance. This will tend to be more severe if the applicant has had a long period of uncertainty about his asylum claim and especially if he is or has been detained on arrival. It is almost never possible to separate the psychological effects of torture from those of exile, uncertainty and worries about relatives still missing or in danger. Many asylum seekers are clinically depressed or even suicidal and require sympathetic handling. They may need to be referred for physical or psychological treatment.

Like any medico-legal report, these ones must be factual, unbiased and authoritative. They should be prepared by doctors who have a knowledge of the local conditions in the country of origin and are aware of the appearances of accidental, deliberate, tribal and self-inflicted wounds (Medical Foundation, 1995).

References and further reading

American Journal of Forensic Medicine and Pathology, vol. 5, no. 4, December 1984. The issue is dedicated to human rights and the forensic sciences, including the recovery and identification of skeletal remains.

American Psychiatric Association (1994) *Diagnostic and Statistical Manual of Mental Disorders*, 4th edition (DSM-IV). Washington, DC: American Psychiatric Association.

Amnesty International UK Section (1995a) *Playing Human Pinball: Home Office Practice in 'Safe Third Country' Asylum cases.* London: Amnesty International UK Section.

Amnesty International UK Section (1995b) *Prisoners without a Voice: Asylum-Seekers Detained in the United Kingdom.* London: Amnesty International UK Section.

Amnesty International UK Section (1996) *Amnesty International's Principal Concerns in Respect of the Asylum & Immigration Bill.* London: Amnesty International UK Section.

'Disappearances' and Political Killings, Human Rights Crisis of the '90s: A Manual for Action, pp. 147–9. Amsterdam: Amnesty International Dutch Section, 1994.

International Rehabilitation Council for Torture Victims (ICRT) and Amnesty International Danish Section Medical Group (1992) *Examining Torture Survivors: Articles and Guidelines. A Reference Book.* Torture supplementum no. 1. Copenhagen: IRCT and Amnesty International Danish Section.

Knight, B. (1991) *Forensic Pathology*, pp. 222–51. London: Arnold.

Manual on the Effective Prevention and Investigation of Extra-legal, Arbitrary and Summary Executions, 1991. New York: United Nations.

Medical Foundation (1995) *Guidelines for the Examination of Survivors of Torture.* London: Medical Foundation for the Care of Victims of Torture.

Miller, C. *et al.* (1995) *Zairian Asylum Seekers in the UK: Their Experiences in Two Countries.* London: Medical Foundation for the Care of Victims of Torture.

Paker, M., Paker, Ö. and Yüksel, Ş. (1992) 'Psychological effects of torture: an empirical study of tortured and non-tortured non-political prisoners'. In M. Başoğlu (ed.) *Torture and Its Consequences*, pp. 72–82. Cambridge: Cambridge University Press.

Petersen, H.D. and Vedel, O.M. (1994) 'Assessment of evidence of human rights violations in Kashmir'. *Forensic Science International* 68, 103–15.

Reyes, H. (1995) 'Torture and its consequences: an ICRC viewpoint'. *Torture* 5 (4), 72–6.

Skinner, M. (1987) 'Planning the archaeological recovery of evidence from recent mass graves'. *Forensic Science International* 34, 267–87.

Tidball-Binz, M. (1991) 'Argentina: forensic investigations of past human rights violations'. *Lancet* 337, 1593–4.

Turner, S. and Gorst-Unsworth, C. (1990) 'Psychological sequelae of torture: a descriptive model'. *British Journal of Psychiatry* 157, 475–80.

Welsh, J. (1992) 'Documenting torture: a human rights approach'. Paper read at the meeting Science of Refugee Mental Health: New Concepts and Methods, Harvard Faculty Club, Cambridge, Mass., 29 September–1 October.

CHAPTER 12

Women, Children and the Family

Gill Hinshelwood

In 1992 Sela was arrested, detained for several hours, questioned, hit, raped and then released.

In 1986 Anya was arrested, detained for 28 days, tortured by various means, questioned, raped repeatedly and released.

Between 1986 and 1990 Zelina was repeatedly taken from the family home by soldiers, driven to their camp, raped, then left by the roadside to find her own way home.

These three outlines of atrocities committed against women and children sound depressingly similar when stated baldly and simply, as they may be when this information is extracted from them. The stories can be multiplied a thousandfold. Women and children from all the countries where torture is practised could give such histories, whether they have fled to seek asylum or remain in their own land. Yet Sela, Anya and Zelina all have stories unique to themselves, and when these are brought to life a complex picture of motives for torture, and the destructive effects of torture on the individual, the family relationships and the community in which they belong, begins to unfold.

Both Sela and her husband had been students and wanted to become teachers. They were politically sympathetic to an opposition group in their Middle Eastern country, he being quite actively so, and also they had experienced racial discrimination from an early age. Sela had identified very much with her father's wishes for her to have a good education, and it was against much opposition from village headmen and villagers that she went away to study. After her husband had been arrested, tortured and detained by police he was expelled from college, so the couple moved back home to their village, and had a baby. Then after more trouble they moved again and he went into hiding. Sela and the child had no permanent home; she stayed with one friend, then with another in 'safe houses'. It was when one of these was raided that she was taken, together with her two-year-old son, to the police station in the middle of the night, hit and slapped in an effort to find out where her husband was (which she did not know), then held down by police while being raped in front of her child. Not long after this they managed to escape to the UK. Then her family problems started. What had happened to Sela was her shameful secret. She never told another person, so the only one with whom she had in common her most shameful secret was – her torturer. All she wanted was to forget the past, yet she was haunted by it every day; everything reminded her of that horrifying night, especially the sexual act, which she could no longer bear. This caused her husband deep distress and suspicion. She thought she would go mad but she did not go mad. Instead, she ailed in body. She ate very little, did not sleep well. She had blocked tear ducts, was constipated, complained of chest pains and difficulty in breathing, lower abdominal pain, sinusitis, leg pains, nightmares; and for all of these she swallowed pills and potions, so that by the time she was brought to the doctors at the Medical Foundation in London she was in a sorry state indeed, a tearful and thin bundle of nerves.

In spite of a very different story, Anya's symptoms were more or less identical. The body's language to communicate and live with the unspeakable is much more simple and primitive than the spoken word. Anya had one more complicating factor. She had been pregnant when she was arrested. The repeated brutality caused death of the fetus in her womb. She had to undergo an operation urgently when she was released from prison, to remove the dead fetus, and this left her with pelvic infection and damage – and a horror of sexual intercourse. Anya was a schoolteacher. She had many criticisms of her Middle Eastern country's ruling dictatorship which were well known among her colleagues, and she was arrested from her classroom at school. She never returned to teach there. The couple fled after more sustained persecution of their race, joining his family in the UK. There persecution of a different order greeted Anya, who was expected to provide her husband with children. Her husband's parents expressed deep distress, anger and suspicion at her failure to do so.

Zelina, from a country in Southern Africa, presented with similar symptoms, similar medications and a very different untold story. She had been 13 years old, living at home with her parents, older brother and some younger ones; the family worked on the land. She went to school and had schoolgirl preoccupations. Soldiers in search of her older brother, suspected of anti-army activities, took her off 'to teach the family a lesson'. The terrified girl was raped at the camp by two soldiers, who promised she would always be theirs. She was returned to the roadside at dawn. Her mother knew what had happened but was unable to provide the support Zelina needed. Zelina's terror increased when her mother tried to kill herself with poison. She had received no sex education and had no idea why her mother was wringing her hands and moaning 'We are ruined.' Thereafter Zelina stopped attending school and withdrew into herself. This did not, however, deter the soldiers, who came at intervals for her. There was one year in particular when the terrorizing of the local population increased. Zelina said that this was 'the year of the babies'. A number of local girls became pregnant. Dead fetuses and babies were found in the bush, but nothing was ever said. Zelina also had a baby. She never loved it, just did her duty, and an aunt took over the care of the young boy. Eventually it became possible to get Zelina out of her country and to the UK. It became second nature for Zelina to hang on to her shameful secret. Zelina was a beautiful young woman and attracted many admirers. She leaned on them to take care of her in an alien land but she was cold and rejected their sexual advances, and they expressed distress, anger and suspicion.

Torture of women and children is widespread; the stated motives can be very different, but the potential for destroying the whole person, the family and the whole community with its political and religious values is surely a known, assumed goal in the collective mind of the torturers.

Is there a difference in the torture of men compared with that of women and children? In other words, once a person is capable of torturing another human being, why should we be surprised that he inflicts the same cruelties on women and children? The majority of torturers are men; this is borne out by the many thousands of testimonies taken. Most (but by no means all) of the stated enemies are men; they may be described as guerrillas, leaders of opposition political movements or trade unionists.

Anya knew she was an enemy of the dictatorial and brutal government of her country because of her outspoken campaigning. She was a member of an 'apparently' official opposition group. She attended rallies, recruited members, contributed to and distributed the organization's literature. She certainly knew about her country's system of punishing dissenters. She also had a strong, perhaps idealized view of her own peaceful and peace-loving beliefs and values. It was this strong sustaining belief which helped her to survive torture. Her torture was brutal. She believes it was directed at the activist in her and also against her, the hated woman who was pregnant, who had had a good education and earned money in her own right, and had dared to challenge men. During the day she was subjected to beatings, *falaka*, electric shocks, cigarette burns. At night she was attacked sexually, degraded, raped. Yet she had no idea of the ability of the torture, particularly the sexual torture to which she was subjected, to get right inside her body and mind and affect her relationship to herself and the outside world, to linger and continue its evil and destructive actions.

Sela believes she knows why she was tortured: both to get information about her husband, who was being sought, and to destroy her husband without even catching him, by sexually assaulting his wife. All this was driven into her with cursings and denigration of femaleness, and her race, seen to be lower than animals. Sela was slapped and pushed around, but the main thrust of her torture was deliberately sexual. It was condoned and performed by the higher-ranking officers at the police station. She was punished for knowing and not knowing, and the resulting feeling of being completely powerless in front of all-powerful officers, and in front of her screaming, helpless two-year-old son, has remained with her, but without words, just as she had no words at that time.

Zelina had been a sheltered, protected child and had in turn protected herself from knowing of grown-up affairs, so she had little idea of sexual matters and little idea of the political problems in her country. Against a background of worsening political tensions and increasing national instability, Zelina and her young friends and cousins were cocooned by their elders. They both knew and yet did not know that very ghastly events were taking place, and somehow they led the idealized life their parents willed on them. Zelina has, in treatment, recently found the words for the feelings that she had, that this 'idyllic' life would come to an end, like a bubble bursting, which it did. But having a feeling locked away was no real preparation for what followed, although Zelina thinks that it was instrumental in keeping her going, in not attempting suicide as some of the other village girls did. Zelina believes that she was repeatedly raped, along with other local girls, as a way of controlling the whole area. Whenever there was an incident involving an attack on the army camp, the whole area was terrorized, houses were raided and occupants beaten up, and young girls were taken and used sexually. Slowly the families who could do so left or sent their daughters away. The effect was total destruction of a community, as surely as if it had been bombed. Family life disintegrated. To a confused and withdrawn Zelina, who was the enemy? The soldiers who called for her and to whom she eventually learnt to submit passively, detaching her mind, going through the motions; or was it her father, mother and brother who did not protect her or even acknowledge that they really knew what was done to her? She developed a theory that she was delivered up to the soldiers as a sacrifice, a peace offering, and kept herself going with the idea that she was the saviour of her family – which she may have been. The 'ideal', protected world that she was brought up in is thus perpetuated in a perverse and contrary reversal.

From the stories of these three women it can be seen that the stated reasons for torturing women and children are to punish them for active subversive behaviour; to obtain information about their menfolk; and to hold a whole family or even a whole community to ransom, to teach them a lesson.

What lesson? The lesson is always 'Our regime is absolutely powerful, and can do anything to anyone. You are absolutely powerless and can do nothing to save yourselves and your family.' These are two unreal, mad and primitive statements, and there is no place for them in civilized, adult living. They are, none the less, a description of the prevailing culture in oppressive dictatorial regimes. The only constructive place for similar but positive statements in reverse is in the situation of the young infant in relation to its mother – a situation that we all struggle to outgrow as soon as possible, because such a state of helpless dependency is so terrifying. When this state of utter dependency on mother in early infancy is lived through successfully we have a belief in our own capacity to survive and also a belief in the nurturing capacity of women. All this is turned upside down by the act of torture. Torturing women kills many birds with one stone for the torturer. It maintains the myth of being powerful directly; it is easier to overpower women and children, it is not so easy for them to run away and they are weaker when caught. When the oppressing authority has been foiled by the escape of a prisoner or by an attack on its troops, for example, women and children are attacked. This helps to repair the slightly dented 'we are all-powerful' image. It is revenge.

Almost all male survivors of torture explain that torture is not only physical abuse. The degrading language, usually defiling the victim's mother, is experienced as one of the worst assaults. The perverse, primitive nature of the act, which affects and binds torturer and victim together in a mental space which is both close and yet utterly distant, pushes them both to a point where to degrade the victim's woman is almost equal to annihilating the man himself. Men scream for their mother during torture, and under such conditions it takes great strength to continue to believe in the good mother when she does not come to the rescue; rather, she is also destroyed by the torturer.

To torture children is generally regarded as a most depraved and degenerate act, yet, in the countries which practise torture, children are certainly not spared. They may be punished in their own right; children jeer at soldiers, throw stones, learn taunting phrases. Slightly older children become very passionate about political and moral issues, belong to student movements. Some are used by adults for taking messages, delivering propaganda leaflets, taking food to people in hiding. For all these reasons and more, children may be abused, imprisoned, killed. In countries where a tribe or whole race is deemed to be second class, less than human, where 'ethnic cleansing' is practised, the child is merely another potential adult of the hated race, to be destroyed. Children are the possessions, the most treasured possessions of the enemy adults, and so the terrorization of children and the destruction of their potential is a most powerful and paralysing force aimed at the whole victim community. To judge from the number of male survivors of torture who flee alone, leaving their wives and children, it would seem that the shift from solely male to male aggression is deemed unthinkable at first in the minds of both the aggressor and oppressed, and that it is in general a feature of the continuation and escalation of the violent disturbances, acting outside on the warring factions as a whole, and internally in the minds of the torturers. Once the unthinkable has been committed, how does it stop?

The ways in which children experience and make sense of the violence inflicted on them depend very much on the stage of mental functioning that they have reached. Almost all will take it absolutely personally, as punishment inflicted for something they have done or not done for their parents, and they will be left with a feeling of guilt and a sense of betrayal, most especially from their mother, who is their source of protection in this world. To see their parents afraid, helpless and attacked has a very powerful and memorable effect on children. Making sense of these unspeakable experiences, in order not to go mad, is the child's main task, and, in the absence of any possibility of speaking about it, this task is coped with at a behavioural level. Often different behaviour patterns emerge in different situations. For example, a child may be over-solicitous to its mother, forever kissing and patting her, and a bully at school. There are endless permutations of the identification children make with their father, their mother and their torturer, giving rise to disturbing behaviour, which further alienates them from their peer group and their creative potential. Sheila Melzak's papers on the effects of atrocities on children, and the treatment of children, give a more in-depth understanding of the long-term work to be done (Melzak and Woodcock, 1991).

Having established that the intention of torture is to damage, spoil, destroy the person, the way in which this is achieved can be looked at in more detail. Sela, Anya and Zelina presented endlessly seeking treatment for something that could not be put into words, so they did not really get any satisfaction. They felt that their important internal organs had been irreparably damaged by something bad that had been forced on them, and they believed that the destructive process continued to ruin them – which it did. They each wanted good medicine to counteract the poison they felt was inside them, and despaired when it did not work. In the absence of words to describe their gross hurt, body language did its best, and perhaps they had partial relief from some of their symptoms: better sleep with hypnotics, less abdominal pain with antacids, and fewer palpitations with beta-blockers, for example. But there was nothing to counteract the huge well of rage and anguish, shame and guilt, which silently festered inside. There is a sense that it took all their efforts to keep this cauldron locked away and out of sight, locked into body organs, stiff muscles, tense head. This effort is with them night and day, they are ever-vigilant, in order to protect their families, friends and acquaintances from harm should any of their violent emotions leak out.

This, of course, has a terrible effect on their relationships. Chronic ill-health in any case has a potentially harmful effect on relationships, but when it is compounded by a torturer lying between a woman and her spouse, a man who is the only one who knows her dreadful secret, the damage is mightily magnified. So the distance widens between the woman and her husband, or her family, which makes it much more difficult for her to be able to take in good experiences from them, to counteract the bad ones. Good experiences would give her a hope that she is not completely damaged, that there remains the possibility of a surge of creativity of life forces within. This is the direction treatment must take.

The effects on a man of the torture, especially the rape, of his wife or children may be equally disastrous. The visible behaviour may vary from culture to culture. In societies where the woman is regarded rather as an obedient possession, the raped woman may simply be abandoned. Some cultures actually believe that it is impossible to penetrate a woman unless she is willing. A raped woman is simply a whore. The men are outraged with their women, who carry the sense of shame and guilt that more appropriately belongs to their torturers. Zelina came from just such a background, and she learnt never to tell her father or brother what had happened to her. It was an unspoken secret she and her mother shared. Anya's more sophisticated husband, and comrade, knew, and suffered with her. He cared for her and understood her, but felt powerless and deskilled and he was never allowed a hint of sexual intimacy with her. In Anya's case, the in-laws somehow took up the persecution of her, and they were never told the truth. Sela carried the secret alone, with the exception of her two-year-old, who she hoped would forget it. She believed the knowledge of her rape would kill her husband. So she took the role of the stronger party, carrying the burden alone, rendering him powerless and impotent, and then despising him. She invested her all in her little son, saying that without him she would have killed herself – strong potential for another broken home.

These three women came from very different cultures and social backgrounds. If they had met before their torture they would have had very little in common to talk about. After these experiences which have changed their lives they have one dominating feature in common: an internal relationship with a torturer with more destructive potential than any of their other relationships – and, without help, one that reaches outside into family and the wider community for a very long time, in some cases for ever.

A very bleak picture has been painted of the long-term destructive effects of torture on individuals, their families and the whole fabric of their societies' culture. Can recovery take place? What sort of help is needed? There is no doubt that when communities are afforded the opportunity to rebuild their lives under conditions of relative peace, normality does slowly return, physical health improves and a more positive outlook on life begins to flourish. This has been documented and is written about eloquently in a number of papers (Summerfield and Toser, 1991; Summerfield, 1995).

Women such as Sela, Anya and Zelina do not die, neither do they have life-threatening conditions. They 'keep going' and address the important issues of their day as best they can: the washing, shopping, cleaning and child-minding, for example, while taking their numerous medications. The quality of their internal world remains poor and there is no sense of joy. And they are representatives of the many women who have been subjected to torture, who have remained in their own countries, who have fled to other neighbouring countries and remain in refugee camps, or have sought asylum in the West. These three women are refugees in the UK and had expectations that Western medicine would cure them. For each of them there was disappointment that after at least a year or two of frequenting doctors, they remain ailing.

The dilemma for them seems to be as follows: they live their lives with the belief that to forget what happened, to erase it completely from their minds, is the answer to recovery and to being as before. However, they allow no means of ridding their minds and bodies of what has invaded them, they keep it buttoned up tightly inside. It is this that relief workers and healers have to address, at a pace set by the women, children and families themselves. There is no place for therapeutic arrogance in the treatment of torture survivors; they have experienced enough arrogance at the hands of torturers to last a lifetime. But there is a place for certain kinds of confidence, a confidence which enables the worker to stay in touch, however frightening it is to get close to torture. The fact that torture breaks up, threatens to fragment, the body and mind is evidenced in the way so many bits of the body and mind are presented to doctors, all isolated from each other, with the consequence that there may be so many medical diagnoses made, also in isolation.

That treating survivors of torture is also frightening can be seen by the way clients are referred to centres such as the Medical Foundation from such a wide range of disciplines: GPs, psychiatrists, clergymen, social workers, teachers, lawyers, landladies and friends. In the cases of Sela, Anya and Zelina, all young women, who had fantasies of irreparable damage, the demonstrable physical disorders were a tendency to gastric hyperacidity in one, an old ear-drum perforation in another, and a persistent fungal infection of a deformed toenail in the third. These are all conditions that can be medically diagnosed and managed, in a confident and thoughtful way, and this proved helpful to them. All their other symptoms obviously caused distress. Medical tests reassuringly told the women that there was nothing wrong, but they were not convinced; indeed, they were more alarmed, since it seemed that they would never feel any better. Work begins with the recognition that unspeakable thoughts and emotions have to have their expression somewhere; that tense muscles may carry all the rage and protest against rapists; that palpitations at night relive the fear of attack. This sooner or later leads to bits of the story being told to another person, with the possibility of putting words to the bad experience, letting someone else feel what it might have been like and taking in a good experience of opening up without being abused; of being listened to, of being considered. It is a painstaking process, and involves acknowledging mistakes on both sides.

Women who have been tortured feel the torture is inside them, and their insides are spoiled, and most particularly their creative reproductive capacity. Many have check-up after check-up, seeking reassurance of normality, but usually without telling the doctor what has happened to them. An important therapeutic tool, once they have mentioned the fact of rape, is a sensitive gynaecological examination, with a full and frank discussion of their fears of damage, and the finite possibilities of damage. Sela was very relieved to learn that she really had not sustained any damage or infection. Anya learnt that she had old tubal scarring, but no active infection. For her, the awareness of the finite damage was preferable to her fantasies. At their worst she imagined her body to be still filled with blood and torturer's semen and dead fetus. She mobilized all her efforts to engage in an assisted fertility programme. Zelina's greatest worry was that she would never be able physically to enjoy a man's company, or love a baby, and she believed that this lack of emotion was caused by gynaecological damage. These ideas only emerged and were available for her to work with during a pelvic examination.

Each of these three women worked towards integration and health in different ways: Zelina in a 'hearth and story-telling' group, Anya in a psychosexual setting, and Sela by attending weekly psychotherapy sessions with her husband. Sela's child attended a children's art therapy group. Most of the women seeking asylum in Britain have been forced to relinquish their material possessions, their former status and way of life, and they feel impoverished in body and mind. They are hungry for help, and, provided that the essence of what is needed (good, meaningful experiences) is kept in mind by the health care worker, women will be able to use a variety of disciplines and practices to build a more solid and positive structure where once it was felt to be chaotic and decayed.

References

Melzak, S. and Woodcock, J. (1991) 'Child refugees who are survivors of repression and its concomitants, including torture'. *Association for Child Psychology and Psychiatry*, Occasional Paper no. 3, 33–7.

Summerfield, D. (1995) 'Raising the dead: war, reparation and the politics of memory'. *British Medical Journal* 311, 496–7.

Summerfield, D. and Toser, L. (1991) '"Low intensity" war and mental trauma in Nicaragua: a study in a rural community'. *Medicine and War* 7, 84–99.

CHAPTER 13

Torture: What Can Be Done?

Piet van Reenen and Dan Jones*

Introduction

Amnesty International's Annual Reports on the state of human rights in the world reveal, year after year, accounts of torture in more than 100 member states of the United Nations – more than half of the world's governments, ranging from the most peaceful and settled democracies with a free press and an independent judiciary to countries riven with internal conflict and to the most repressive of military juntas. Each of these 100 accounts concerns an unacceptable and illegal pattern of action by a government. A deeper study of these AI reports over the past quarter of a century shows that the severest torture tends to be concentrated in about 45 states, among which 14 countries feature particularly prominently. The pattern of torture has changed to some extent over the period of AI's existence. New trends are emerging, including its increasing use (especially rape) as a weapon of war (e.g. in Rwanda and the former Yugoslavia), and new patterns of torture and other cruel treatment that are being targeted at common criminals, and ethnic minorities.

After such a catalogue of appalling human rights abuses in the preceding chapters, the reader must be wondering what action can possibly be taken to stop torture. This chapter examines some practical and pragmatic measures that may help to put a stop to the torturer. It considers the role of non-governmental human rights organizations like AI in combating torture. It looks at the possibilities of intervention and spells out what action can be taken to deal with the perpetrators.

Torture is universally condemned by states, but is also carried out by them. In most cases it takes place in secret. However, that secrecy is difficult to maintain. Torture is rarely the work of a single individual; normally a large number of people are involved. A government which tortures needs a complex system to carry out its torture programme. Torturers have to be selected, and trained – often as members of an élite corps within the military, police or prison staff, or as unofficial squads or paramilitary groups operating under the protection of the security forces.

Within these services staffing arrangements need to be in place – a personnel structure with its own command arrangements and career prospects. Formal or informal arrangements providing impunity have to be in place – those involved being reassured that their actions will be protected from above, and that they will not be held personally responsible for the things that they are undertaking on behalf of the state.

Plans have to be drawn up and approved, secret intelligence operations organized, orders given. Victims have to be arrested, and detained somewhere. The buildings where torture takes place have to be maintained by caretakers and guards. Torture equipment has to be bought and installed. Wages and bills have to be paid. Medical staff may be involved. There may be a trial involving all the paraphernalia of court with lawyers and judges who may know what is happening and fail to intervene. If the victim of torture unfortunately dies, undertakers and members of the clergy may need to be called in, or specialist staff to get rid of the body.

The pages of this book reflect the findings of AI's 30 years of careful research into torture round the world. The phenomenon has been studied in depth and AI now knows a great deal about its aetiology, the background which creates it, the situations that allow it to flourish, and its perpetrators. In 1972 this research led to AI's first worldwide campaign describing and condemning torture. The denunciations had a major impact on governments. It was followed by the UN General Assembly's passing of the UN Declaration on Torture.

AI organized an even bigger Campaign against Torture in 1984–5 in which the organization greatly expanded its impact on international circles. AI had moved from denunciation to demands for specific measures by governments to stop the practice of torture. It drew up a 12-point Program for the Prevention of Torture, a recipe of practical measures for states to carry out in order to stop torture. They are as relevant today as they were when they were first drawn up, and continue to form the basis of AI's approaches to governments on this issue.

Amnesty International 12-point Program for the Prevention of Torture

1. Official condemnation of torture

The highest authorities of every country should demonstrate their total opposition to torture. They should make clear to all law enforcement personnel that torture will not be tolerated under any circumstances.

2. Limits on detention incommunicado

Torture often takes place while the victims are held incommunicado, unable to contact people outside who could help them or find out what is happening to them. Governments should adopt safeguards to ensure that detention incommunicado does not become an opportunity for torture. It is vital that all prisoners be brought before a judicial authority promptly after being taken into custody and that relatives, lawyers and doctors have prompt and regular access to them.

3. No secret detention

In some countries torture takes place in secret centres, often after victims have been made to 'disappear'. Governments should ensure that prisoners are held in publicly recognized places, and that accurate information about their whereabouts is made available to relatives and lawyers.

4. Safeguards during interrogation and custody

Governments should keep procedures for detention and interrogation under regular review. All prisoners should be promptly told of their rights, including the right to lodge complaints about their treatment. There should be regular independent visits of inspection to places of detention. An important safeguard against torture would be the separation of authorities responsible for detention from those in charge of interrogation.

5. Independent investigation of reports of torture

Governments should ensure that all complaints and reports of torture are impartially and effectively investigated. The methods and findings of such investigations should be made public. Complainants and witnesses should be protected from intimidation.

6. No use of statements extracted under torture

Governments should ensure that confessions or other evidence obtained through torture may never be invoked in legal proceedings.

7. Prohibition of torture in law

Governments should ensure that acts of torture are punishable offences under the criminal law. In accordance with international law, the prohibition of torture must not be suspended under any circumstances, including states of war or other public emergency.

8. Prosecutions of alleged torturers

Those responsible for torture should be brought to justice. This principle should apply wherever they happen to be, wherever the crime was committed and whatever the nationality of the perpetrators or victims. There should be no 'safe haven' for torturers.

9. Training procedures

It should be made clear during the training of all officials involved in the custody, interrogation or treatment of prisoners that torture is a criminal act. They should be instructed that they are obliged to refuse to obey any order to torture.

10. Compensation and rehabilitation

Victims of torture and their dependants should be entitled to obtain financial compensation. Victims should be provided with appropriate medical care or rehabilitation.

11. International response

Governments should use all available channels to intercede with governments accused of torture. Intergovernmental mechanisms should be established and used to investigate reports of torture urgently and take effective action against it. Governments should ensure that military, security and police transfers or training do not facilitate the practice of torture.

12. Ratification of international instruments

All governments should ratify international instruments containing safeguards and remedies against torture, including the International Covenant on Civil and Political Rights and its Optional Protocol, which provides for individual complaints.

How torture actually takes place varies from country to country, and an analysis of each country situation is an important first step in planning appropriate action against torture. Different parts of AI's programme are appropriate for different situations. Overall, any international strategy to combat torture around the world needs to address three different human rights scenarios: preventive programmes appropriate for work in countries where no torture is taking place; denunciatory programmes appropriate for work in countries where torture is being carried out; and rehabilitative programmes appropriate for work in countries recovering from a period in which torture has taken place.

Preventive programmes

In a country situation where there is no evidence of the use of torture, or cruel, inhuman and degrading treatment or punishment of prisoners, preventive programmes against torture are still needed and relevant. Recent world history and AI's own records show all too clearly that today's democratic and law-abiding states can become tomorrow's pariah countries where human rights are flouted and torture is rampant. Equally, today's torturer state can become tomorrow's bastion of justice. These preventive programmes work against any resort to torture by strengthening the safeguards and barriers against it, and by increasing the effectiveness of domestic human rights organizations.

The divide between countries where torture is not practised and those where it is practised is often a grey area. Common sense tells us that in countries where social and political violence are the norm, police methods of law enforcement, crowd control and detention are also likely to be violent. This situation will be regarded as normal and acceptable. From there it is a short step to the drift into outright cruel, inhuman and degrading treatment and torture. In many countries the population, while not liking the situation, regard it with resignation as inevitable.

Any campaign against torture necessitates public education about its nature, its monitoring and detection, and the introduction of safeguards to prevent it. Their main elements consist of:

- *a human rights education programme to develop public awareness and appreciation of human rights. Knowledge of these rights and the laws and practices which circumscribe them can build community resistance to any resort to torture, and enable people to campaign for their rights and to work against their abuse. Human rights education should be an element in the educational curriculum of every state. Public information about torture abroad can help develop public understanding and resistance to any resort to torture at home;*

- *the strengthening of practical measures, laws and structures that stop torture, and the ratification of international treaties and conventions dealing with torture. The prohibition of torture in law should ensure that all acts of torture are punishable offences that cannot be excused with the usual defence of 'I was only obeying orders'. The ban on torture can never be suspended, even in emergency situations, including war;*

- *government condemnation of torture, making it clear to all law enforcement personnel in public statements that torture in any form will not be tolerated under any circumstances, and that anyone responsible for torture will be brought to justice;*

- *regulations, professional codes of conduct, disciplinary rules and ethical codes for government officials and professional staff which should include explicit references to the illegality of torture and their responsibility for its prevention;*

- *the professional training of law enforcement and security personnel at all levels to ensure that torture is recognized as an illegal act;*

- *prompt access to detainees for lawyers, medical staff and family members;*

- *the effective and independent monitoring of all places of detention and interrogation. Torture mostly takes place where prisoners are held in secret in unacknowledged places of custody or are interrogated while in detention incommunicado;*

- *keeping accurate records of the whereabouts of all detainees, who should be held only in publicly recognized places of detention and be promptly brought before a judge;*

- *action to stop the manufacture and export of the technology of repression to torturing states and the transfer abroad of equipment and expertise for carrying out torture.*

Denunciatory programmes

Here the programmes of action confront the situation where torture is actually taking place, in a deteriorating human rights situation. In this situation:

- *the government's use of torture is exposed and denounced;*

- *the government is challenged to condemn torture explicitly and publicly and to take measures to prevent its use;*

- *the perpetrators of torture – governments, the military, and the police – are warned about the limited benefit that can be gained from the use of torture – that evidence obtained through torture is not only illegal but also notoriously unreliable;*

- *they are warned of negative personal consequences that can follow a resort to torture, including public contempt, feelings of guilt and psychological problems;*

- *the perpetrators can also face the possibility of exposure, condemnation and subsequent prosecution. Criminal proceedings may ensue from the commission of this offence in the perpetrators' own country, or (through the extraterritorial jurisdiction that applies to torture) anywhere in the world;*

- *human rights monitors including political activists, human rights defenders and prominent journalists need to collect information about the structures within which the torturers operate, the personnel involved, the secret centres where torture is suspected of taking place. This information may be published, and, as a consequence, the human rights monitors themselves may be at risk of arrest or even torture, and may need international support. Measures to protect human rights monitors include AI's Urgent Action scheme, which generates thousands of appeals to governments if a human rights defender is at risk; the escort assistance to human rights monitors offered by the international peace brigades; or the proposed Human Rights Defenders at Risk Scheme in Turkey, where human rights monitors carry notices that AI will make their arrest public and campaign for their release;*

- *safe channels will be needed by human rights monitors so they can send out information about torture safely – a precondition for the launch of any international action against it;*

- in the most extreme torturing states torture takes place in the context of general political repression or internal conflict. A state of emergency often operates, on grounds of 'national security', or armed opposition. Human rights are suspended; detention is likely to take place by units not identifiable as police or army in unknown locations; prolonged imprisonment, political killings or 'disappearances' occur. The struggle against torture in such circumstances is inevitably linked to efforts to end other forms of human rights abuse. Torture becomes an issue in any campaign against 'disappearances', and 'disappearance' figures in any campaign against torture. The scope for action within such a situation becomes more and more limited as 'total control' is exercised by the state and all dissent is crushed. In these circumstances action tends to move over to a response by outsiders.

- detailed information on torture is needed if outsiders are to direct effective attention to the torturers and those responsible for their activities. Such evidence can become a realistic deterrent, warning perpetrators that they will be brought to account. Safe channels need to be established to pass out such information to enable it to be publicized and denounced at home (if possible) and abroad, leading to national and international demands to put an end to such violations, including condemnation by the UN's Special Rapporteurs and Working Groups, and pressure on the UN itself to draw firm conclusions about the pattern of violations.

Rehabilitative programmes

In the period after torture has been used, measures need to address the consequences for the victims, the task of bringing the offenders to justice, and ways to prevent repetition. Repression can last a long time. But it does not last for ever. Eventually a more humane government comes forward. The question then is how to clear up the mess. How are the victims to be taken care of? What is to be done about the violators? How can returning refugees be accepted in the new society? How can one-time enemies learn to coexist? How are the feelings of revenge to be channelled?

The following measures form the programmes of rehabilitation:

- It is crucial to record carefully exactly what took place in order that the sense of injustice about the past is addressed. Lawyers and medical personnel and other professionals need to document the role played by their fellow professionals during the period of repression for professional and educational purposes.

- Redress should be provided for the victims. Medical and psychiatric help is needed for torture victims, who will be afflicted not only with physical *effects but also with severe psychological ones, requiring access to specialized medical and psychiatric help. Financial reparation to the victims is also needed.*

- *One of the best forms of reconciliation for the victims will result from the punishment of the perpetrators (Bronkhorst, 1995). Those responsible for torture should be brought to justice wherever they are, wherever the crime was committed and whatever the nationality of the perpetrators or victims. There should be no 'safe haven' for torturers. Ending impunity and bringing human rights violators to justice is an important part of the process of the return to the rule of law at the end of a period of repression.*

- *Bringing suspected torturers to justice needs to be done in a proper manner with appropriate safeguards to avoid the wrong persons being arrested, unfair trials and summary punishment with the exclusion of the death penalty as a form of punishment.*

- *Sometimes the outbreak of peace and reconciliation is accompanied by amnesties for previous human rights violators, or their being granted immunity from prosecution. The human rights movement would unconditionally reject the idea of the perpetrators of violations being allowed to get away with their crimes, and the green light that this gives to other perpetrators.*

- *Once a period of repression has stopped, the preservation and consolidation of institutions and other arrangements can help to prevent future violations. Norms should be ensured to impede resort to torture: the creation of a constitution that excludes human rights violations, the establishment of a system of political decision-making that links up with these principles, an independent judiciary, a police force and an army familiar with the central values of the constitution and human rights.*

Torture and the role of professional bodies

Personnel from a range of professional backgrounds become involved in torture. A programme of action against torture needs to address this, to organize professional education and training programmes to stop torture, and develop ways to expose, resist and campaign against such involvement. Many relevant professional organizations, particularly legal and medical organizations, have a good track record of acts of international solidarity in the past and in supporting human rights defenders. Action suggested here depends on the commitment and activism of individuals within local, national and international professional organizations, and specialist human rights groups like AI's lawyers' and medical networks, military professions' groups or journalists' networks.

The wider human rights movement should ensure that the human rights education and professional training programmes suggested here for the governments of any countries targeted in any campaign against torture are in place at home.

The organization and funding of such training in countries where it does not yet exist can be part of bilateral or multilateral aid programmes to targeted countries.

Medical personnel

The training of health professionals should always include explicit consideration of ethical principles and the Hippocratic Oath, or its modern equivalent, the World Medical Association's Declaration of Geneva, 1983, and its Declaration of Tokyo, 1973, with its prohibition on torture.

Medical professionals need training to recognize the symptoms of torture — psychological as well as physical — and to know about its treatment. Such training is of particular importance and relevance for medical personnel in countries where torture or other cruel, inhuman or degrading punishment is taking place, for medical staff coming from such countries for training, and for those going abroad to work in such countries. It is also needed by those who work with asylum seekers and refugees from such countries, among whom there may be victims of torture. In appropriate countries international agencies or appropriate aid programmes should provide such training.

The existence of an independent organization of medical professionals with its own disciplinary codes and regulations is an important safeguard against torture. Such professional bodies can provide significant support if a government orders medical personnel to assist in human rights violations. Professional medical codes should explicitly forbid participation in torture or cruel, inhuman and degrading treatment or punishment and include disciplinary sanctions against those who participate in such actions, and an obligation on medical professionals to report indications of torture in confidence to their professional organization (where this is in the best interest of the victim).

Medical professionals are particularly at risk when they work for government structures such as the police, the army or the prison system. Under repressive governments they can be subjected to great pressure to co-operate in torture. They need to be made explicitly aware of their right and responsibility to refuse to participate in torture and cruel treatment (BMA, 1989).

Professional medical organizations can help medical personnel withstand pressures to become involved in torture. If they have independent status rather than being in government service they are in a much better position to resist. In the UK armed forces, medical personnel may appeal to an independent body if asked to do something contrary to medical ethics. Such appeals procedures should be devised for medical personnel working anywhere for the police, military, the prison system and psychiatric institutes.

Medical personnel should be encouraged to organize human rights groups to promote human rights within their profession and to combat abuses of these rights in their own country or abroad. AI has set up such groups and medical networks in many countries.

In a deteriorating human rights situation, medical professionals have an important role in ascertaining whether torture is actually taking place, and entering any evidence in official records. The independence of forensic medical personnel will need to be defended. Timely warnings can have a strong moral appeal to medical staff, particularly those working for the security services and being pressured to participate in torture, with their attention being drawn to the symptoms of torture, and the risk and the cost of their participation in torture being pointed out.

When torture is taking place on a widespread basis, medical associations should appeal to their members to refuse all co-operation with torture. In such a situation professional medical groups are likely to have lost any independence.

Medical bodies abroad could give moral and financial support to those who refuse to co-operate with torture, and their associations. At the end of a period of repression, medical professionals can play a valuable role in providing facilities for physical and psychiatric care for torture victims. Action can be taken by professional medical associations to discipline any medical staff responsible for helping in the perpetration of torture.

Lawyers

Training in human rights law should be available for all lawyers. Lawyers need to know the basic human rights conventions, the provisions of the UN Basic Principles on the Role of Lawyers (1990) and the UN Basic Principles on the Independence of the Judiciary.

Lawyers working in the human rights field need practical training about torture, evidence it has taken place, its sequelae, the behaviour of victims and the best way to obtain information from them about their experiences.

Lawyers' training should include the specifics of human rights legislation. The right not to be tortured is a universal one. Differences in human rights practice, culture and legislation deny this right in some countries. Discussions on this issue should take place with local jurists and politicians, and academic studies should be carried out into the compatibility of universal human rights and local legal provisions.

The organization of independent professional associations of lawyers should be promoted. Their disciplinary codes should include an obligation to report any evidence, suspicions or allegations of torture to an independent organization. Lawyers' organizations that campaign for human rights, such as the AI lawyers' networks, should promote similar groups in countries where these do not yet exist.

Where there is an increased incidence of torture in a country, local lawyers concerned about human rights need to be alerted as they may be able to provide valuable information about violations. They will need contact with international human rights bodies collecting information on human rights abuse such as AI and the UN Special Rapporteur on Torture.

In the face of increasing use of torture, lawyers, judges and law professors can exert considerable influence as the guardians of the constitutional principles of the state. They can speak out against the use of torture and warn the government and the general public about its risks, and work to combat it. They themselves may also be under threat, and will need the help of professional associations abroad, as will their professional associations, if they still exist.

Following a period of repression, lawyers have a special responsibility to see that the rule of law is re-established and that adequate or new legislation is introduced. The perpetrators of human rights abuses need to be brought to court and fairly tried.

Police

Knowledge of human rights should be an integral part of police education in every country, part of police training in the principles of law and criminal justice, and an essential element in practical police training. Such training should include knowledge of the international treaties that prohibit the ill-treatment of prisoners and the use of violence and torture laid out in clear internal guidelines for all forces. In countries where such arrangements do not yet exist, human rights education material for police training should be devised, and adapted as appropriate to particular country situations linking human rights and police work. The Council of Europe (Alderson, 1992), and human rights organizations such as AI in Brazil and the Netherlands, have produced such modules. A valuable model for such training was recently organized by the United Nations Development Programme for the police of Mongolia.

As an essential part of their training, police officers need to learn that they retain individual responsibility for any act of torture, or for any cruel, inhuman or degrading treatment or punishment of a detainee that they carry out. No order to carry out such acts can relieve them of their individual responsibility inside and outside their own country. Law enforcement officials should be taught their right and obligation to refuse an illegal order to carry out an act of torture. This should be spelt out in national criminal legislation and in disciplinary rules.

The limits of what is permissible to detectives who undertake interrogation in criminal investigations should be made unambiguously clear in their training, including such safeguards as the separation of interrogation and custody, regular external supervision of interrogation rooms and places of detention, and the prohibition of interrogation by a single individual or at night. All prisoners should be promptly told of their rights, including that of lodging complaints about their treatment.

Special training is needed for police officers who work with asylum seekers, to help them to recognize potential torture victims, and to help referral to specialist centres for their treatment that may exist.

Such human rights training should be an inherent part of any UN or intergovernmental police support programme. Police who are to be sent abroad in this role need human rights training themselves. They should be able to train local police in human rights, paying particular attention to the prevention of torture. The Dutch Section of AI has drafted short guidelines on human rights called *Basic Rules of Law Enforcement* which fit into the pocket of a uniform, and which were used in Mozambique by the UN Civpol project.

In order to combat torture by the police, independent bodies need to be available to supervise, inspect and investigate the police, to guarantee the correct treatment of suspects in police custody, to detect acts of torture and to punish those responsible. This may be an independent ombudsman, a complaints centre, or a unit or organization, independent of the police, with the power to initiate a judicial inquiry.

In many countries police have special cells at their disposal and torture often occurs in these cells when a suspect is in police custody. Effective guidelines and procedures need to be drawn up that restrict opportunities for ill-treatment and torture in police cells.

Police professional associations and trade unions can play a role in promoting and safeguarding human rights within the police, and act as a barrier against extreme requirements by governments on the police.

Police officers and members of the military often attend international meetings and congresses. These could provide opportunities to confront the practice of torture in a country through confrontation with its representatives, demonstrations or other actions that may involve members of the police or military who are also members of human rights organizations during such meetings.

Military

As with police training, military training should emphasize the fact that torture is a crime and that no order or emergency situation relieves military personnel of their individual responsibility for any human rights abuse in which they are involved. They are personally answerable. They have a right and responsibility to refuse an illegal order to torture.

With the rapid increase of international peacekeeping operations under the umbrella of the UN, human rights training for the military has become a necessity. The Dutch Section of AI has produced a book, *Peace Keeping and Human Rights* (Amnesty International, 1994) for use during training of UN military personnel. Peacekeepers require operational training to recognize abuses and gather evidence to bring human rights violators to justice — skills needed at the time of writing in Rwanda and Bosnia.

After a period of repression has come to an end, the process of getting justice for the victims of torture and abuse will often require a clean-up of the police and the military. Those officers who have contributed actively to torture or were responsible for it must be brought to court. Those who, while not directly responsible, failed to intervene might be excluded from re-employment. Special units responsible for repression should be identified and disbanded.

Military training may include techniques for resisting interrogation techniques, methods akin to torture, and torture equipment that may be used by an 'enemy'. For this purpose torture may be practised on military personnel. Training in these techniques also may be part of military assistance programmes between countries. Such training should be ended, the equipment forbidden and instruction books in these techniques taken out of circulation.

Journalists

Revelations about torture and human rights violations can be an important part of the work of the investigative journalist. Human rights education should be included in journalists' training. Their value depends on the quality of their research and their freedom to exercise their independence. These qualities need to be safeguarded and strengthened by an independent press.

If the human rights situation begins to deteriorate, journalists will have a crucial part to play in the prevention of torture. Public warnings of the dangers of torture will need broadcasting once human rights abuses begin to occur. Human rights activists should be able to provide journalists with local information and with foreign examples of torture and its aftermath. When human rights violations begin to occur on a major scale, articles on torture may need to be published in foreign newspapers or transmitted on television programmes abroad. It may be important for local journalists to build up a network of trusted foreign colleagues at their disposal. As the human rights situation deteriorates the role of the journalist in compiling evidence about human rights abuses and that of newspapers daring to publish such information becomes more important but also more hazardous. Even when journalists cannot get their human rights stories printed, their investigative skills and information may be made available to foreign colleagues on a confidential basis or to non-governmental organizations (NGOs) such as AI. Journalists who warn against possible torture or reveal incidents of human rights violations may be threatened; colleagues and professional writers' bodies abroad, such as International PEN, can provide powerful support.

At the end of a repressive regime, the press and journalists gain or regain a reasonable degree of independence and freedom. A free press has a considerable power to influence respect for human rights and journalists have an important part in the public discussion on justice. Journalists can investigate, record and expose the human rights abuses that took place, contributing to national discussion and reflection on these violations. At the same time extra pressure is generated on the government to ensure that justice is done. Foreign associations of journalists and human rights NGOs can assist this process.

References

Alderson, J. (1992) *Human Rights and the Police*. Strasbourg: Council of Europe.

Amnesty International (1984) *Torture in the Eighties*. London: Amnesty International.

Amnesty International (1994) *Peace Keeping and Human Rights: Materials for Military Training Course*. London: Amnesty International.

Amnesty International (1994) *Basic Rules of Law Enforcement: Commentary and Materials Prepared for the Mozambican Police and ONUMOZ Civilian Police Monitors*. London: Amnesty International.

British Medical Association (1989) *Medicine Betrayed*. London: BMA.

Bronkhorst, D. (1995) *Truth and Reconciliation*. Amsterdam: Amnesty International Netherlands.

* This chapter was adapted by Dan Jones, from a paper written by Piet van Reenan.

Index